Moon Girl and Devil Dinosaur

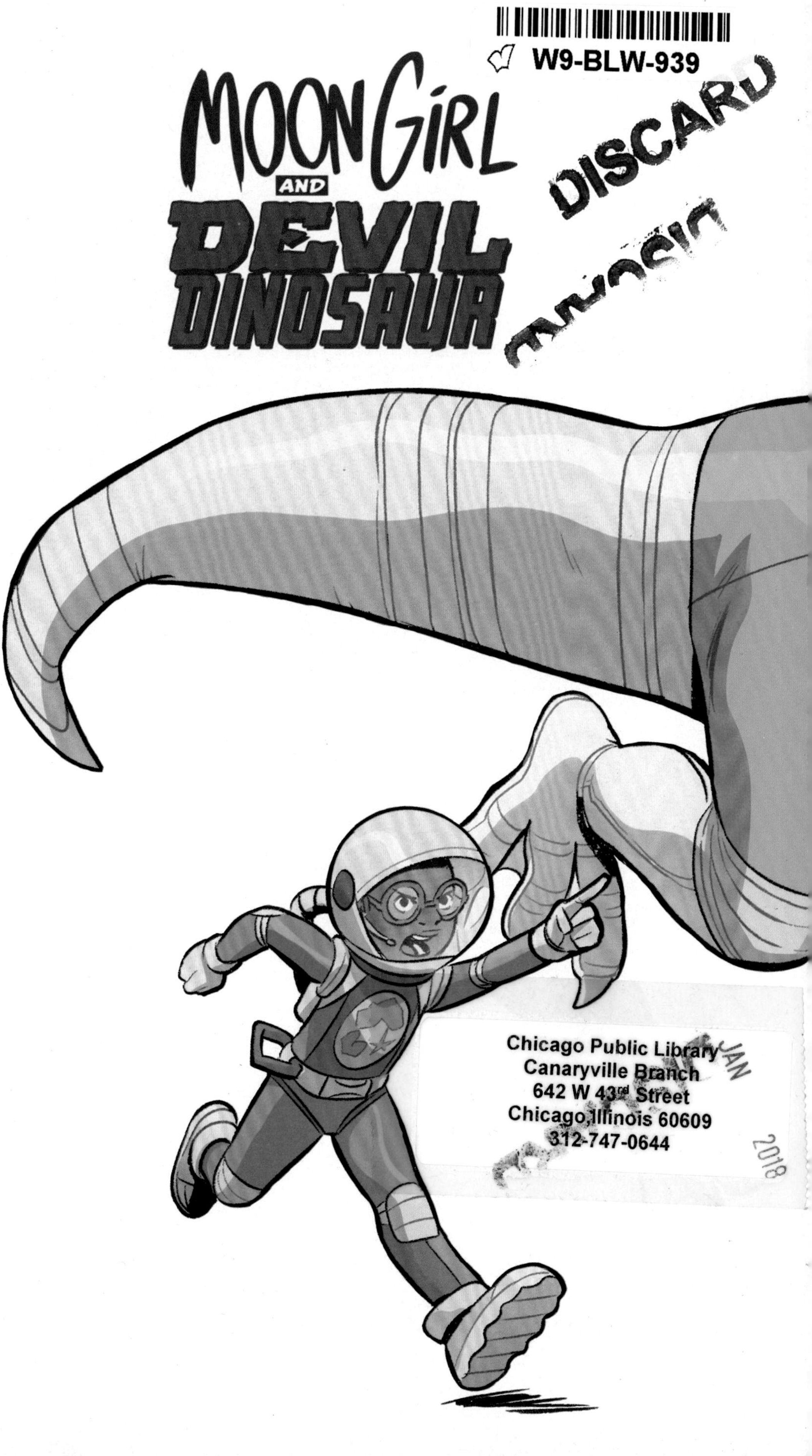

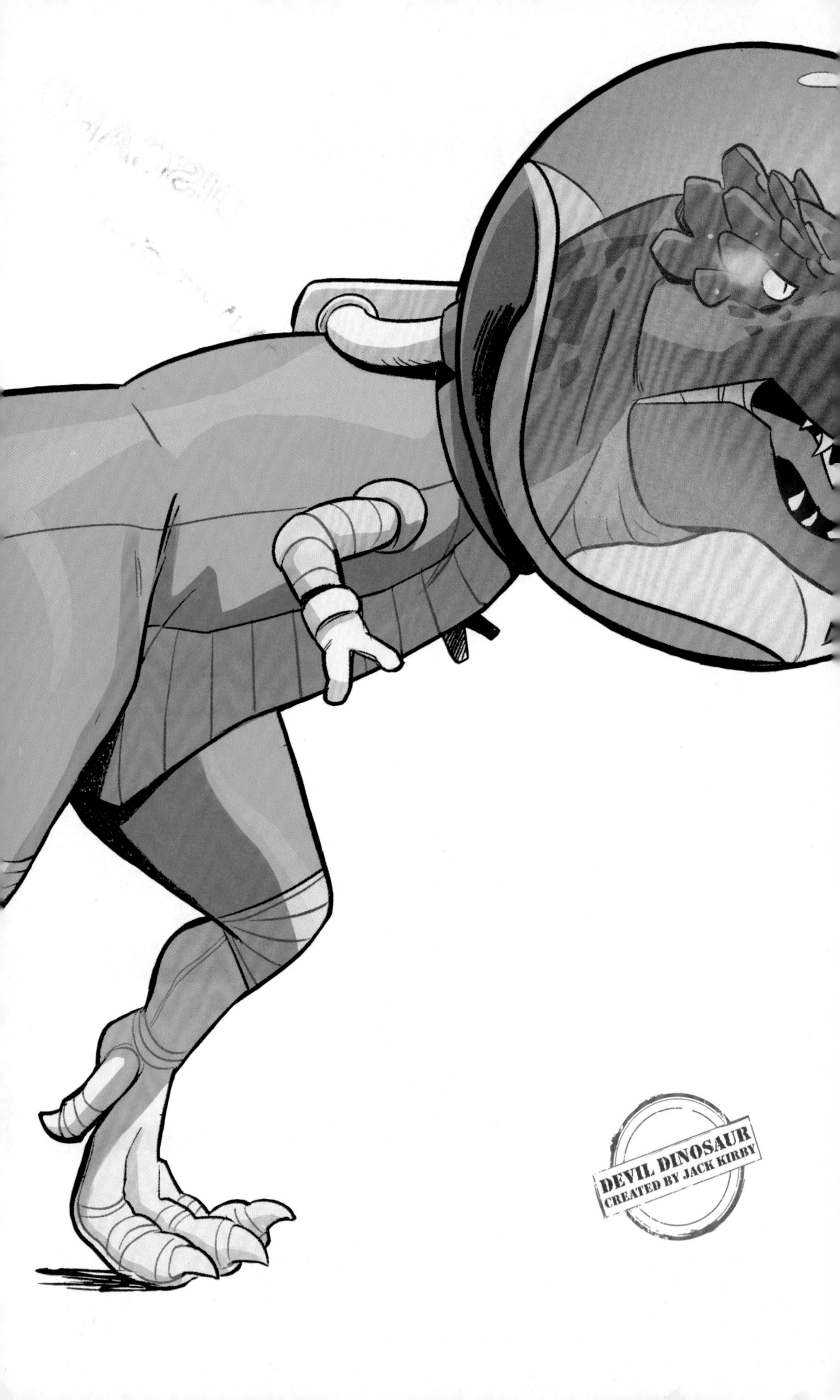
DEVIL DINOSAUR
CREATED BY JACK KIRBY

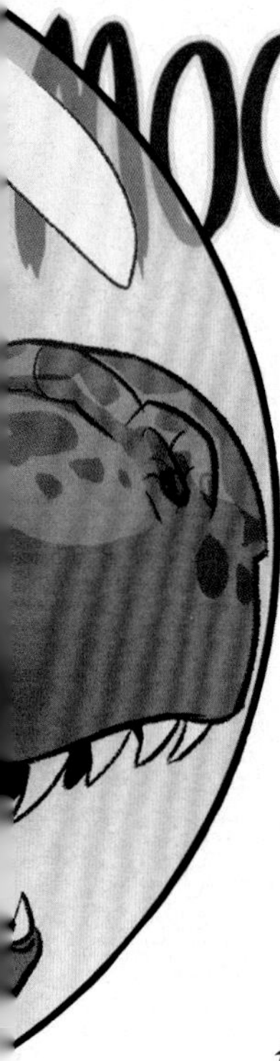

MOON GIRL AND DEVIL DINOSAUR

GIRL-MOON

Brandon Montclare
WRITER

Natacha Bustos
ARTIST

Tamra Bonvillain
COLOR ARTIST

Ray-Anthony Height
ARTIST, "SIGN ON THE DOTTED LINE..."

Dominike "Domo" Stanton
ARTIST, "THINK FAST!"

Michael Shelfer
ARTIST, "BLINDS"

VC's Joe Caramagna (#19) & Travis Lanham (#20-24)
LETTERERS

Natacha Bustos
COVER ART

Chris Robinson
ASSISTANT EDITOR

Mark Paniccia
EDITOR

COLLECTION EDITOR: Jennifer Grünwald
ASSISTANT EDITOR: Caitlin O'Connell
ASSOCIATE MANAGING EDITOR: Kateri Woody
EDITOR, SPECIAL PROJECTS: Mark D. Beazley
VP, PRODUCTION & SPECIAL PROJECTS: Jeff Youngquist
SVP PRINT, SALES & MARKETING: David Gabriel
BOOK DESIGNER: Jay Bowen

EDITOR IN CHIEF: Axel Alonso
CHIEF CREATIVE OFFICER: Joe Quesada
PRESIDENT: Dan Buckley
EXECUTIVE PRODUCER: Alan Fine

MOON GIRL AND DEVIL DINOSAUR VOL. 4: GIRL-MOON. Contains material originally published in magazine form as MOON GIRL AND DEVIL DINOSAUR #19-24. First printing 2017. ISBN# 978-1-302-90535-4. Published by MARVEL WORLDWIDE, INC., a subsidiary of MARVEL ENTERTAINMENT, LLC. OFFICE OF PUBLICATION: 135 West 50th Street, New York, NY 10020. Copyright © 2017 MARVEL No similarity between any of the names, characters, persons, and/or institutions in this magazine with those of any living or dead person or institution is intended, and any such similarity which may exist is purely coincidental. **Printed in Canada.** DAN BUCKLEY, President, Marvel Entertainment; JOE QUESADA, Chief Creative Officer; TOM BREVOORT, SVP of Publishing; DAVID BOGART, SVP of Business Affairs & Operations, Publishing & Partnership; C.B. CEBULSKI, VP of Brand Management & Development, Asia; DAVID GABRIEL, SVP of Sales & Marketing, Publishing; JEFF YOUNGQUIST, VP of Production & Special Projects; DAN CARR, Executive Director of Publishing Technology; ALEX MORALES, Director of Publishing Operations; SUSAN CRESPI, Production Manager; STAN LEE, Chairman Emeritus. For information regarding advertising in Marvel Comics or on Marvel.com, please contact Jonathan Parkhideh, VP of Digital Media & Marketing Solutions, at jparkhideh@marvel.com. For Marvel subscription inquiries, please call 888-511-5480. Manufactured between 11/3/2017 and 12/4/2017 by SOLISCO PRINTERS, SCOTT, QC, CANADA.

10 9 8 7 6 5 4 3 2 1

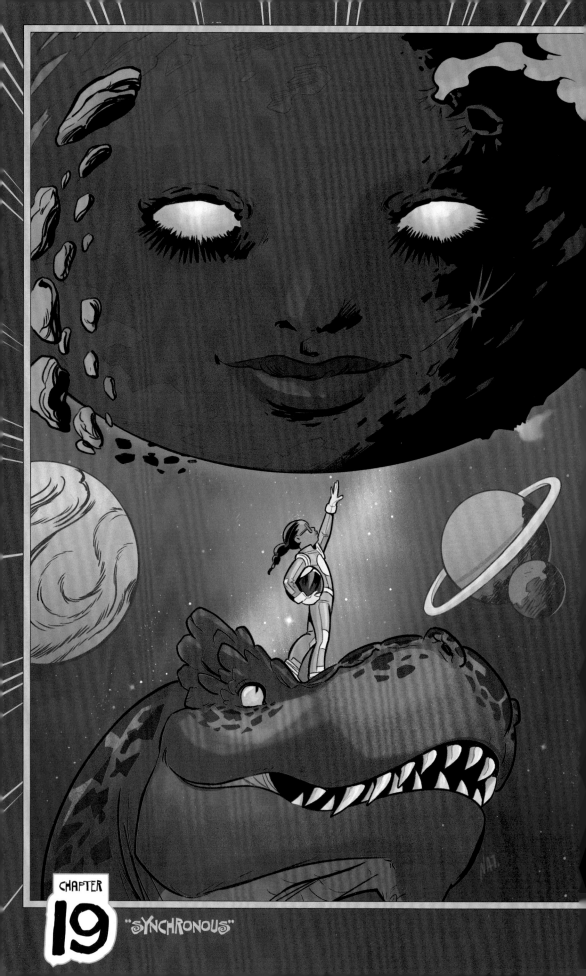

CHAPTER
19 "SYNCHRONOUS"

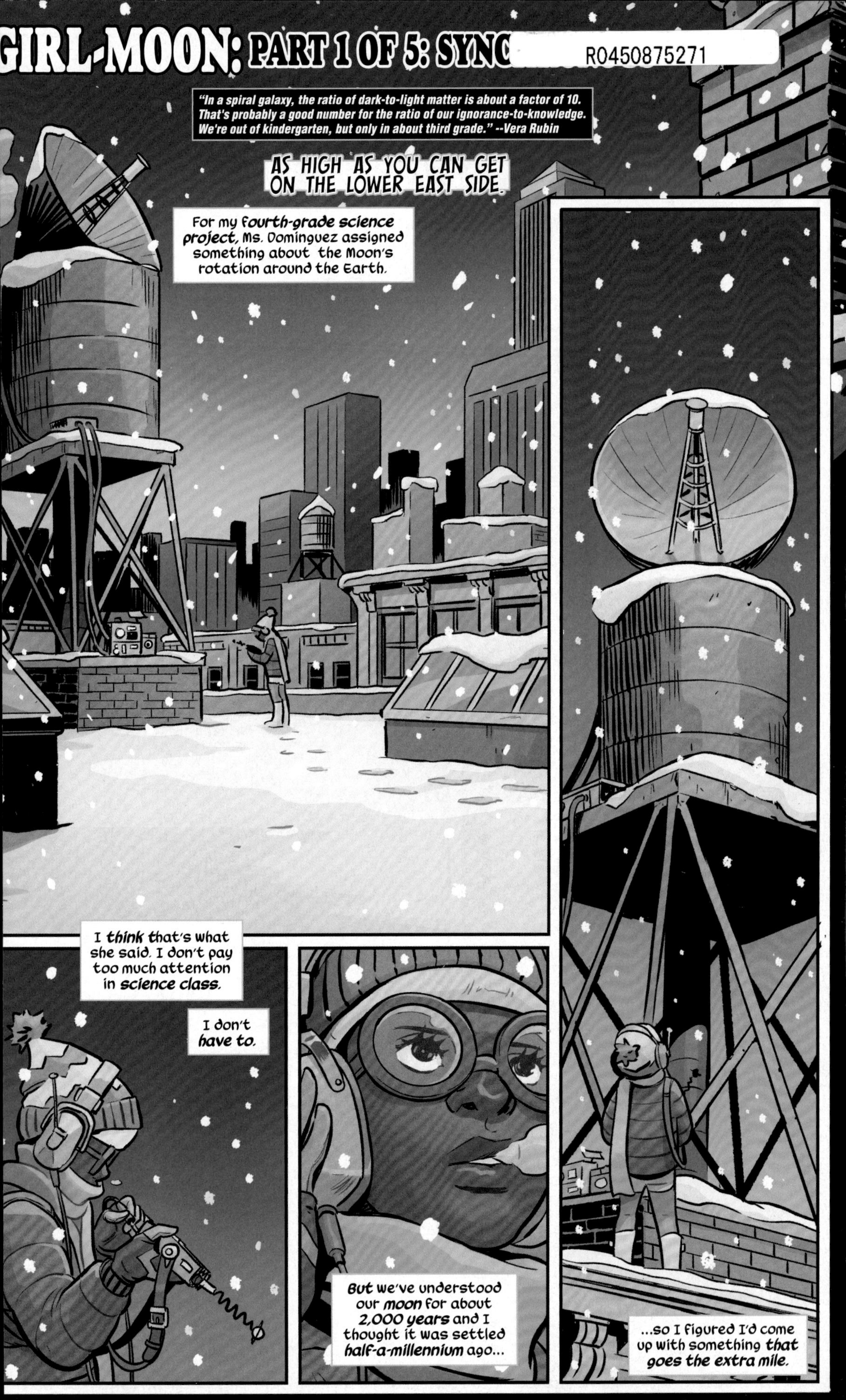
GIRL-MOON: PART 1 OF 5: SYNC
"In a spiral galaxy, the ratio of dark-to-light matter is about a factor of 10. That's probably a good number for the ratio of our ignorance-to-knowledge. We're out of kindergarten, but only in about third grade." --Vera Rubin
AS HIGH AS YOU CAN GET ON THE LOWER EAST SIDE.
For my fourth-grade science project, Ms. Dominguez assigned something about the Moon's rotation around the Earth.
I think that's what she said. I don't pay too much attention in science class.
I don't have to.
But we've understood our moon for about 2,000 years and I thought it was settled half-a-millennium ago...
...so I figured I'd come up with something that goes the extra mile.

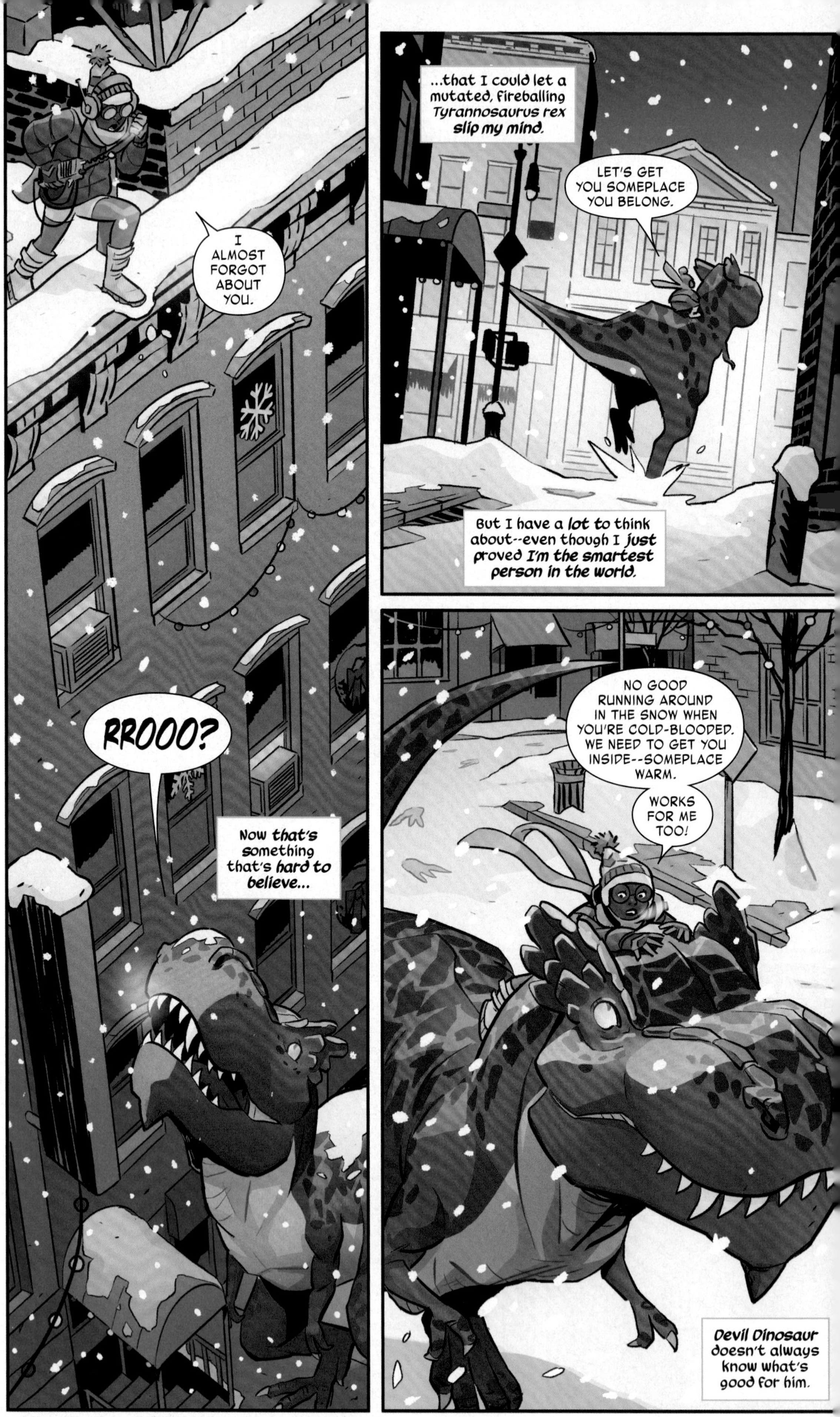
I ALMOST FORGOT ABOUT YOU.
RROOO?
Now that's something that's hard to believe...
...that I could let a mutated, fireballing Tyrannosaurus rex slip my mind.
LET'S GET YOU SOMEPLACE YOU BELONG.
But I have a lot to think about--even though I just proved I'm the smartest person in the world.
NO GOOD RUNNING AROUND IN THE SNOW WHEN YOU'RE COLD-BLOODED. WE NEED TO GET YOU INSIDE--SOMEPLACE WARM.
WORKS FOR ME TOO!
Devil Dinosaur doesn't always know what's good for him.

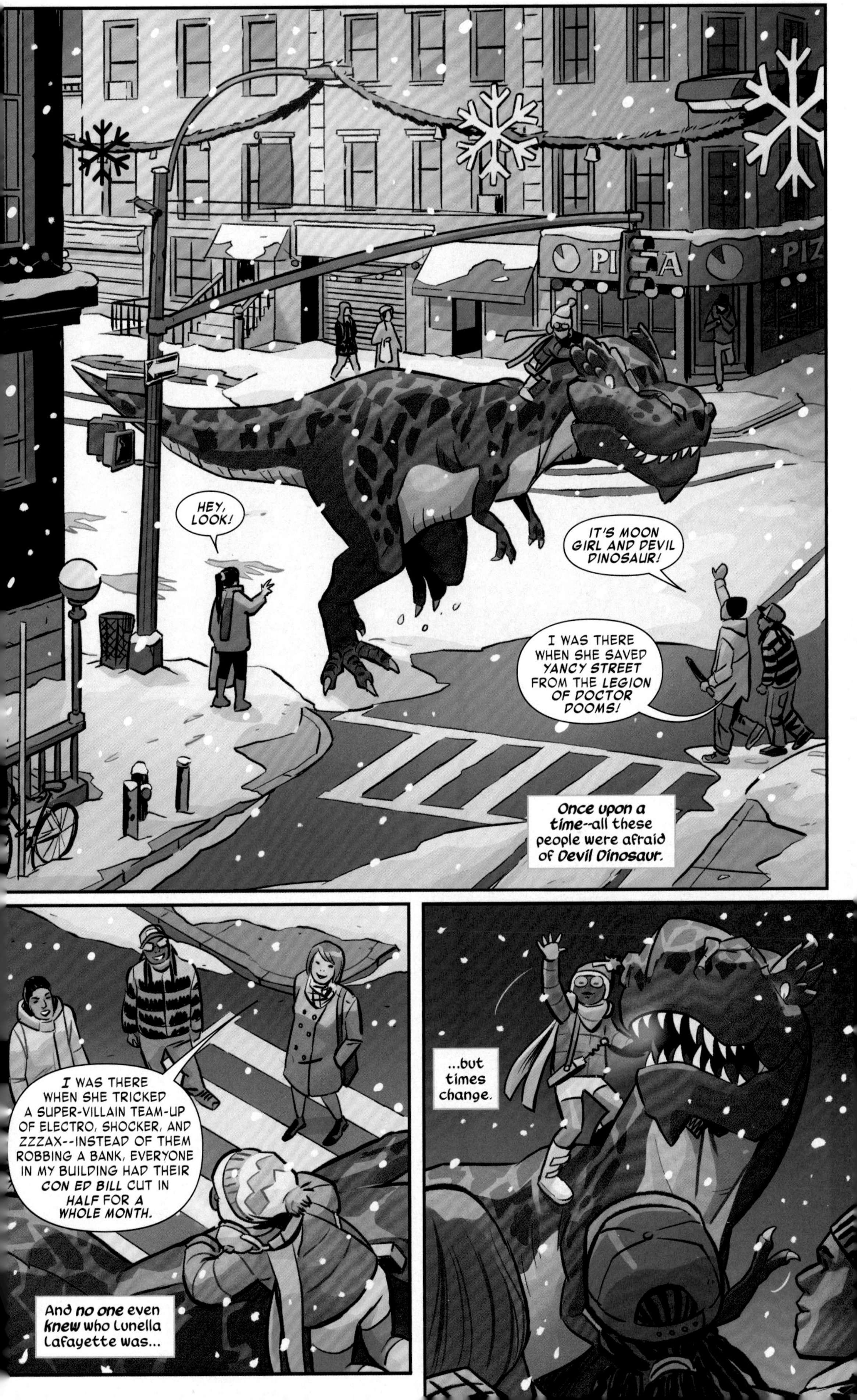

HEY, LOOK!
IT'S MOON GIRL AND DEVIL DINOSAUR!
I WAS THERE WHEN SHE SAVED YANCY STREET FROM THE LEGION OF DOCTOR DOOMS!
Once upon a time--all these people were afraid of Devil Dinosaur.
I WAS THERE WHEN SHE TRICKED A SUPER-VILLAIN TEAM-UP OF ELECTRO, SHOCKER, AND ZZZAX--INSTEAD OF THEM ROBBING A BANK, EVERYONE IN MY BUILDING HAD THEIR CON ED BILL CUT IN HALF FOR A WHOLE MONTH.
And no one even knew who Lunella Lafayette was...
...but times change.

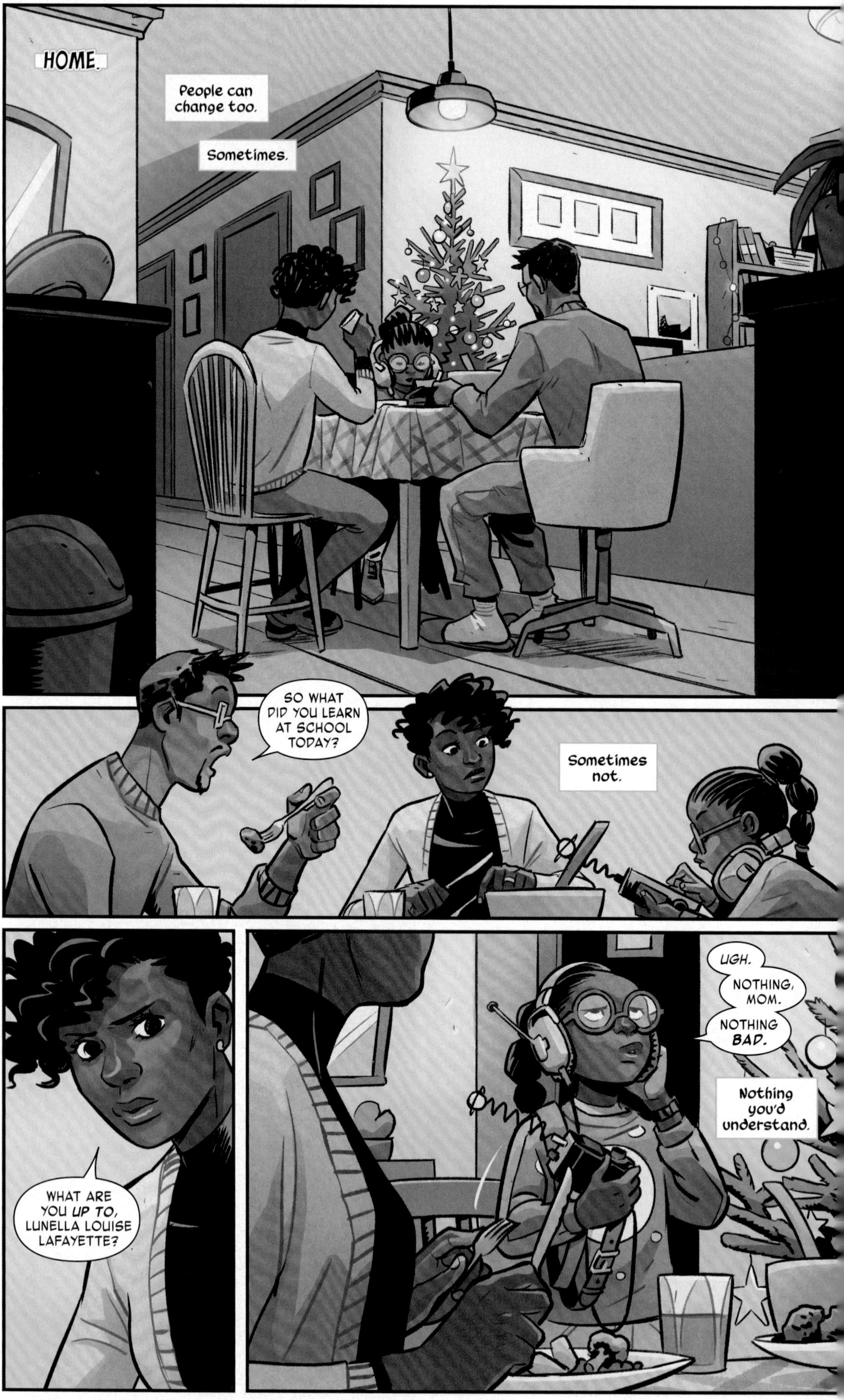
HOME.
People can change too.
Sometimes.
SO WHAT DID YOU LEARN AT SCHOOL TODAY?
Sometimes not.
WHAT ARE YOU *UP TO*, LUNELLA LOUISE LAFAYETTE?
UGH.
NOTHING, MOM.
NOTHING *BAD*.
Nothing you'd understand.

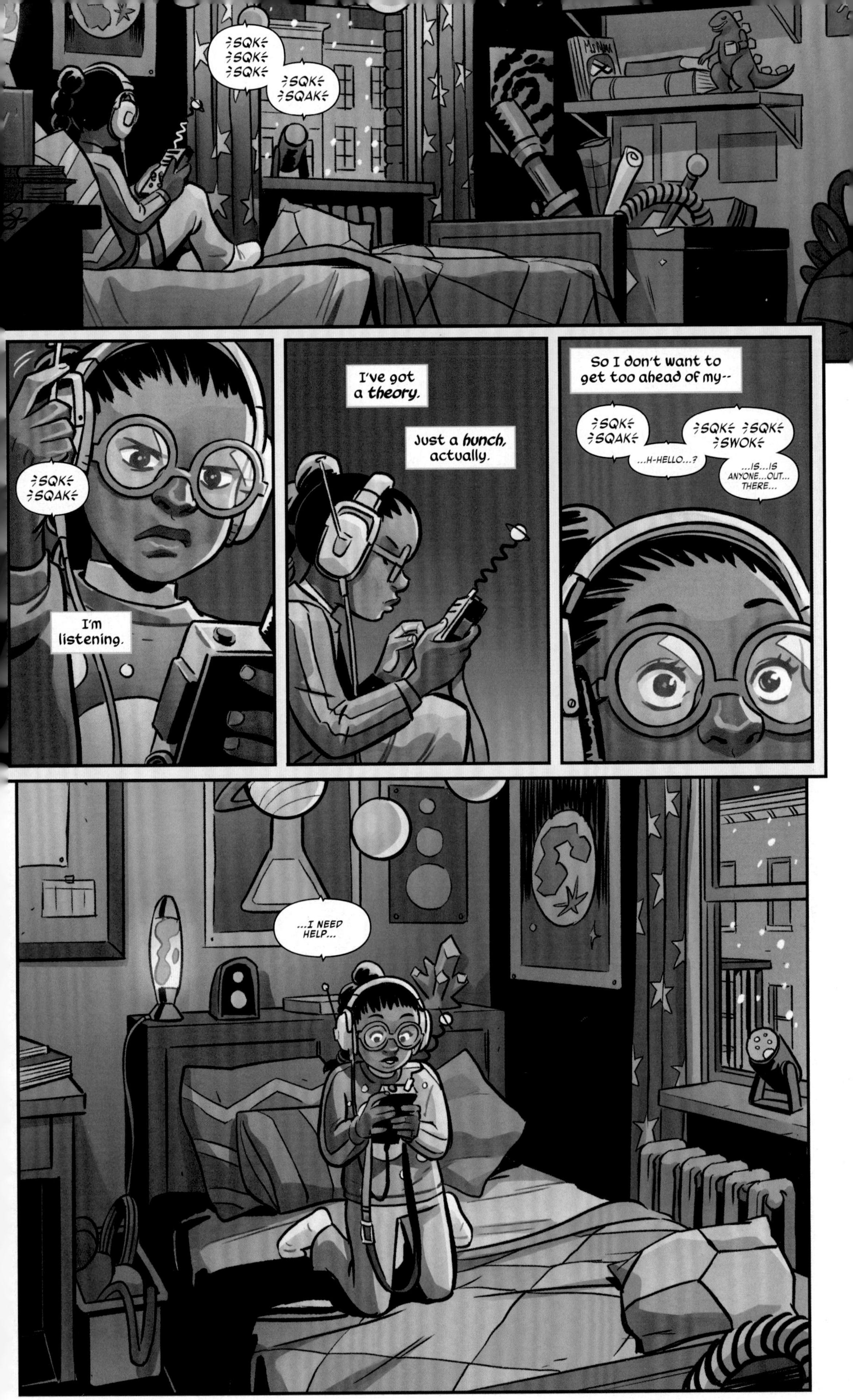

⇉SQK⇇ ⇉SQK⇇ ⇉SQK⇇
⇉SQK⇇ ⇉SQAK⇇
⇉SQK⇇ ⇉SQAK⇇
I'm listening.
I've got a *theory*.
Just a *hunch*, actually.
So I don't want to get too ahead of my--
⇉SQK⇇ ⇉SQAK⇇
...H-HELLO...?
⇉SQK⇇ ⇉SQK⇇ ⇉SWOK⇇
...IS...IS ANYONE...OUT... THERE...
...I NEED HELP...

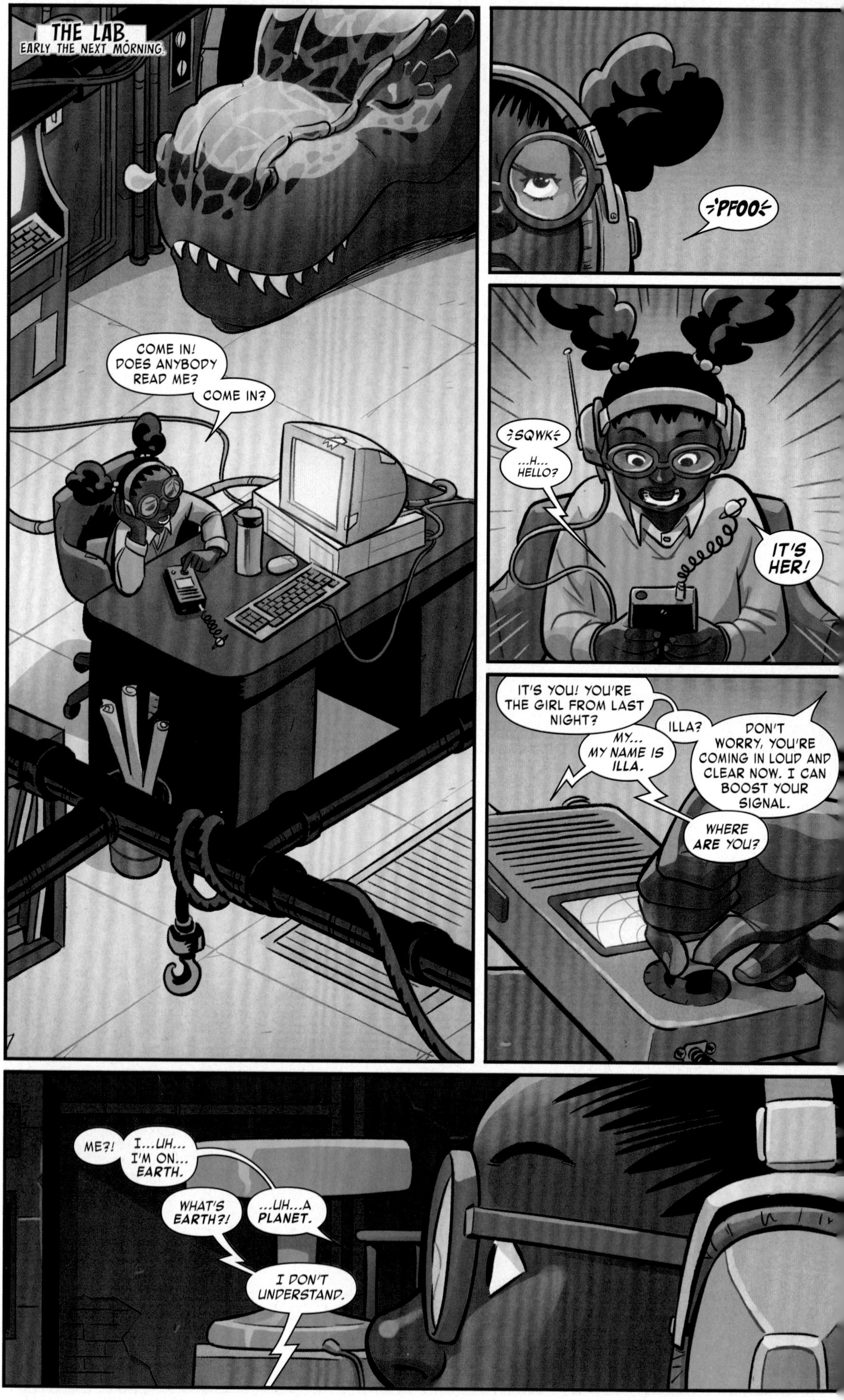
THE LAB.
EARLY THE NEXT MORNING.
COME IN! DOES ANYBODY READ ME?
COME IN?
PFOO
SQWK
...H... HELLO?
IT'S HER!
IT'S YOU! YOU'RE THE GIRL FROM LAST NIGHT?
MY... MY NAME IS ILLA.
ILLA?
DON'T WORRY, YOU'RE COMING IN LOUD AND CLEAR NOW. I CAN BOOST YOUR SIGNAL.
WHERE ARE YOU?
ME?!
I...UH... I'M ON... EARTH.
WHAT'S EARTH?!
...UH...A PLANET.
I DON'T UNDERSTAND.

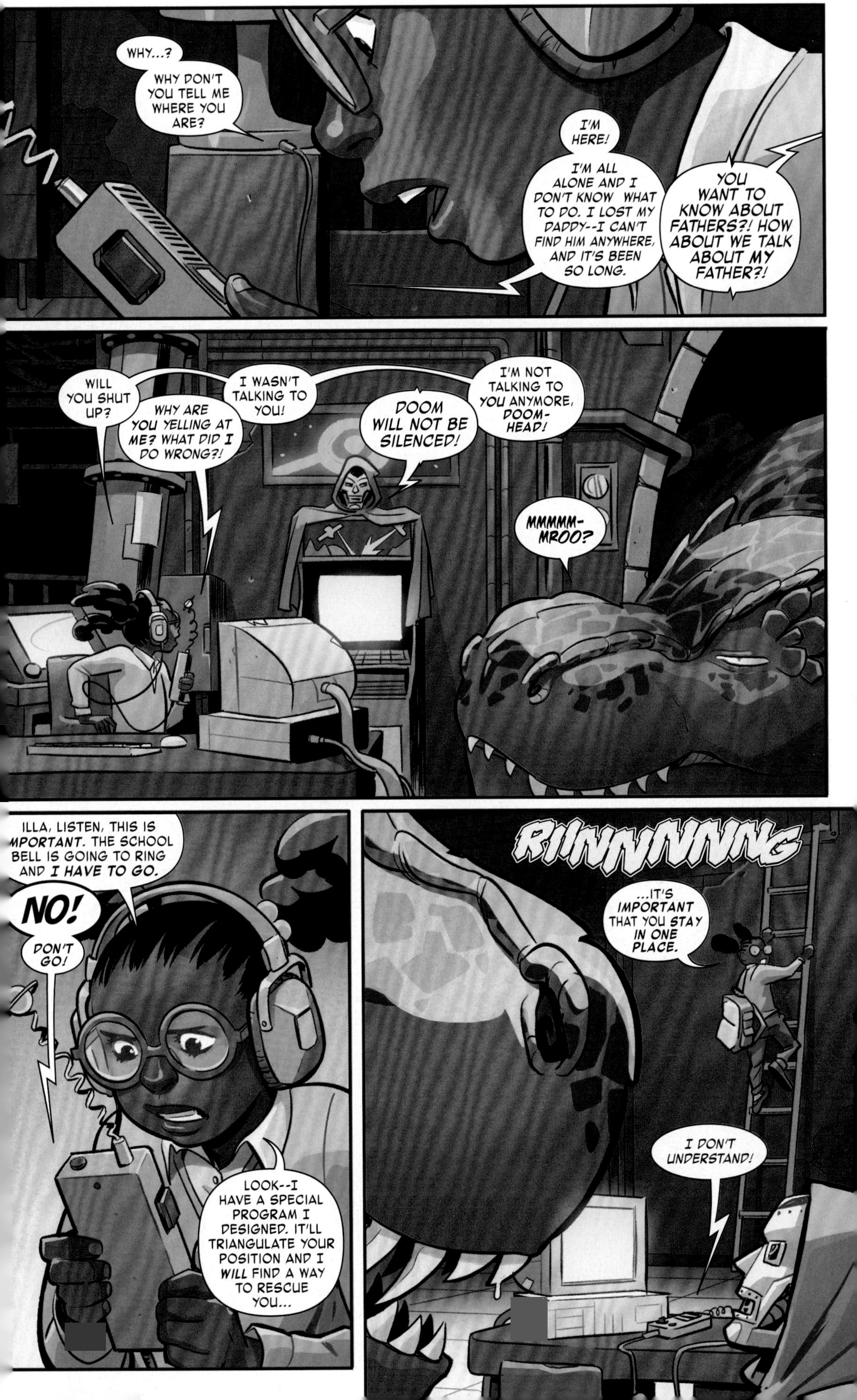
WHY...?
WHY DON'T YOU TELL ME WHERE YOU ARE?
I'M HERE!
I'M ALL ALONE AND I DON'T KNOW WHAT TO DO. I LOST MY DADDY--I CAN'T FIND HIM ANYWHERE, AND IT'S BEEN SO LONG.
YOU WANT TO KNOW ABOUT FATHERS?! HOW ABOUT WE TALK ABOUT MY FATHER?!
WILL YOU SHUT UP?
WHY ARE YOU YELLING AT ME? WHAT DID I DO WRONG?!
I WASN'T TALKING TO YOU!
DOOM WILL NOT BE SILENCED!
I'M NOT TALKING TO YOU ANYMORE, DOOM-HEAD!
MMMMM-MROO?
ILLA, LISTEN, THIS IS MPORTANT. THE SCHOOL BELL IS GOING TO RING AND I HAVE TO GO.
NO!
DON'T GO!
LOOK--I HAVE A SPECIAL PROGRAM I DESIGNED. IT'LL TRIANGULATE YOUR POSITION AND I WILL FIND A WAY TO RESCUE YOU...
RIINNNNNG
...IT'S IMPORTANT THAT YOU STAY IN ONE PLACE.
I DON'T UNDERSTAND!

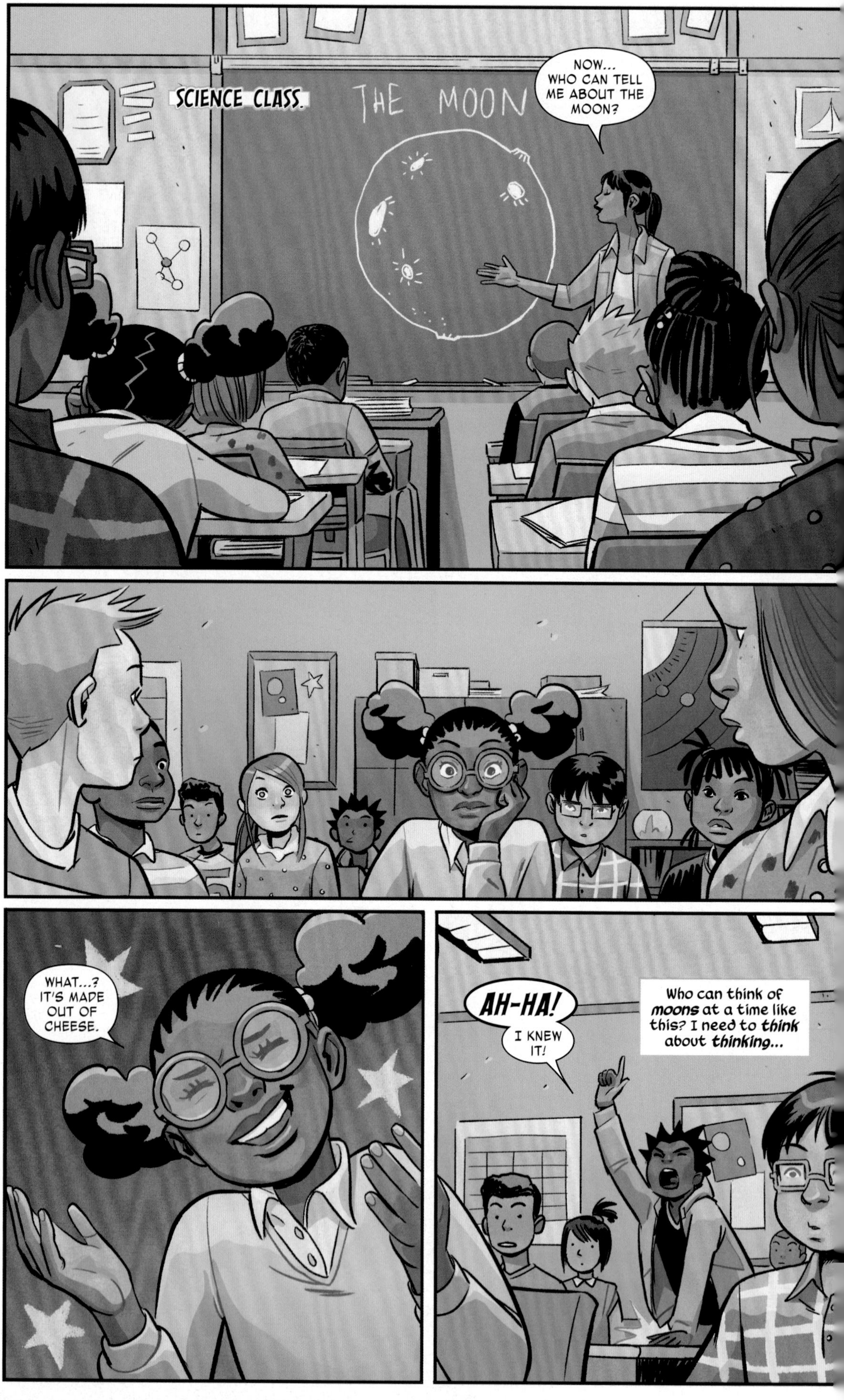
SCIENCE CLASS.
THE MOON
NOW... WHO CAN TELL ME ABOUT THE MOON?
WHAT...? IT'S MADE OUT OF CHEESE.
AH-HA! I KNEW IT!
Who can think of moons at a time like this? I need to think about thinking...

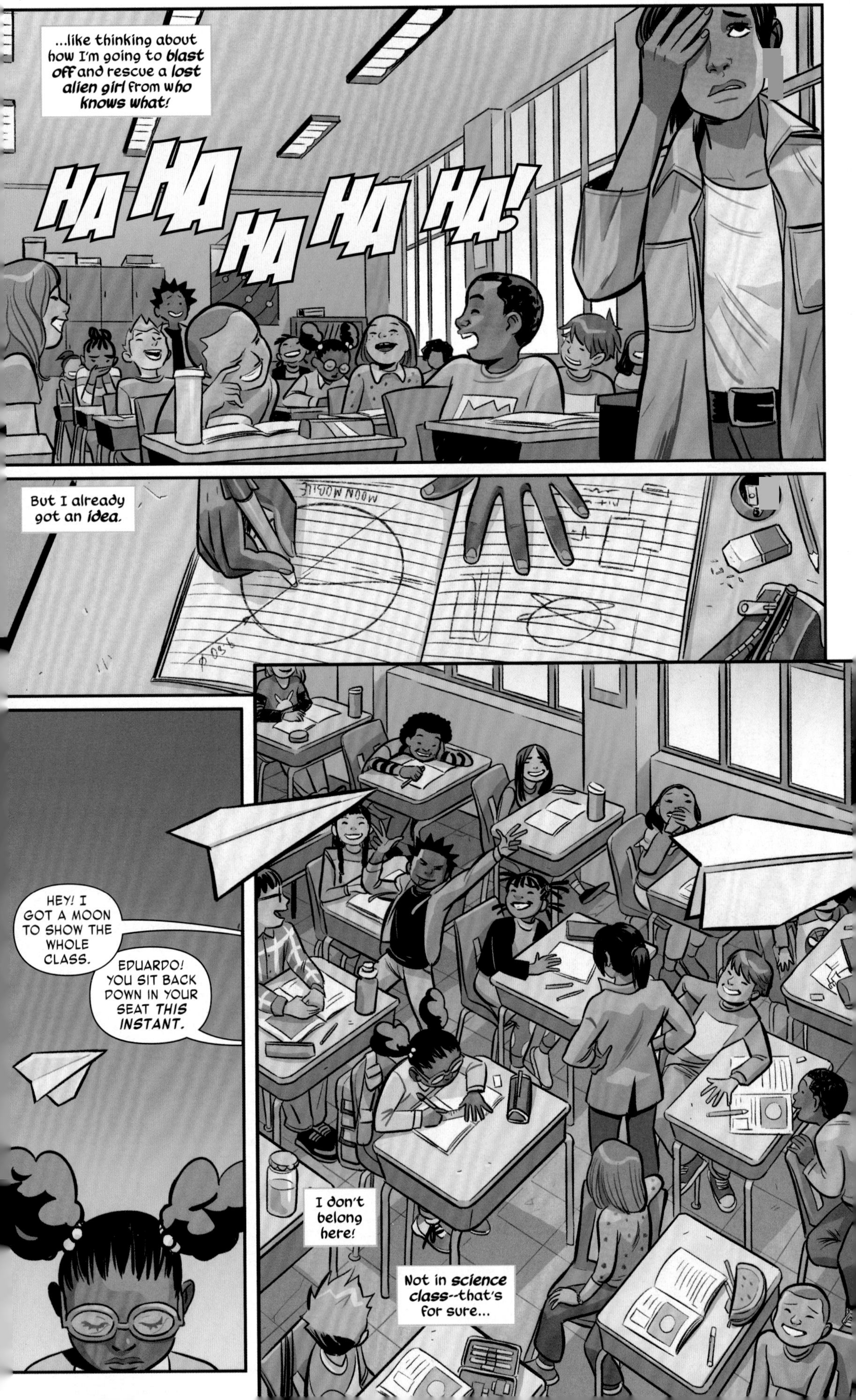
...like thinking about how I'm going to *blast off* and rescue a *lost alien girl* from *who knows what!*
HA HA HA HA HA!
But I already got an *idea.*
HEY! I GOT A MOON TO SHOW THE WHOLE CLASS.
EDUARDO! YOU SIT BACK DOWN IN YOUR SEAT *THIS INSTANT.*
I don't belong here!
Not in *science class*--that's for sure...

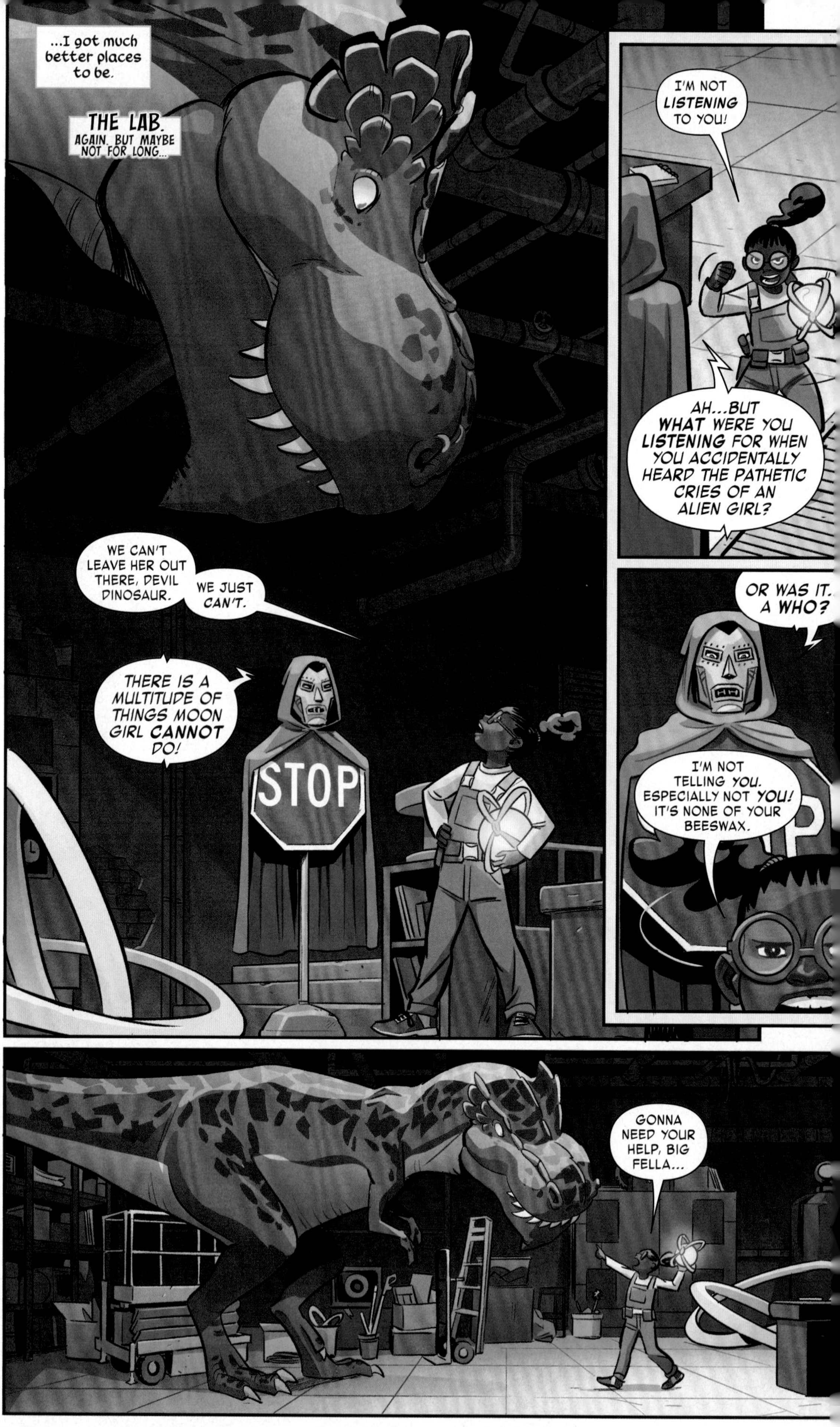

...I got much better places to be.
THE LAB. AGAIN. BUT MAYBE NOT FOR LONG...
I'M NOT LISTENING TO YOU!
AH...BUT WHAT WERE YOU LISTENING FOR WHEN YOU ACCIDENTALLY HEARD THE PATHETIC CRIES OF AN ALIEN GIRL?
WE CAN'T LEAVE HER OUT THERE, DEVIL DINOSAUR.
WE JUST CAN'T.
THERE IS A MULTITUDE OF THINGS MOON GIRL CANNOT DO!
STOP
OR WAS IT... A WHO?
I'M NOT TELLING YOU. ESPECIALLY NOT YOU! IT'S NONE OF YOUR BEESWAX.
GONNA NEED YOUR HELP, BIG FELLA...

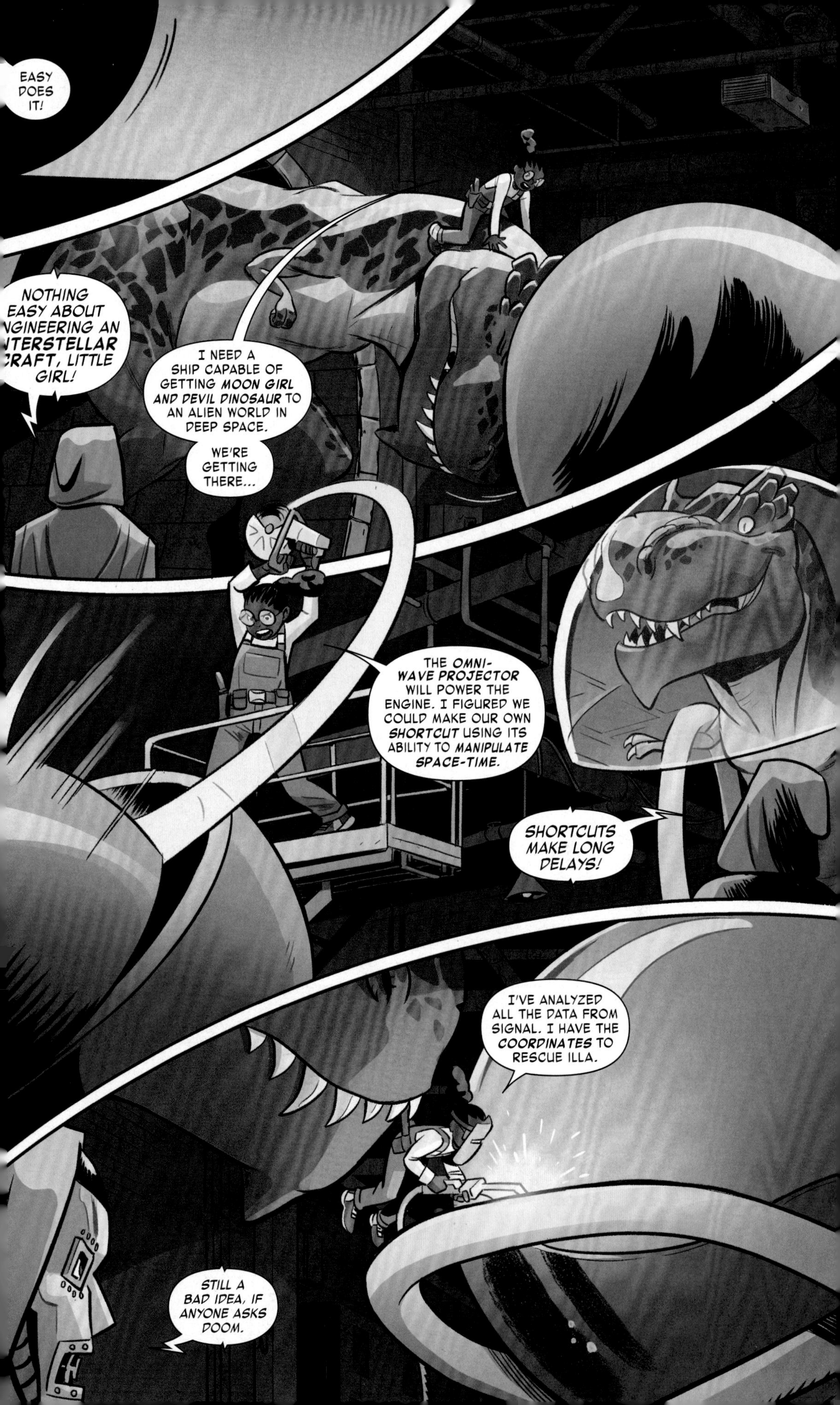

EASY DOES IT!
NOTHING EASY ABOUT NGINEERING AN NTERSTELLAR RAFT, LITTLE GIRL!
I NEED A SHIP CAPABLE OF GETTING MOON GIRL AND DEVIL DINOSAUR TO AN ALIEN WORLD IN DEEP SPACE.
WE'RE GETTING THERE...
THE OMNI-WAVE PROJECTOR WILL POWER THE ENGINE. I FIGURED WE COULD MAKE OUR OWN SHORTCUT USING ITS ABILITY TO MANIPULATE SPACE-TIME.
SHORTCUTS MAKE LONG DELAYS!
I'VE ANALYZED ALL THE DATA FROM SIGNAL. I HAVE THE COORDINATES TO RESCUE ILLA.
STILL A BAD IDEA, IF ANYONE ASKS DOOM.

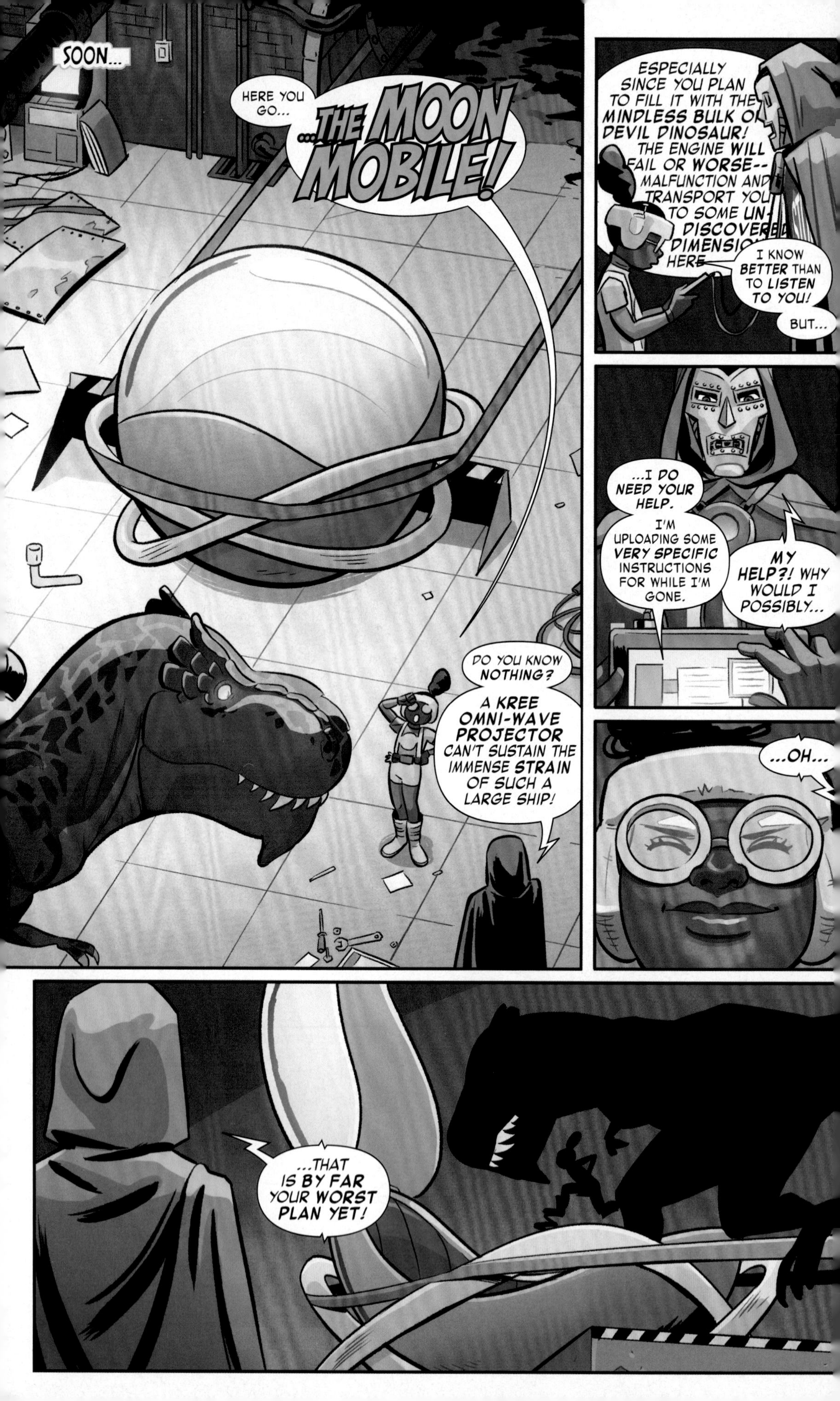
SOON...
HERE YOU GO...
...THE MOON MOBILE!
DO YOU KNOW NOTHING?
A KREE OMNI-WAVE PROJECTOR CAN'T SUSTAIN THE IMMENSE STRAIN OF SUCH A LARGE SHIP!
ESPECIALLY SINCE YOU PLAN TO FILL IT WITH THE MINDLESS BULK OF DEVIL DINOSAUR! THE ENGINE WILL FAIL OR WORSE-- MALFUNCTION AND TRANSPORT YOU TO SOME UN-DISCOVERED DIMENSION HERE
I KNOW BETTER THAN TO LISTEN TO YOU!
BUT...
...I DO NEED YOUR HELP.
I'M UPLOADING SOME VERY SPECIFIC INSTRUCTIONS FOR WHILE I'M GONE.
MY HELP?! WHY WOULD I POSSIBLY...
...OH...
...THAT IS BY FAR YOUR WORST PLAN YET!

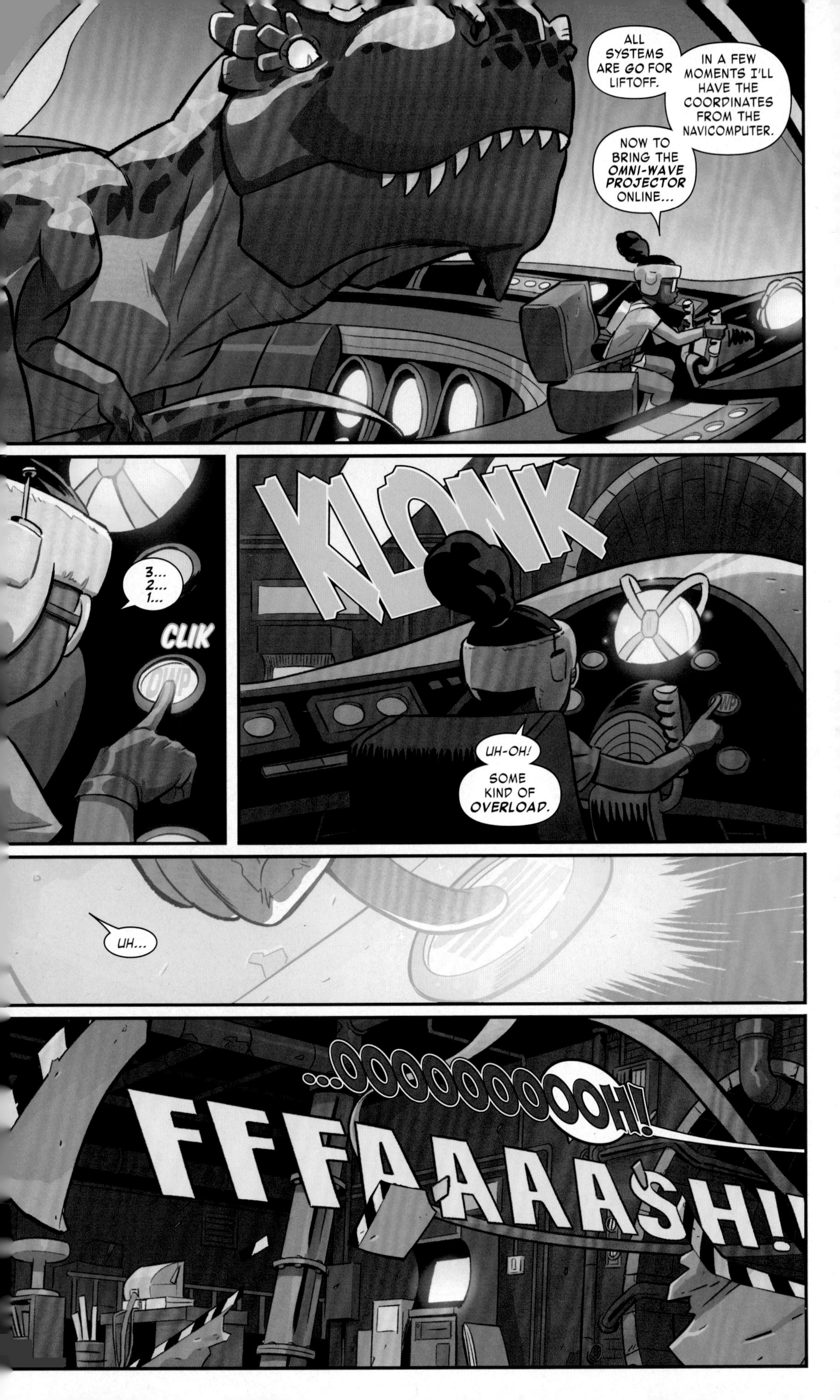
ALL SYSTEMS ARE GO FOR LIFTOFF.
IN A FEW MOMENTS I'LL HAVE THE COORDINATES FROM THE NAVICOMPUTER.
NOW TO BRING THE OMNI-WAVE PROJECTOR ONLINE...
3... 2... 1...
CLIK
KLONK
UH-OH!
SOME KIND OF OVERLOAD.
UH...
...OOOOOOOOOOH!
FFFAAAASH!!

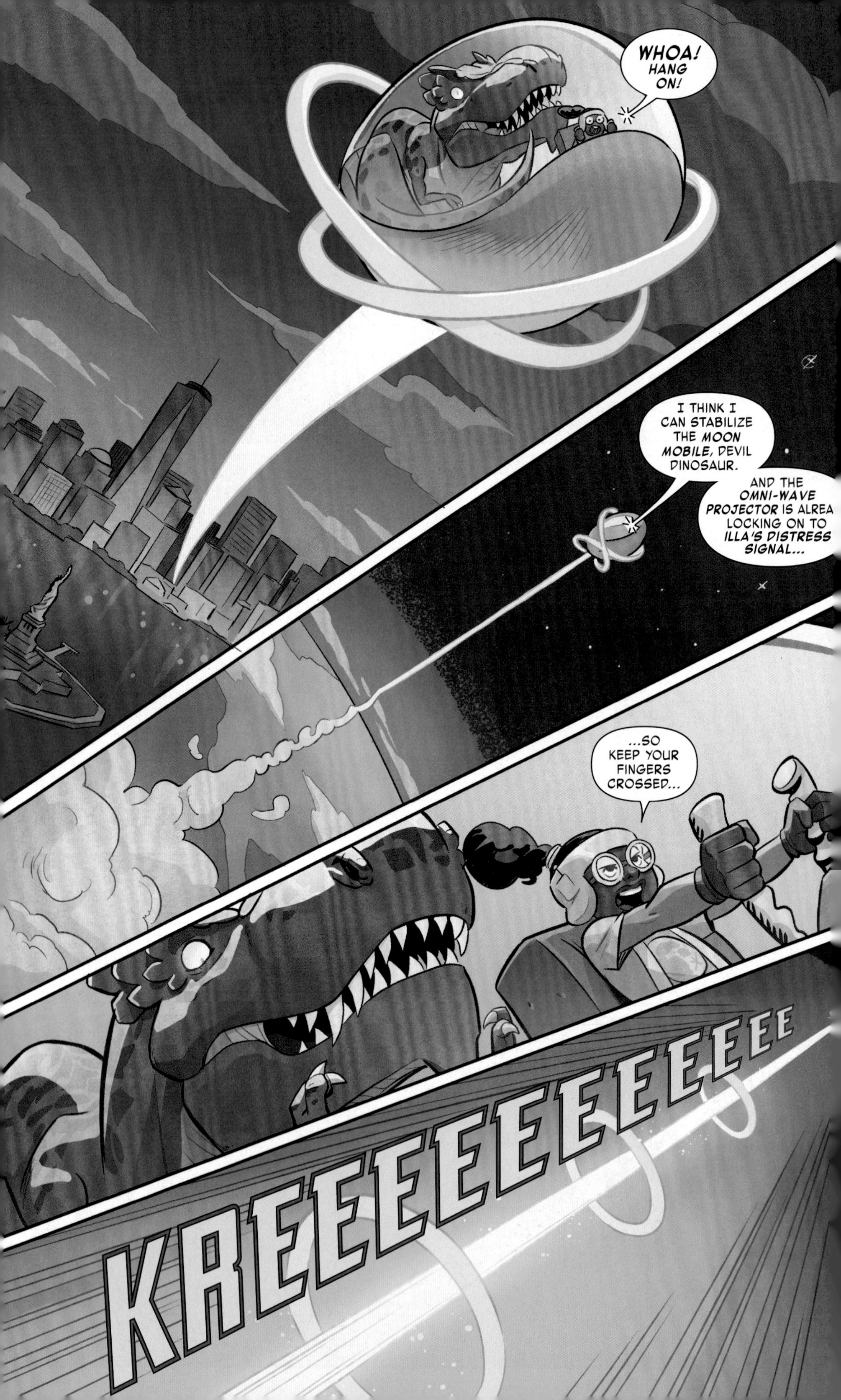
WHOA! HANG ON!
I THINK I CAN STABILIZE THE MOON MOBILE, DEVIL DINOSAUR.
AND THE OMNI-WAVE PROJECTOR IS ALREA LOCKING ON TO ILLA'S DISTRESS SIGNAL...
...SO KEEP YOUR FINGERS CROSSED...
KREEEEEEEEEEEE

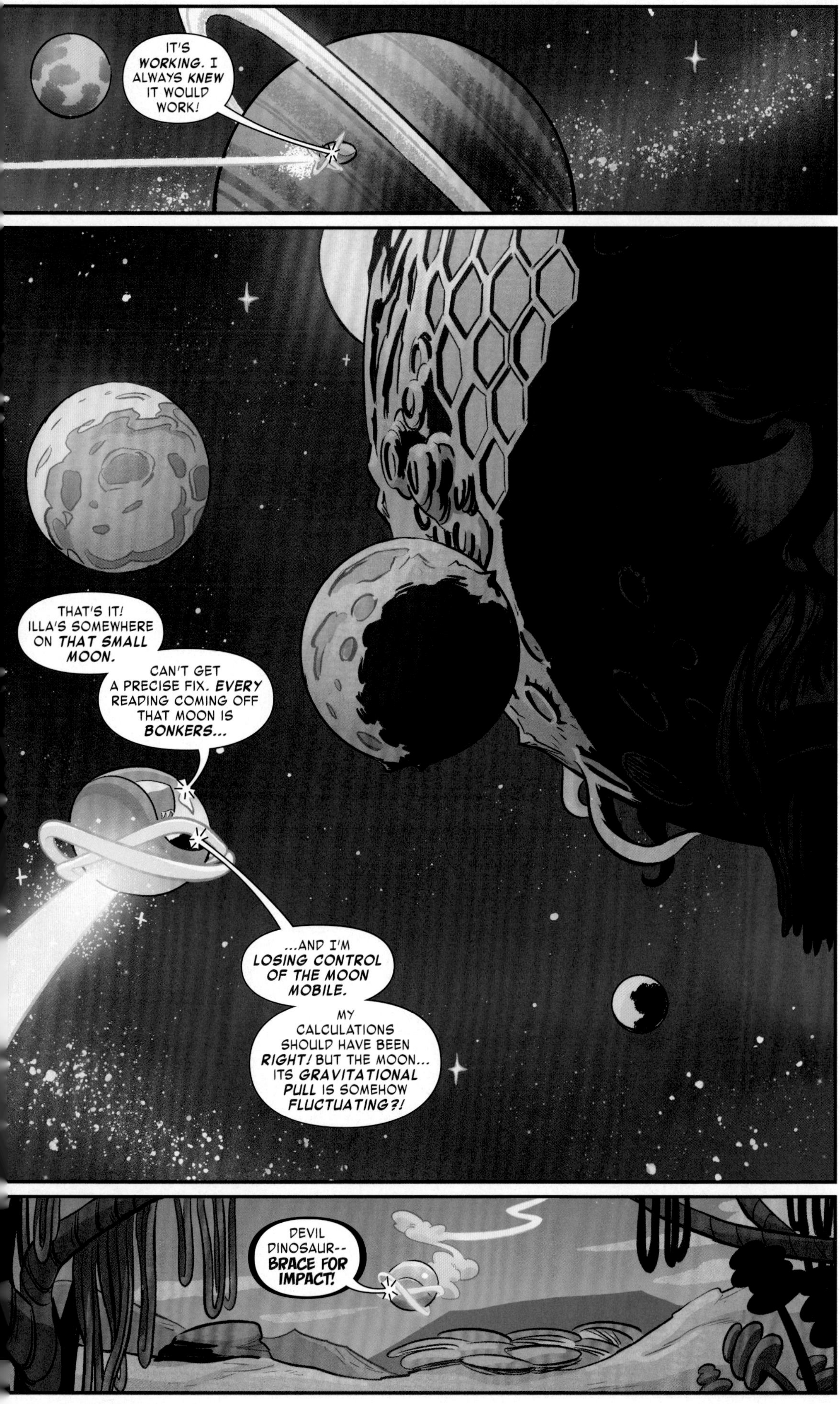

IT'S *WORKING.* I ALWAYS *KNEW* IT WOULD WORK!
THAT'S IT! ILLA'S SOMEWHERE ON *THAT SMALL MOON.*
CAN'T GET A PRECISE FIX. *EVERY* READING COMING OFF THAT MOON IS ***BONKERS...***
...AND I'M ***LOSING CONTROL OF THE MOON MOBILE.***
MY CALCULATIONS SHOULD HAVE BEEN ***RIGHT!*** BUT THE MOON... ITS ***GRAVITATIONAL PULL*** IS SOMEHOW ***FLUCTUATING?!***
DEVIL DINOSAUR-- **BRACE FOR IMPACT!**

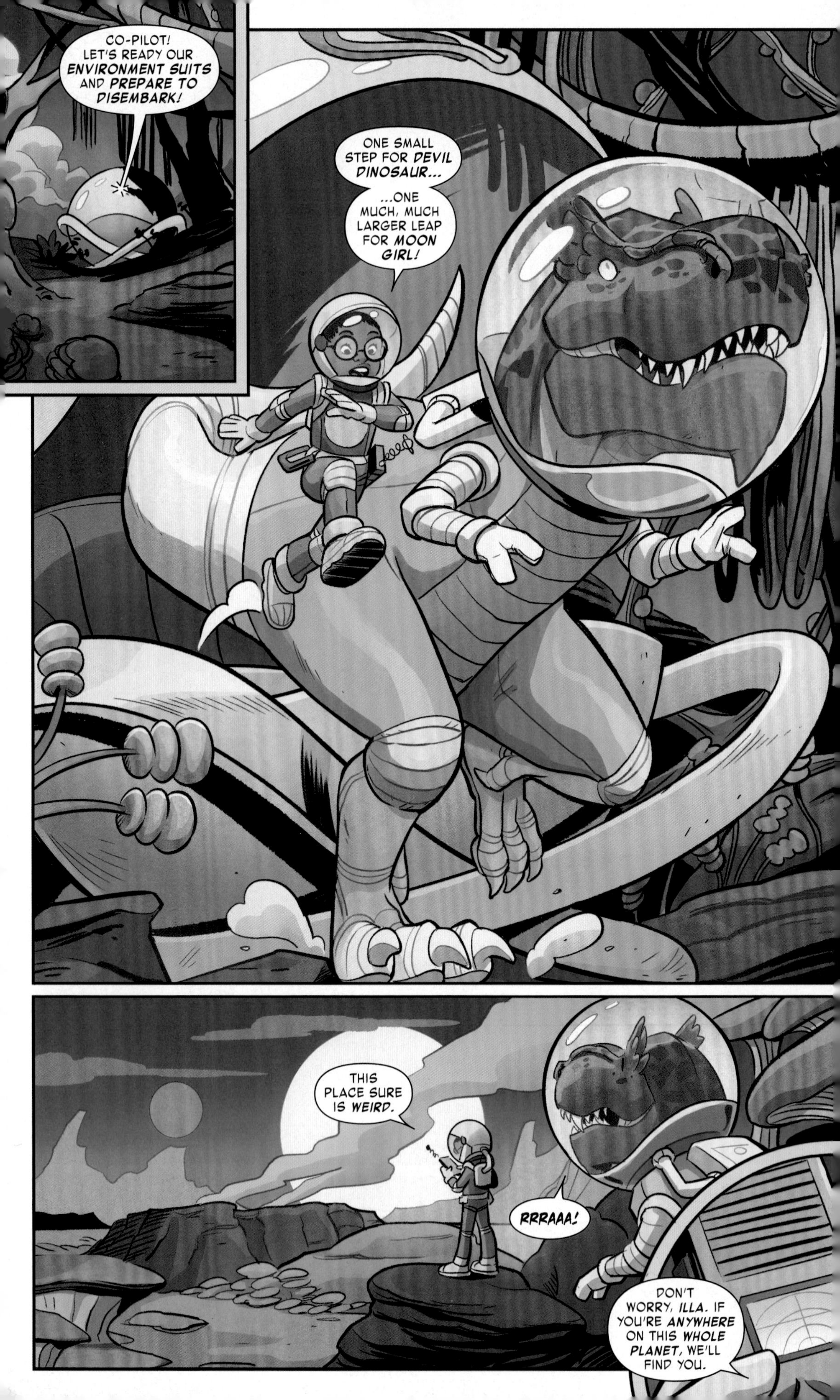
CO-PILOT! LET'S READY OUR ENVIRONMENT SUITS AND PREPARE TO DISEMBARK!
ONE SMALL STEP FOR DEVIL DINOSAUR...
...ONE MUCH, MUCH LARGER LEAP FOR MOON GIRL!
THIS PLACE SURE IS WEIRD.
RRRAAA!
DON'T WORRY, ILLA. IF YOU'RE ANYWHERE ON THIS WHOLE PLANET, WE'LL FIND YOU.

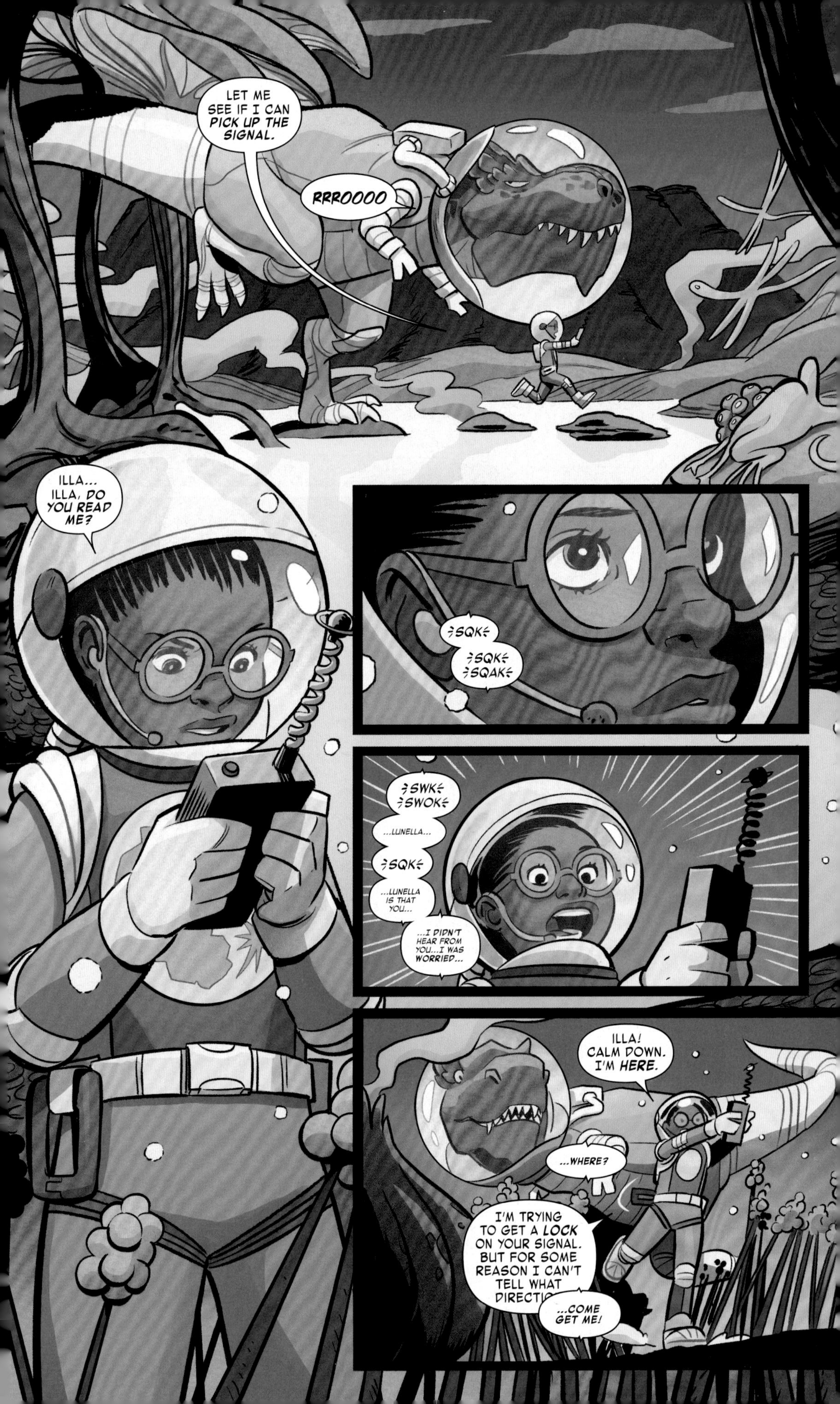
LET ME SEE IF I CAN PICK UP THE SIGNAL.
RRROOOO
ILLA... ILLA, DO YOU READ ME?
SQK
SQK SQAK
SWK SWOK
...LUNELLA...
SQK
...LUNELLA IS THAT YOU...
...I DIDN'T HEAR FROM YOU...I WAS WORRIED...
ILLA! CALM DOWN. I'M HERE.
...WHERE?
I'M TRYING TO GET A LOCK ON YOUR SIGNAL. BUT FOR SOME REASON I CAN'T TELL WHAT DIRECTIO
...COME GET ME!

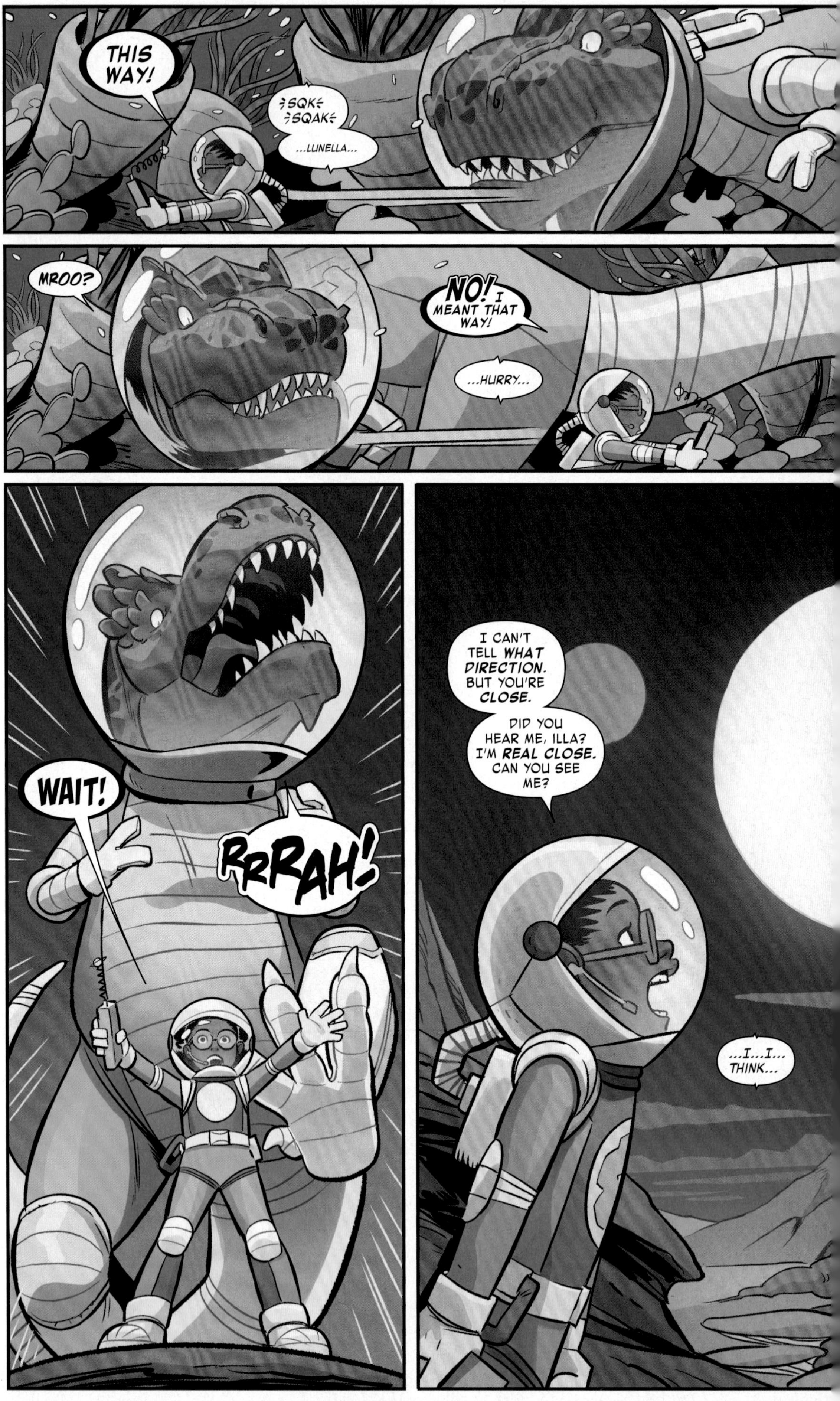
THIS WAY!
SQK SQAK
...LUNELLA...
MROO?
NO! I MEANT THAT WAY!
...HURRY...
WAIT!
RRRAH!
I CAN'T TELL WHAT DIRECTION. BUT YOU'RE CLOSE.
DID YOU HEAR ME, ILLA? I'M REAL CLOSE. CAN YOU SEE ME?
...I...I... THINK...

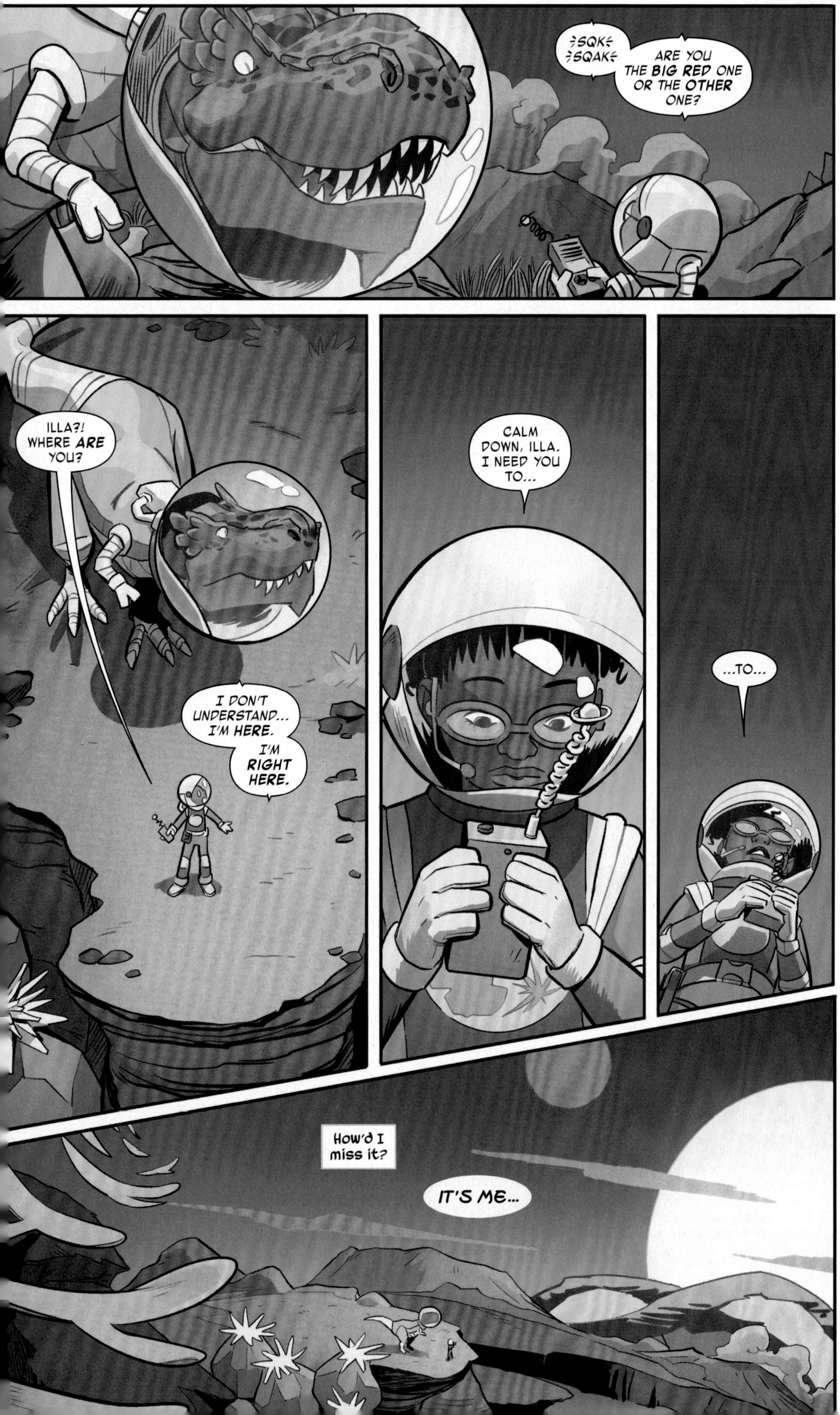

SQK SQAK
ARE YOU THE BIG RED ONE OR THE OTHER ONE?
ILLA?! WHERE ARE YOU?
I DON'T UNDERSTAND... I'M HERE.
I'M RIGHT HERE.
CALM DOWN, ILLA. I NEED YOU TO...
...TO...
How'd I miss it?
IT'S ME...

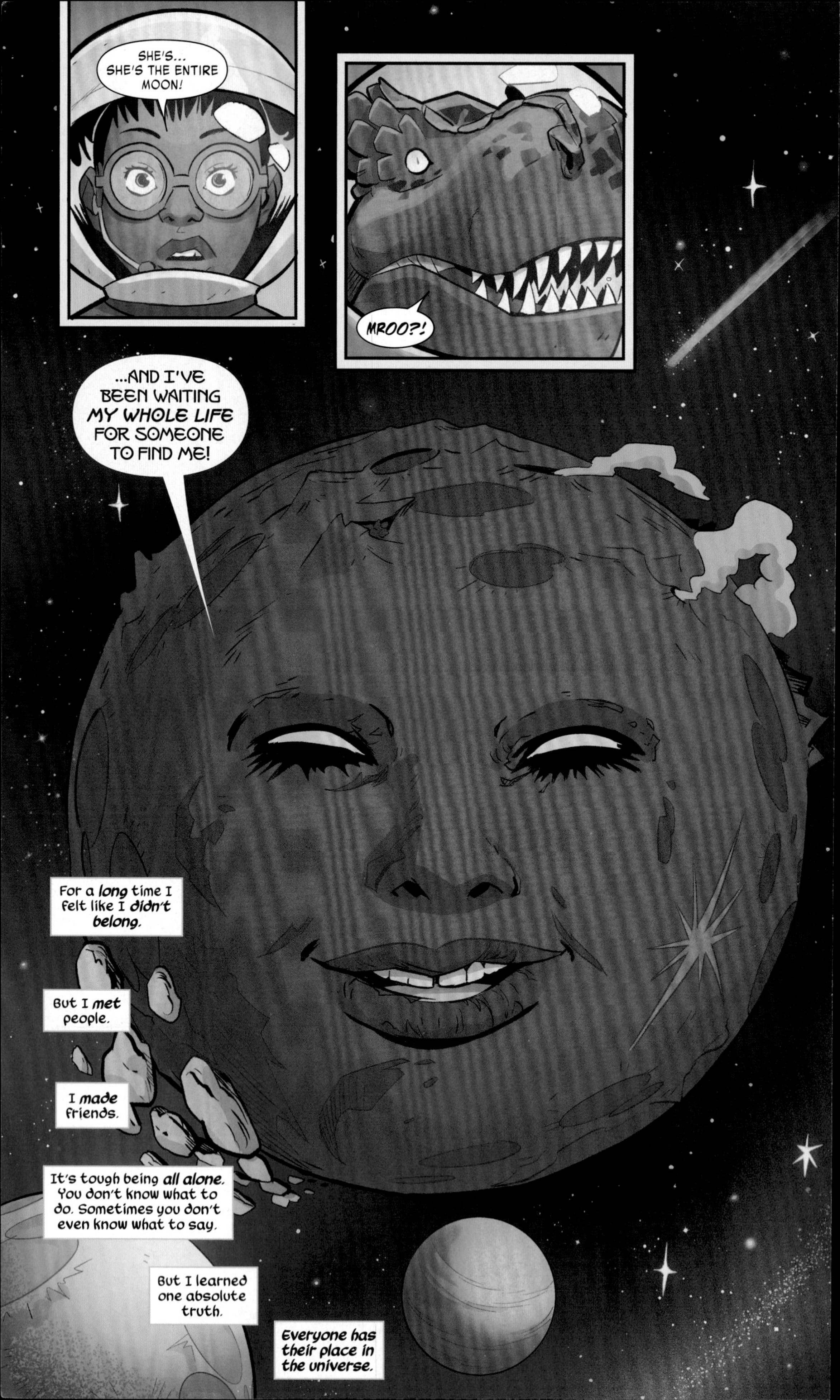

SHE'S... SHE'S THE ENTIRE MOON!
MROO?!
...AND I'VE BEEN WAITING MY WHOLE LIFE FOR SOMEONE TO FIND ME!
For a long time I felt like I didn't belong.
But I met people.
I made friends.
It's tough being all alone. You don't know what to do. Sometimes you don't even know what to say.
But I learned one absolute truth.
Everyone has their place in the universe.

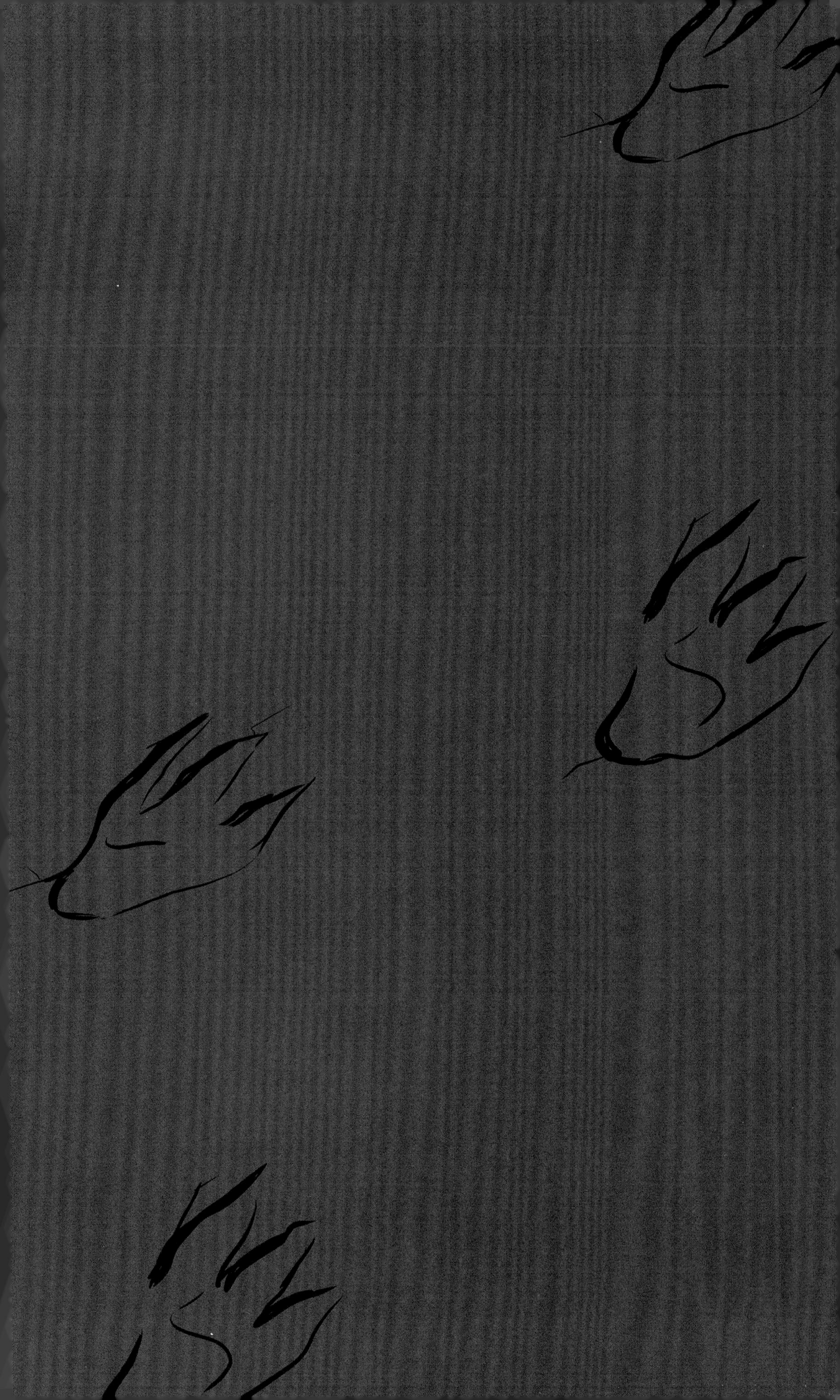

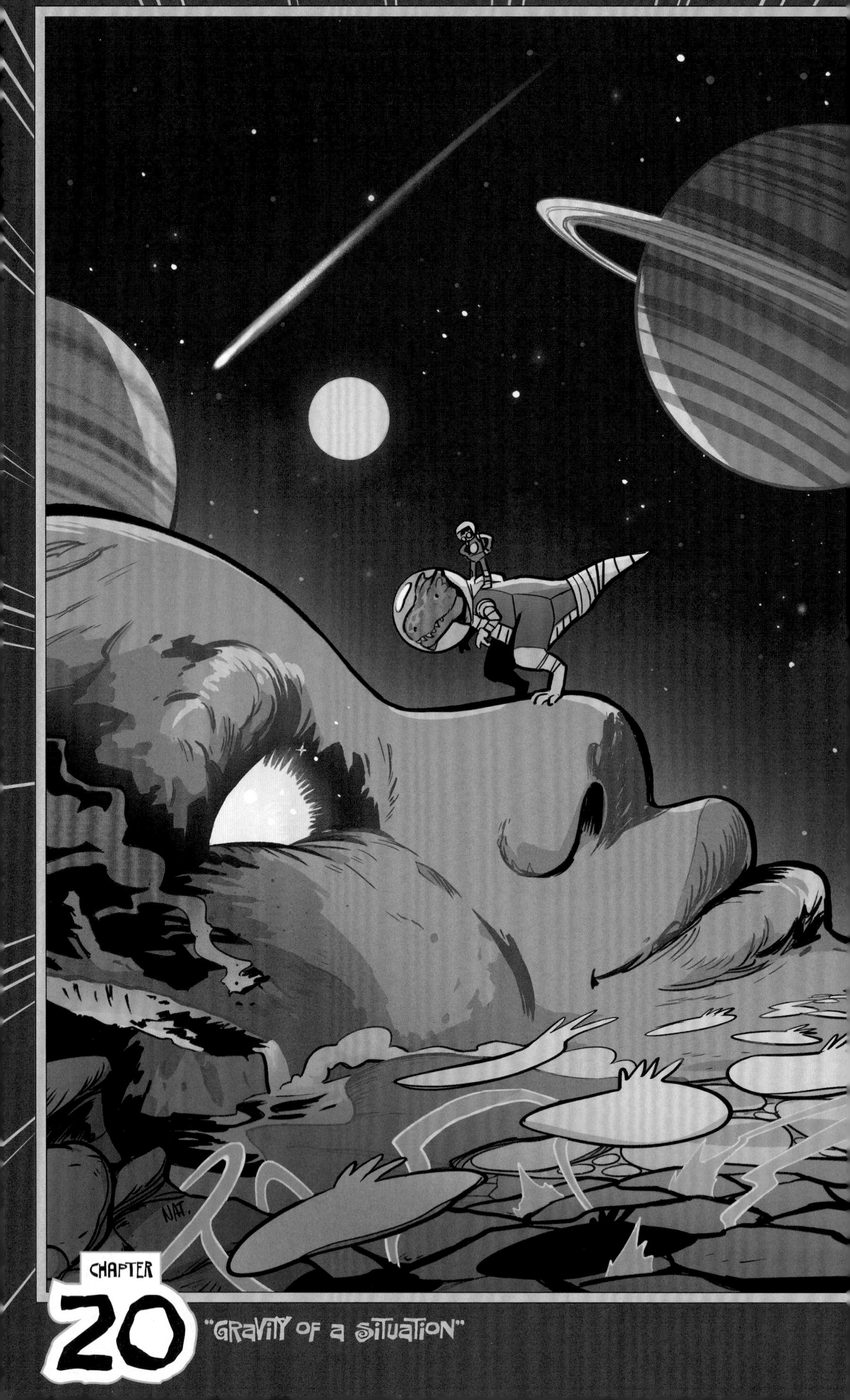

CHAPTER 20

"GRAVITY OF A SITUATION"

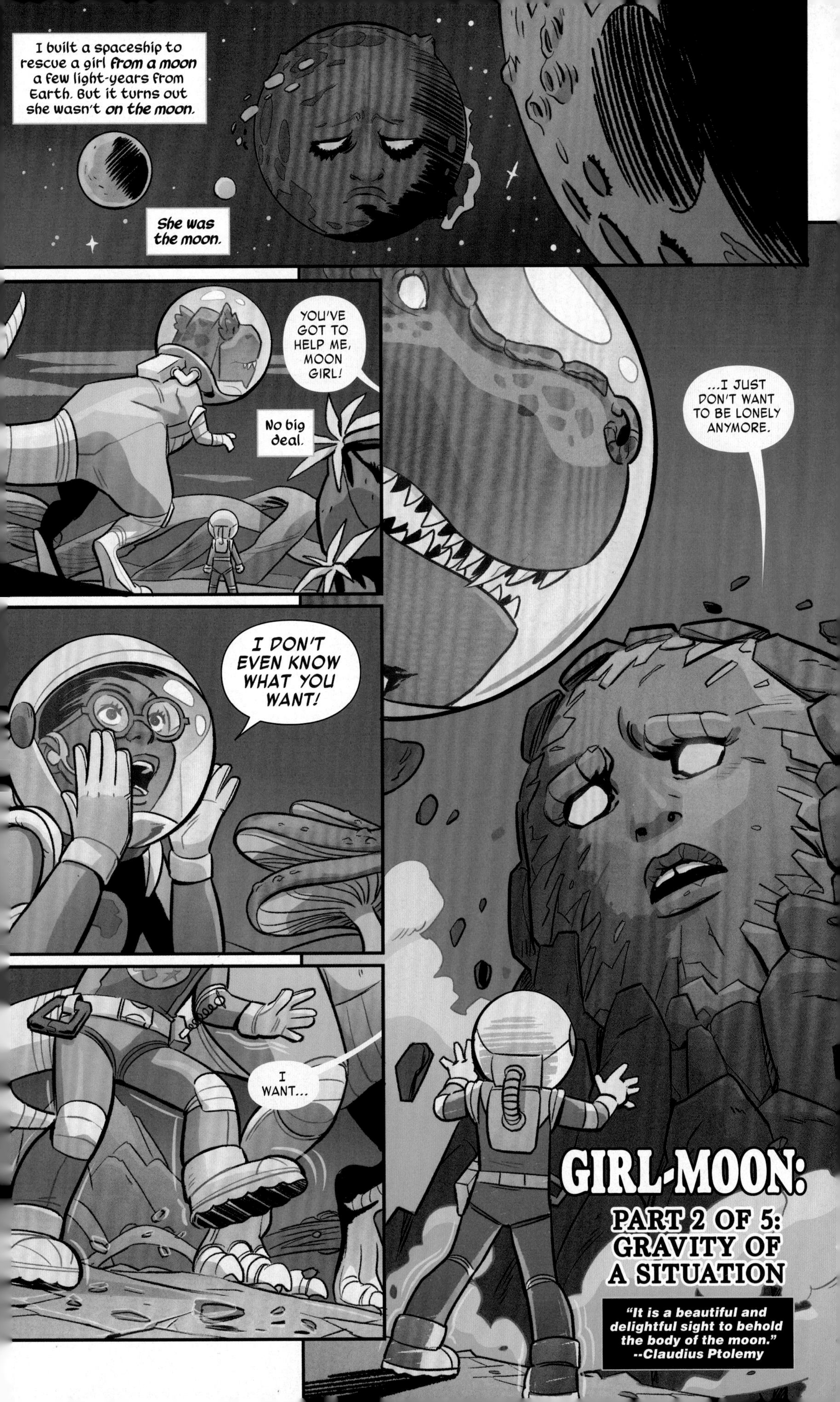

I built a spaceship to rescue a girl *from a moon* a few light-years from Earth. But it turns out she wasn't *on the moon.*
She was the moon.
YOU'VE GOT TO HELP ME, MOON GIRL!
No big deal.
I DON'T EVEN KNOW WHAT YOU WANT!
I WANT...
...I JUST DON'T WANT TO BE LONELY ANYMORE.
GIRL-MOON:
PART 2 OF 5: GRAVITY OF A SITUATION
"It is a beautiful and delightful sight to behold the body of the moon." --Claudius Ptolemy

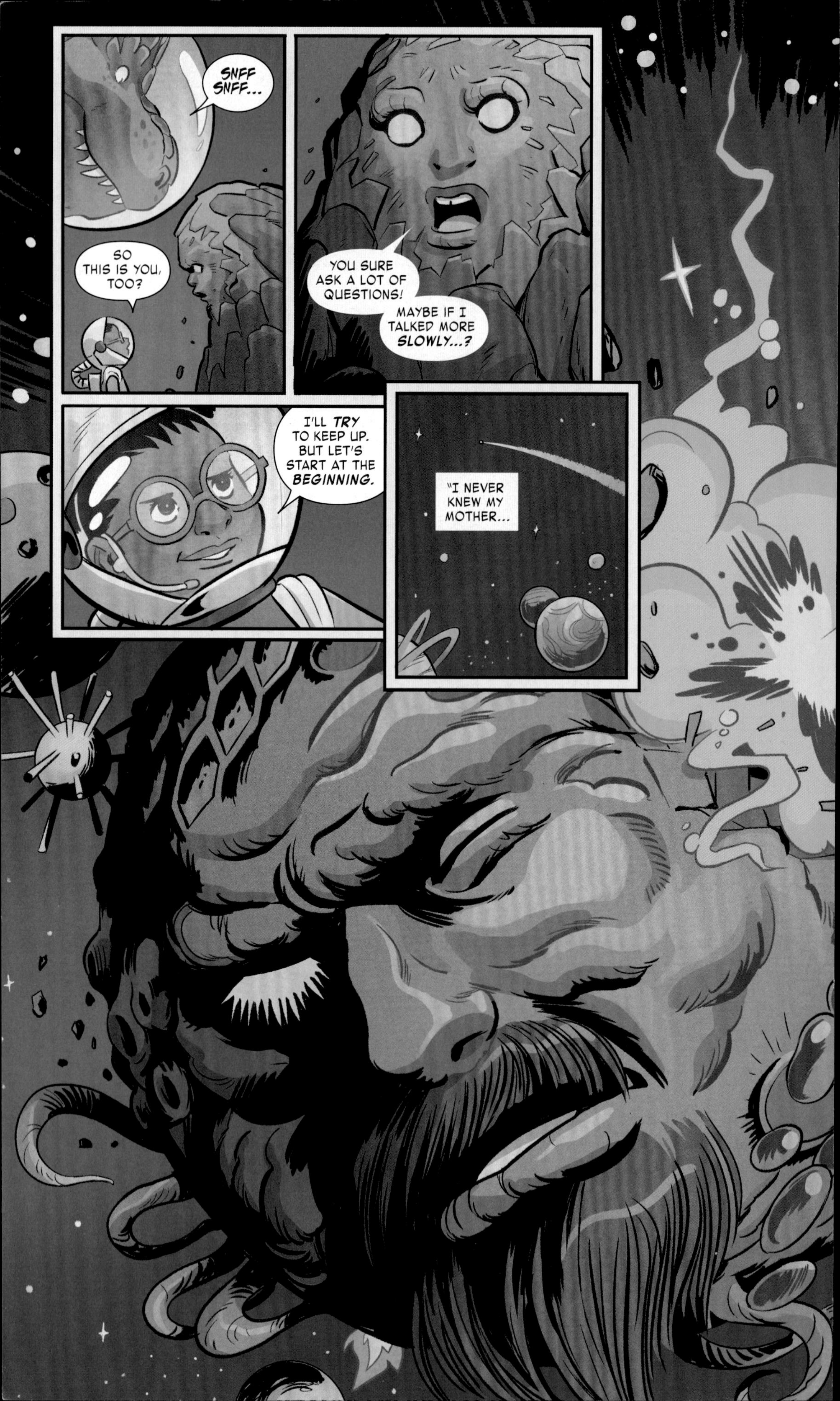
SNFF SNFF...
SO THIS IS YOU, TOO?
YOU SURE ASK A LOT OF QUESTIONS!
MAYBE IF I TALKED MORE SLOWLY...?
I'LL TRY TO KEEP UP. BUT LET'S START AT THE BEGINNING.
"I NEVER KNEW MY MOTHER...

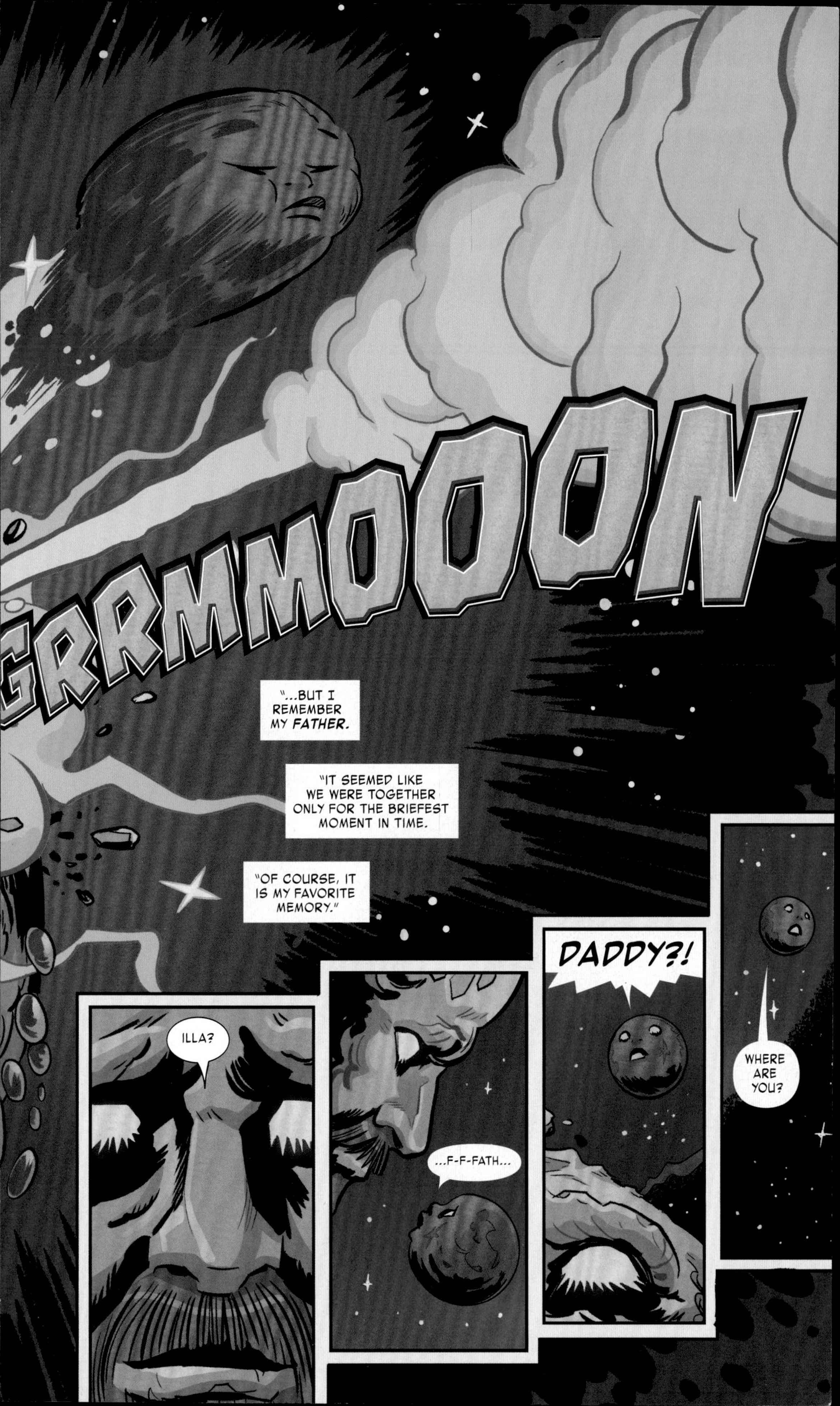
GRRMMOOON
"...BUT I REMEMBER MY FATHER.
"IT SEEMED LIKE WE WERE TOGETHER ONLY FOR THE BRIEFEST MOMENT IN TIME.
"OF COURSE, IT IS MY FAVORITE MEMORY."
ILLA?
...F-F-FATH...
DADDY?!
WHERE ARE YOU?

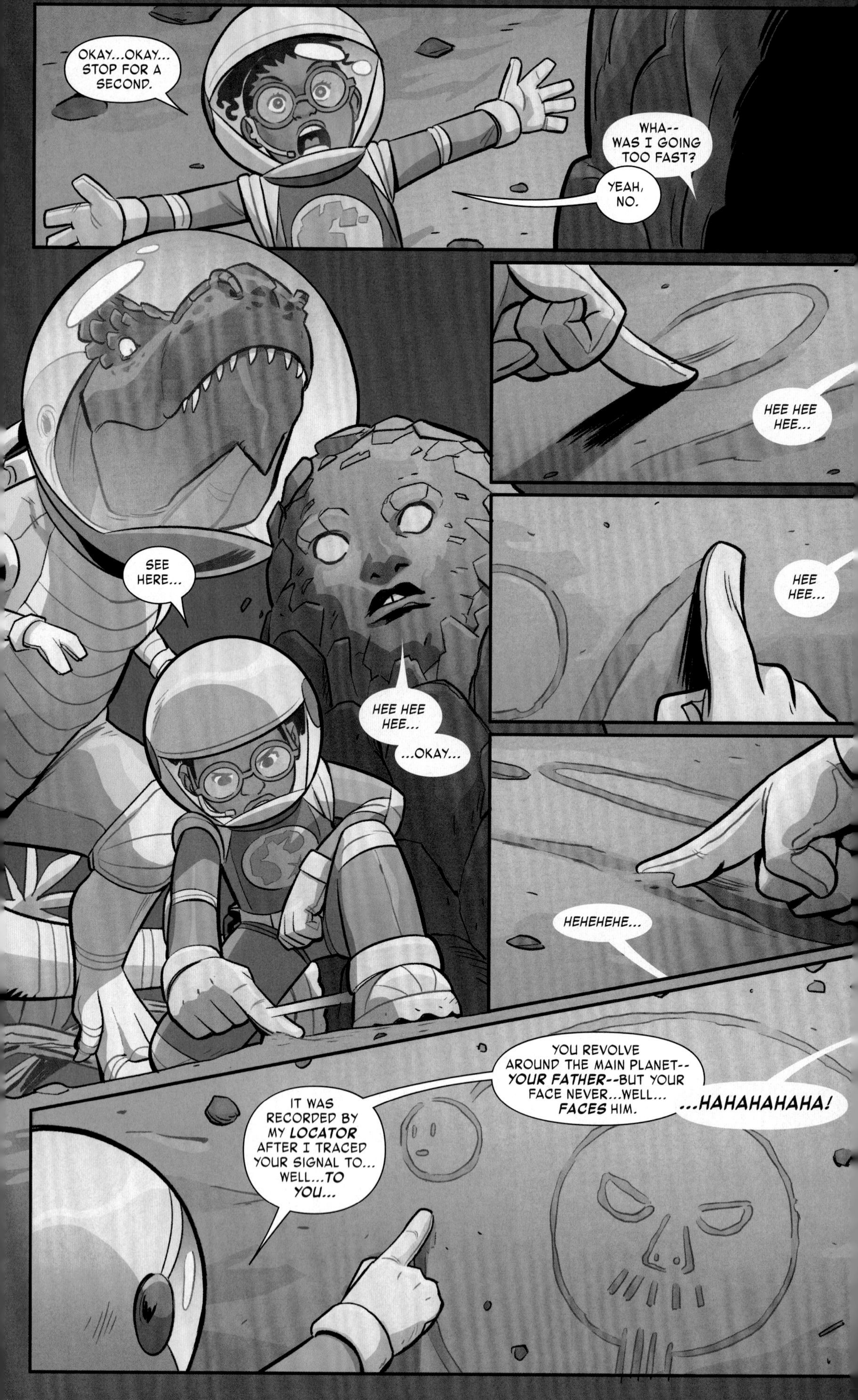
OKAY...OKAY... STOP FOR A SECOND.
WHA-- WAS I GOING TOO FAST?
YEAH, NO.
SEE HERE...
HEE HEE HEE...
...OKAY...
HEE HEE HEE...
HEE HEE...
HEHEHEHE...
IT WAS RECORDED BY MY *LOCATOR* AFTER I TRACED YOUR SIGNAL TO... WELL...*TO YOU...*
YOU REVOLVE AROUND THE MAIN PLANET-- *YOUR FATHER*--BUT YOUR FACE NEVER...WELL... *FACES* HIM.
...HAHAHAHAHA!

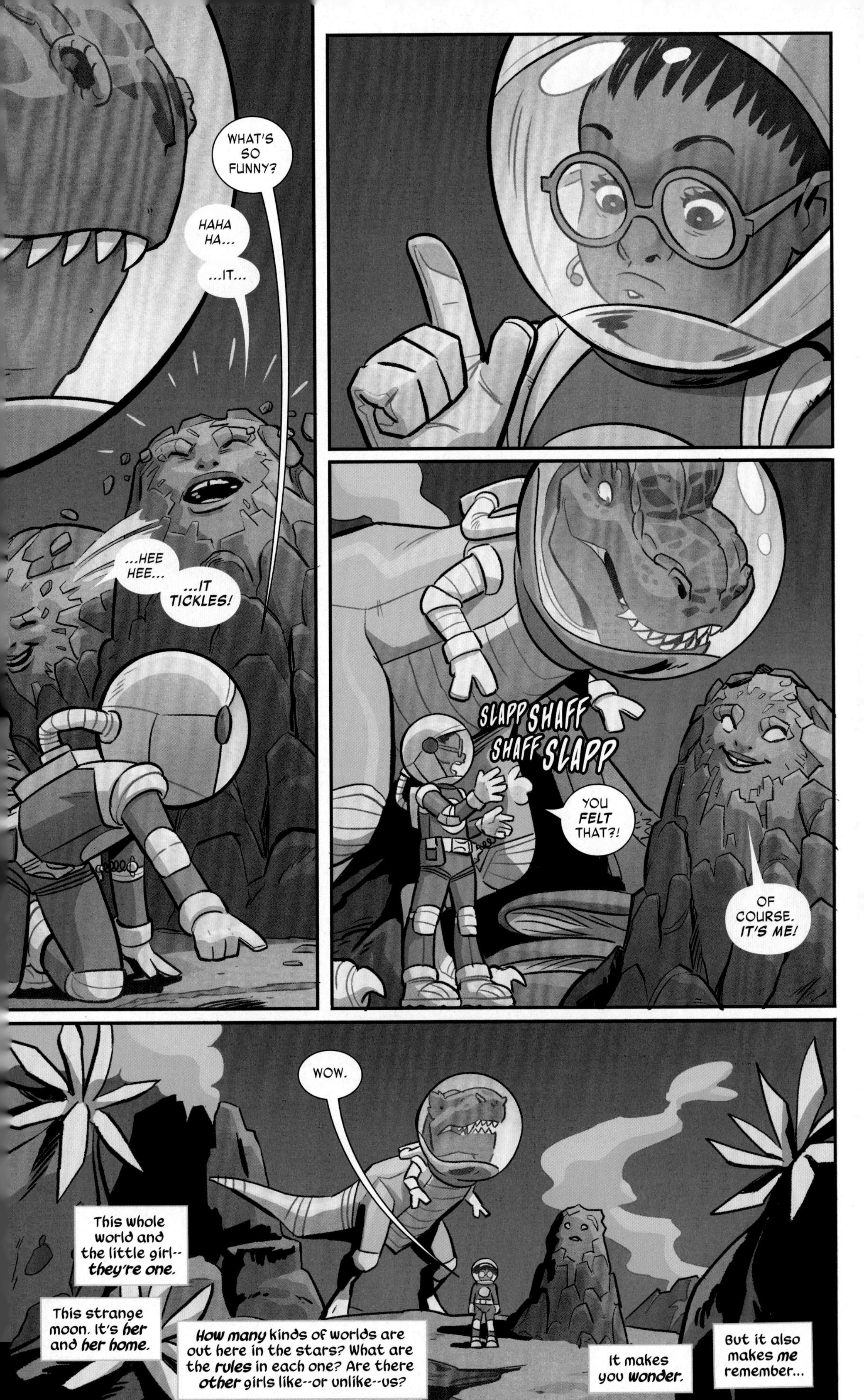

WHAT'S SO FUNNY?
HAHA HA...
...IT...
...HEE HEE...
...IT TICKLES!
SLAPP SHAFF SHAFF SLAPP
YOU FELT THAT?!
OF COURSE. IT'S ME!
WOW.
This whole world and the little girl-- they're one.
This strange moon. It's her and her home.
How many kinds of worlds are out here in the stars? What are the rules in each one? Are there other girls like--or unlike--us?
It makes you wonder.
But it also makes me remember...

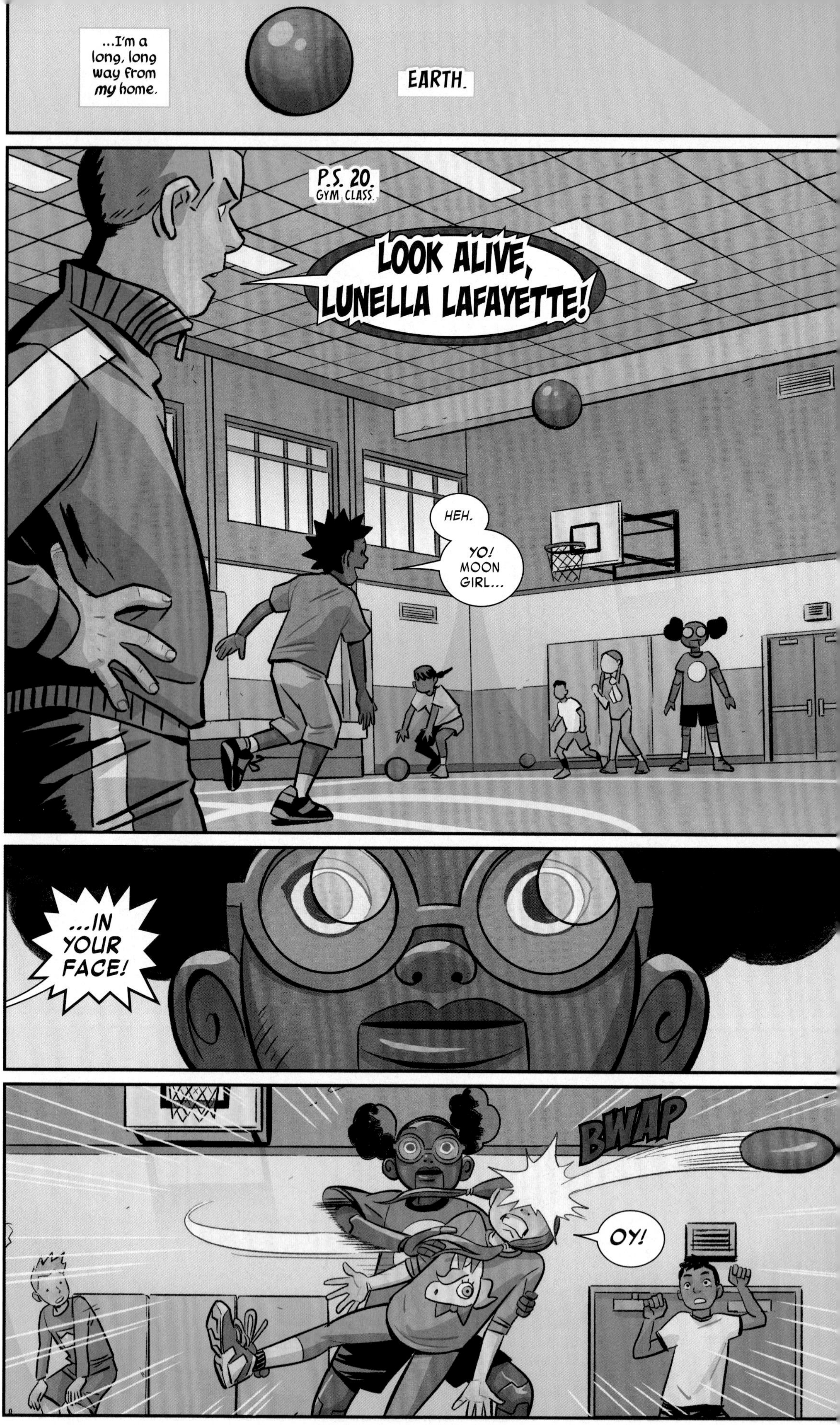
...I'm a long, long way from *my* home.
EARTH.
P.S. 20. GYM CLASS.
LOOK ALIVE, LUNELLA LAFAYETTE!
HEH.
YO! MOON GIRL...
...IN YOUR FACE!
BWAP
OY!

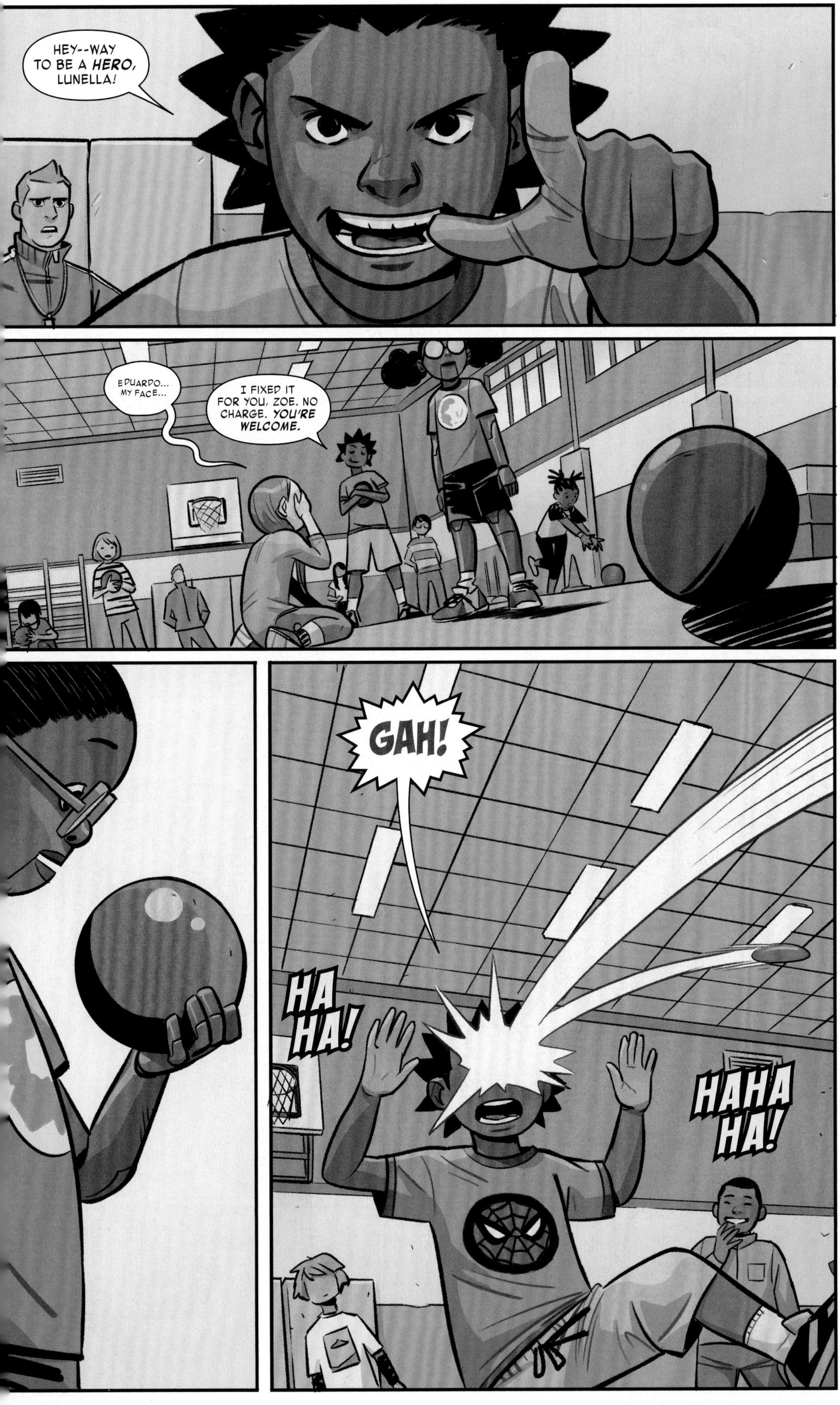
HEY--WAY TO BE A *HERO,* LUNELLA!
EDUARDO... MY FACE...
I FIXED IT FOR YOU, ZOE. NO CHARGE. *YOU'RE WELCOME.*
GAH!
HA HA!
HAHA HA!

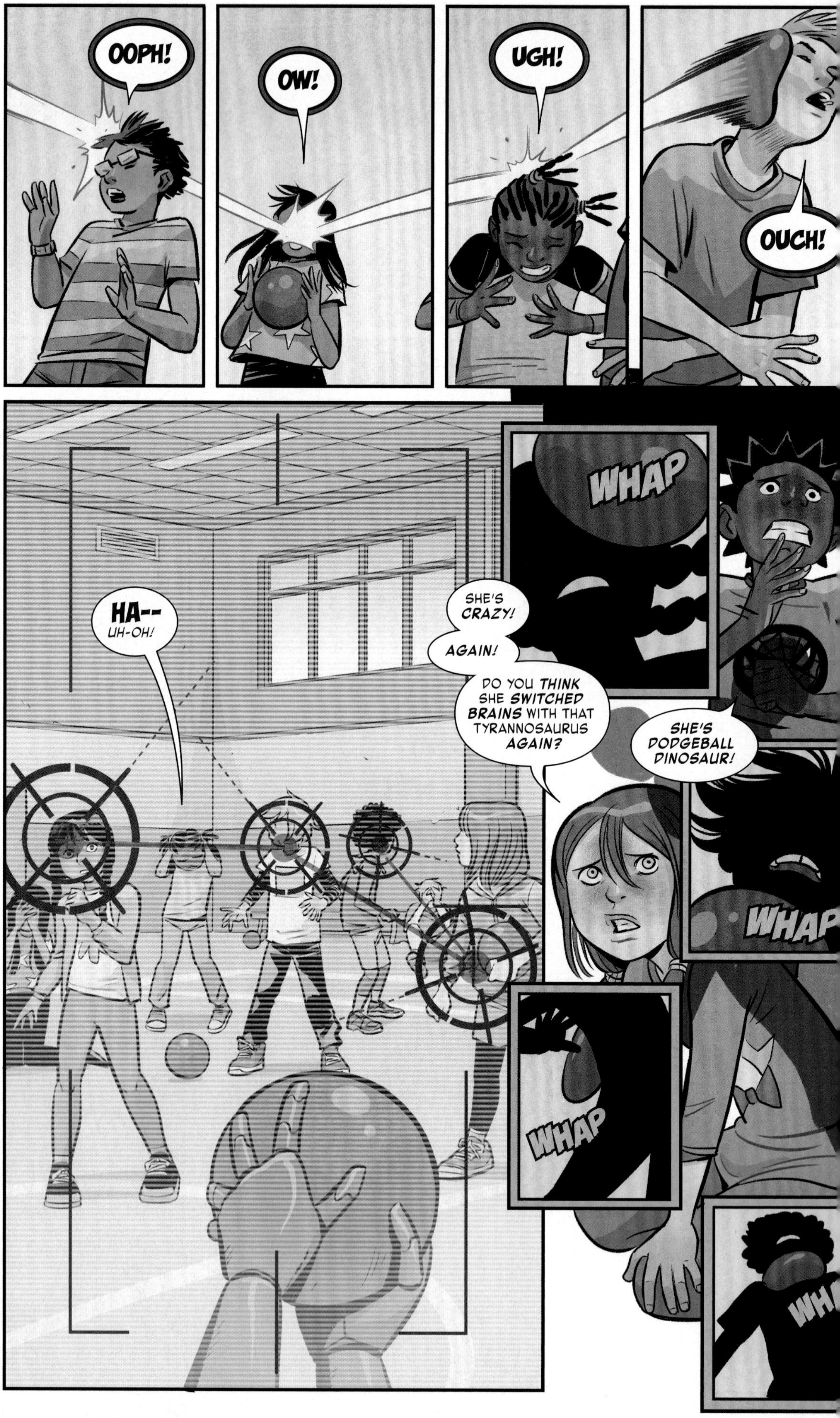
OOPH!
OW!
UGH!
OUCH!
HA-- UH-OH!
WHAP
SHE'S CRAZY!
AGAIN!
DO YOU THINK SHE SWITCHED BRAINS WITH THAT TYRANNOSAURUS AGAIN?
SHE'S DODGEBALL DINOSAUR!
WHAP
WHAP

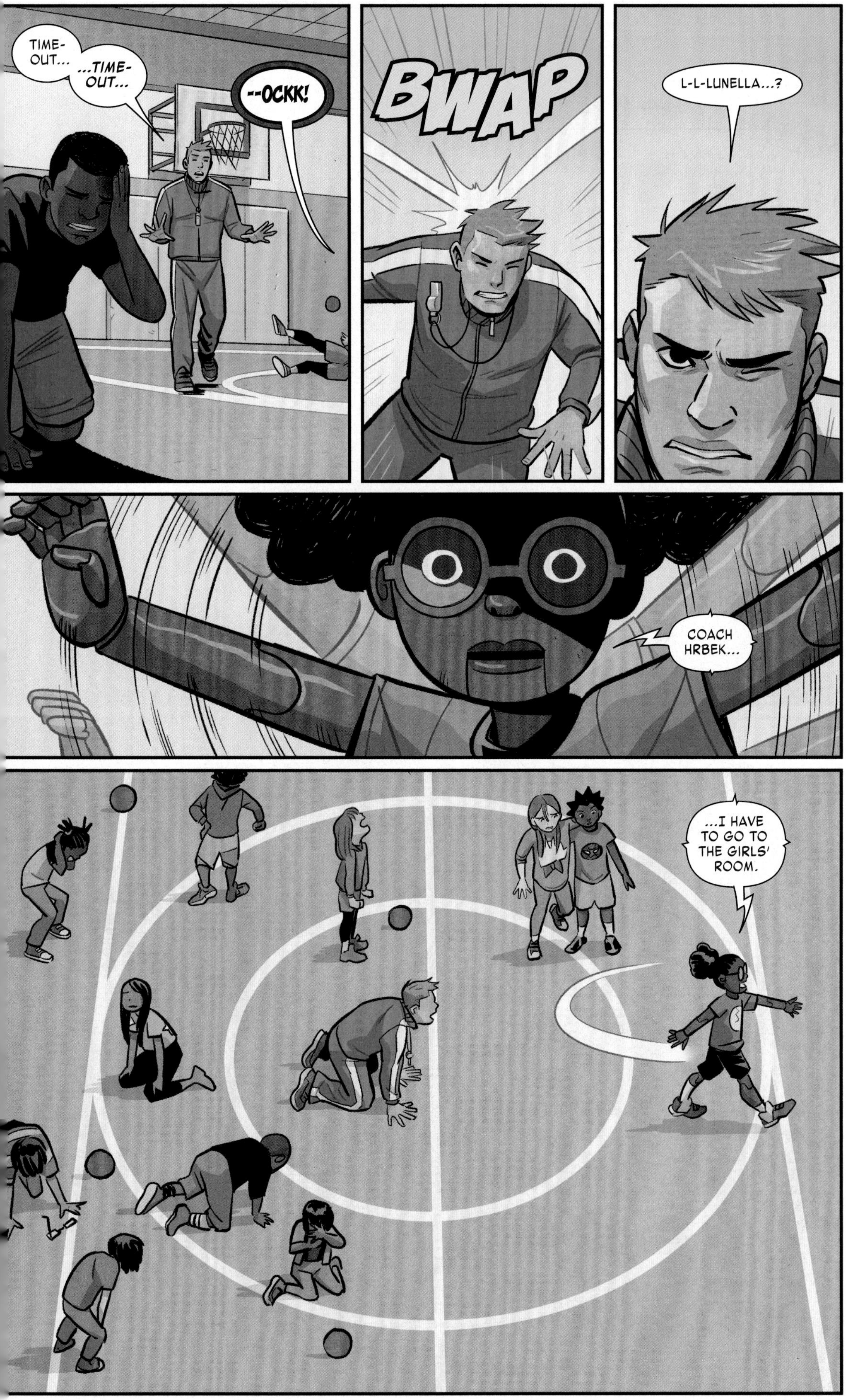

TIME-OUT...
...TIME-OUT...
--OCKK!
BWAP
L-L-LUNELLA...?
COACH HRBEK...
...I HAVE TO GO TO THE GIRLS' ROOM.

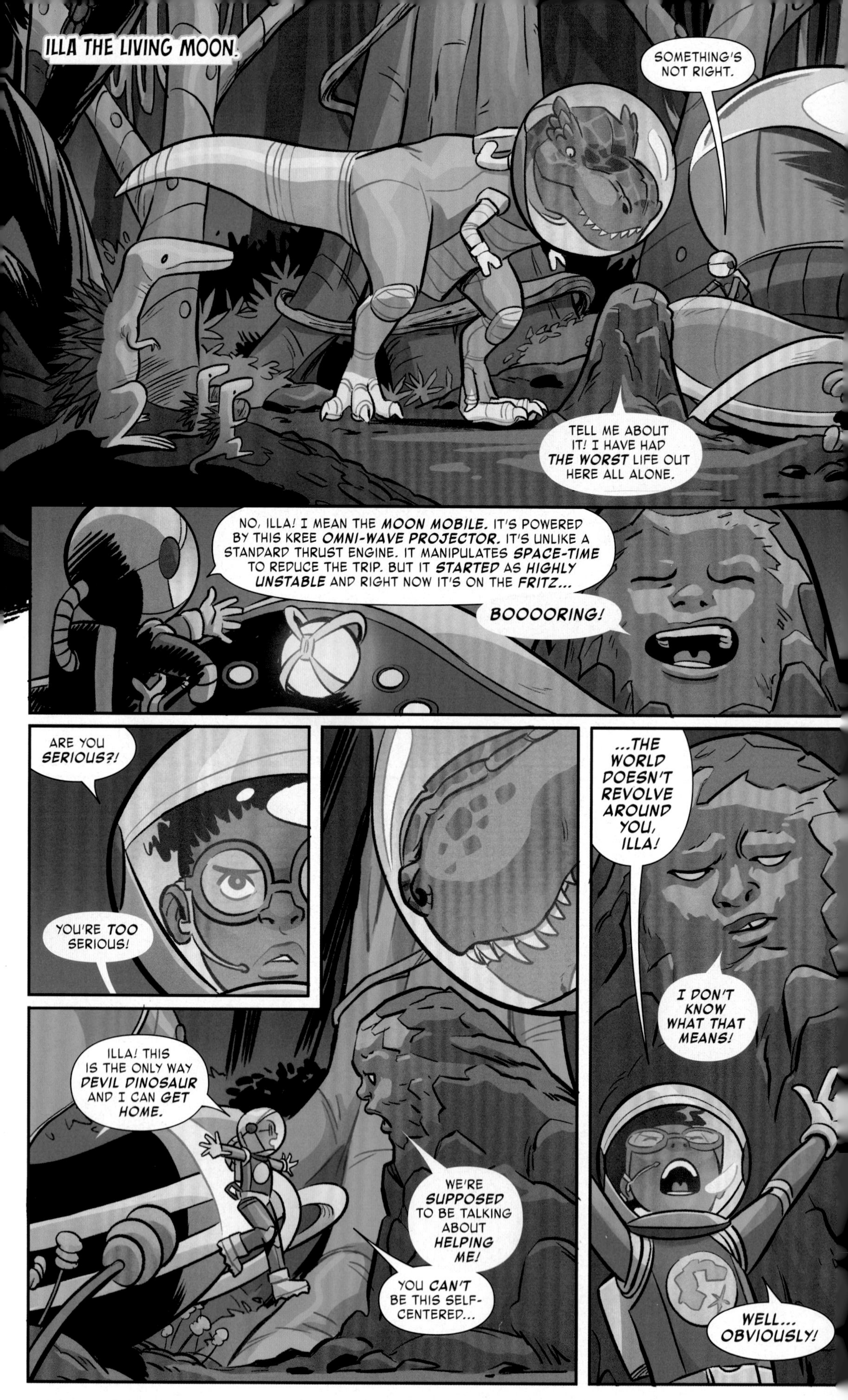
ILLA THE LIVING MOON.
SOMETHING'S NOT RIGHT.
TELL ME ABOUT IT! I HAVE HAD THE WORST LIFE OUT HERE ALL ALONE.
NO, ILLA! I MEAN THE MOON MOBILE. IT'S POWERED BY THIS KREE OMNI-WAVE PROJECTOR. IT'S UNLIKE A STANDARD THRUST ENGINE. IT MANIPULATES SPACE-TIME TO REDUCE THE TRIP. BUT IT STARTED AS HIGHLY UNSTABLE AND RIGHT NOW IT'S ON THE FRITZ...
BOOOORING!
ARE YOU SERIOUS?!
YOU'RE TOO SERIOUS!
ILLA! THIS IS THE ONLY WAY DEVIL DINOSAUR AND I CAN GET HOME.
WE'RE SUPPOSED TO BE TALKING ABOUT HELPING ME!
YOU CAN'T BE THIS SELF-CENTERED...
...THE WORLD DOESN'T REVOLVE AROUND YOU, ILLA!
I DON'T KNOW WHAT THAT MEANS!
WELL... OBVIOUSLY!

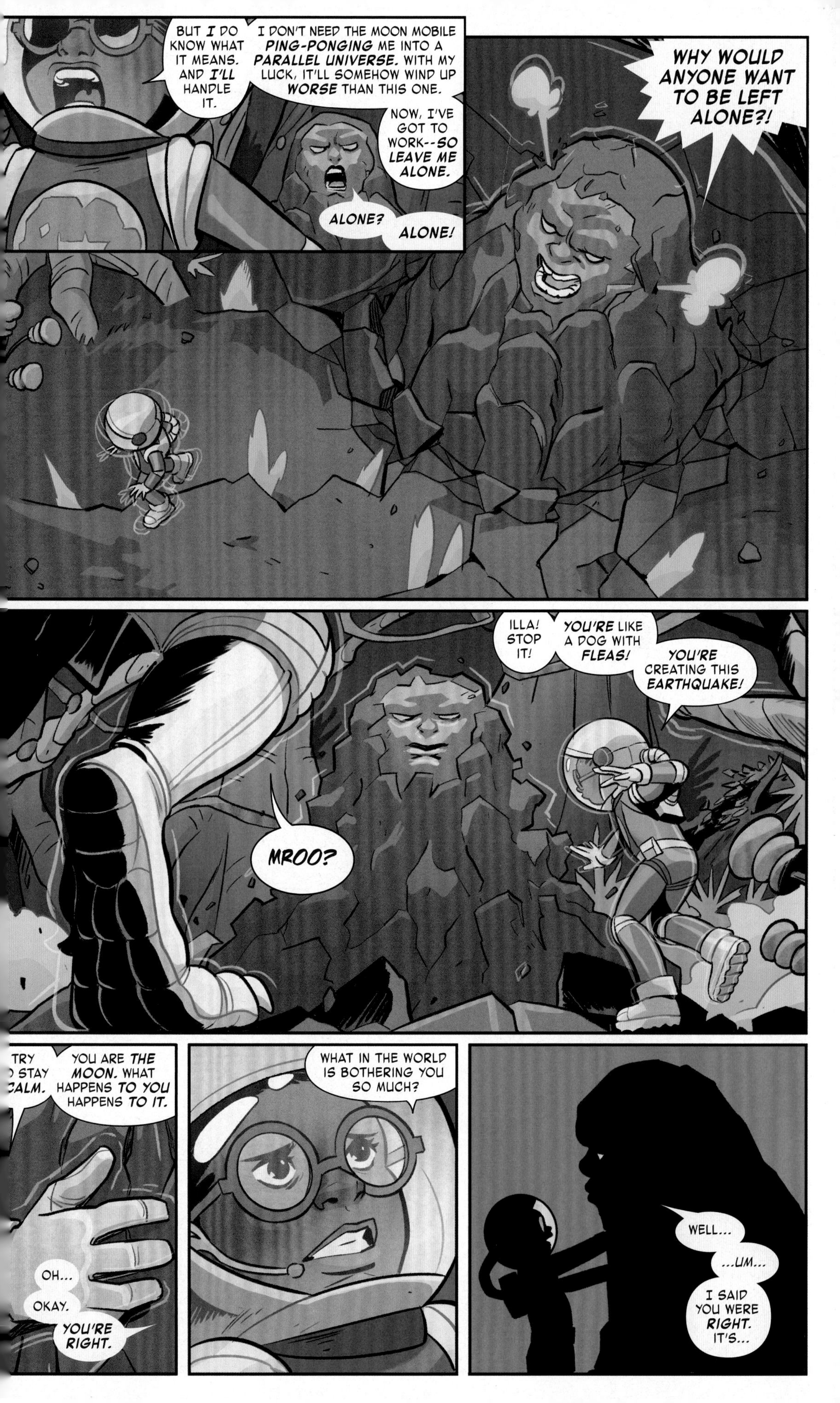
BUT I DO KNOW WHAT IT MEANS. AND I'LL HANDLE IT.
I DON'T NEED THE MOON MOBILE PING-PONGING ME INTO A PARALLEL UNIVERSE. WITH MY LUCK, IT'LL SOMEHOW WIND UP WORSE THAN THIS ONE.
NOW, I'VE GOT TO WORK--SO LEAVE ME ALONE.
ALONE?
ALONE!
WHY WOULD ANYONE WANT TO BE LEFT ALONE?!
ILLA! STOP IT!
YOU'RE LIKE A DOG WITH FLEAS!
YOU'RE CREATING THIS EARTHQUAKE!
MROO?
TRY STAY CALM.
YOU ARE THE MOON. WHAT HAPPENS TO YOU HAPPENS TO IT.
OH...
OKAY.
YOU'RE RIGHT.
WHAT IN THE WORLD IS BOTHERING YOU SO MUCH?
WELL...
...UM...
I SAID YOU WERE RIGHT. IT'S...

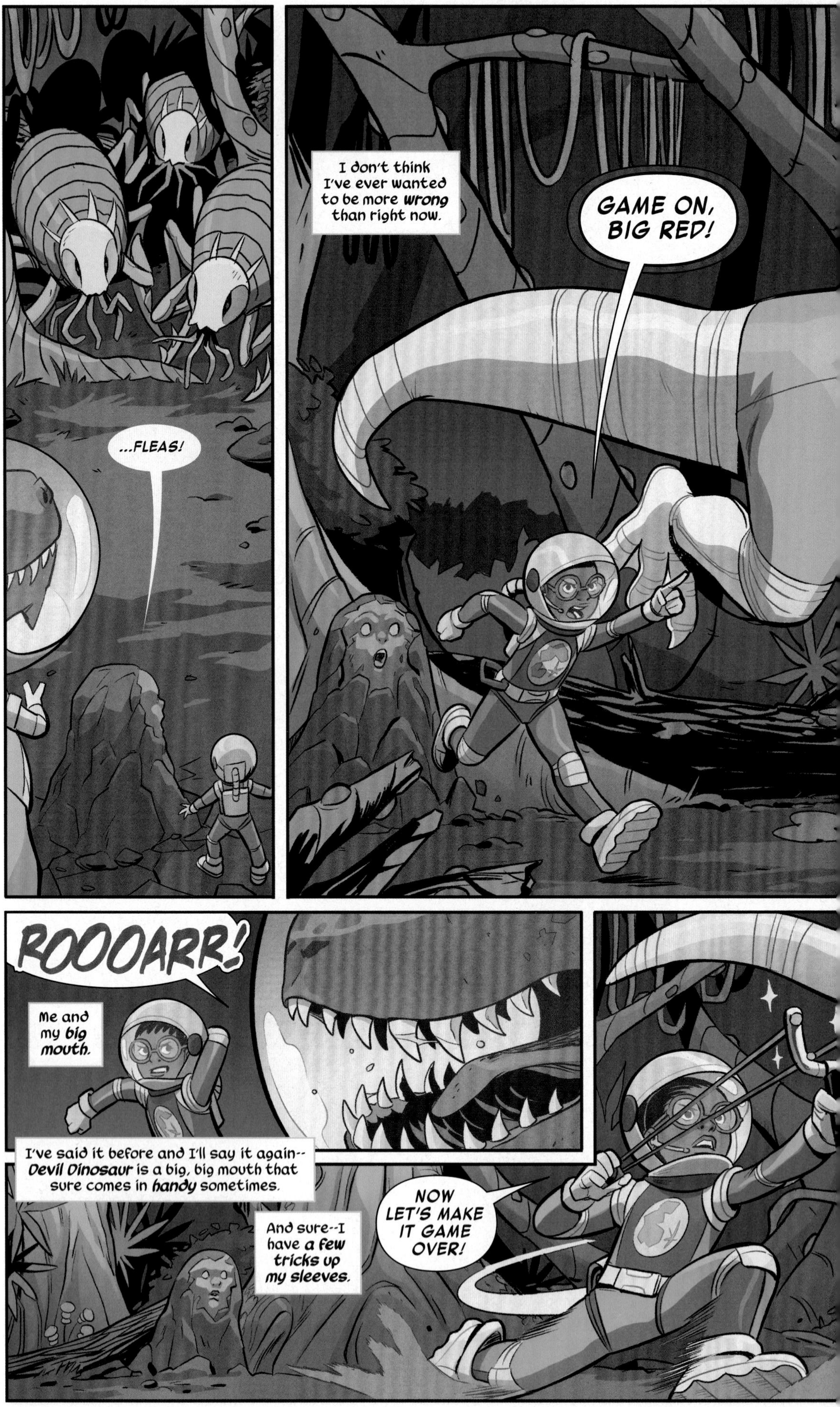
...FLEAS!
I don't think I've ever wanted to be more *wrong* than right now.
GAME ON, BIG RED!
ROOOARR!
Me and my *big mouth.*
I've said it before and I'll say it again-- *Devil Dinosaur* is a big, big mouth that sure comes in *handy* sometimes.
And sure--I have *a few tricks up my sleeves.*
NOW LET'S MAKE IT GAME OVER!

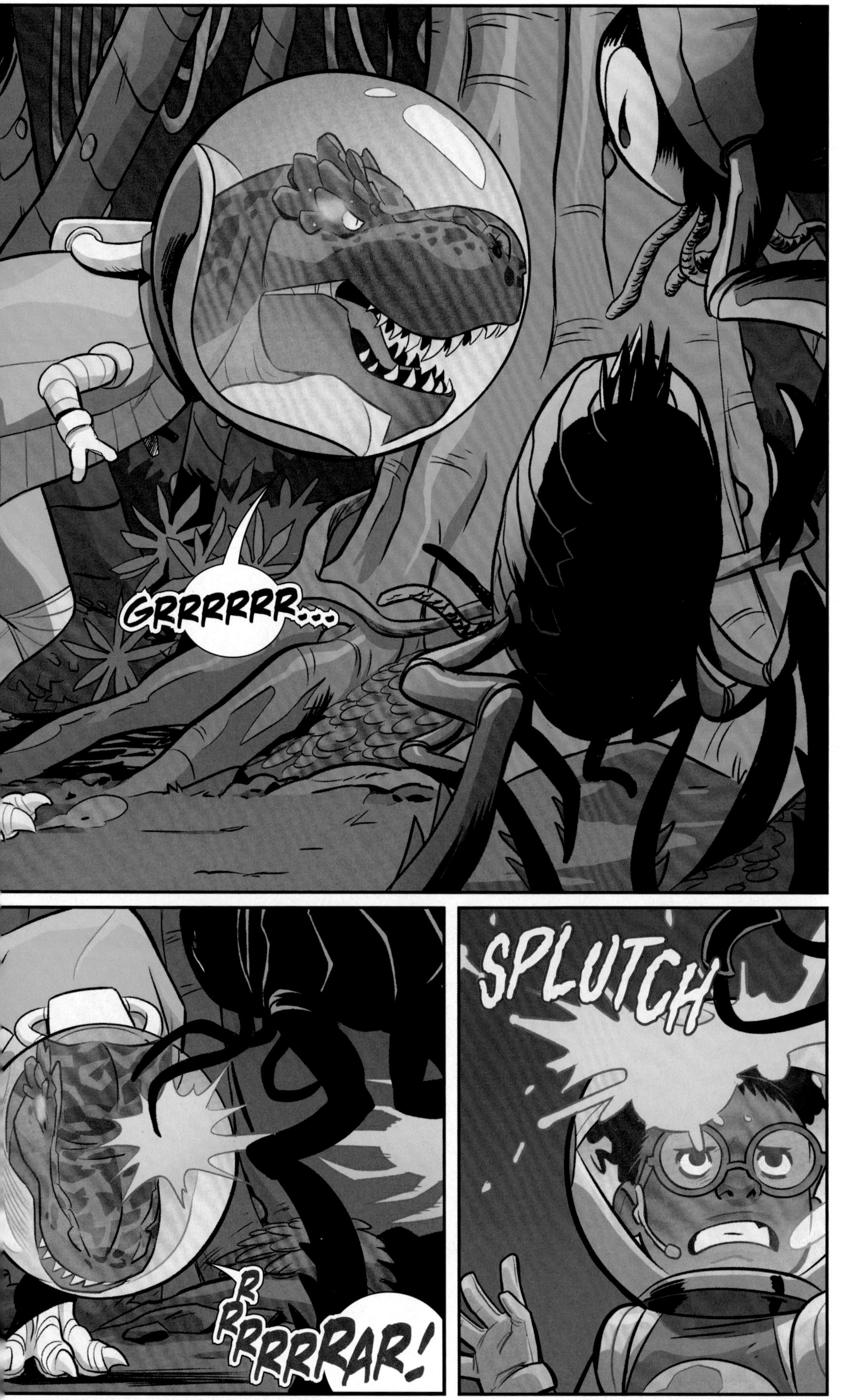

GRRRRRR...
RRRRRRRAR!
SPLUTCH

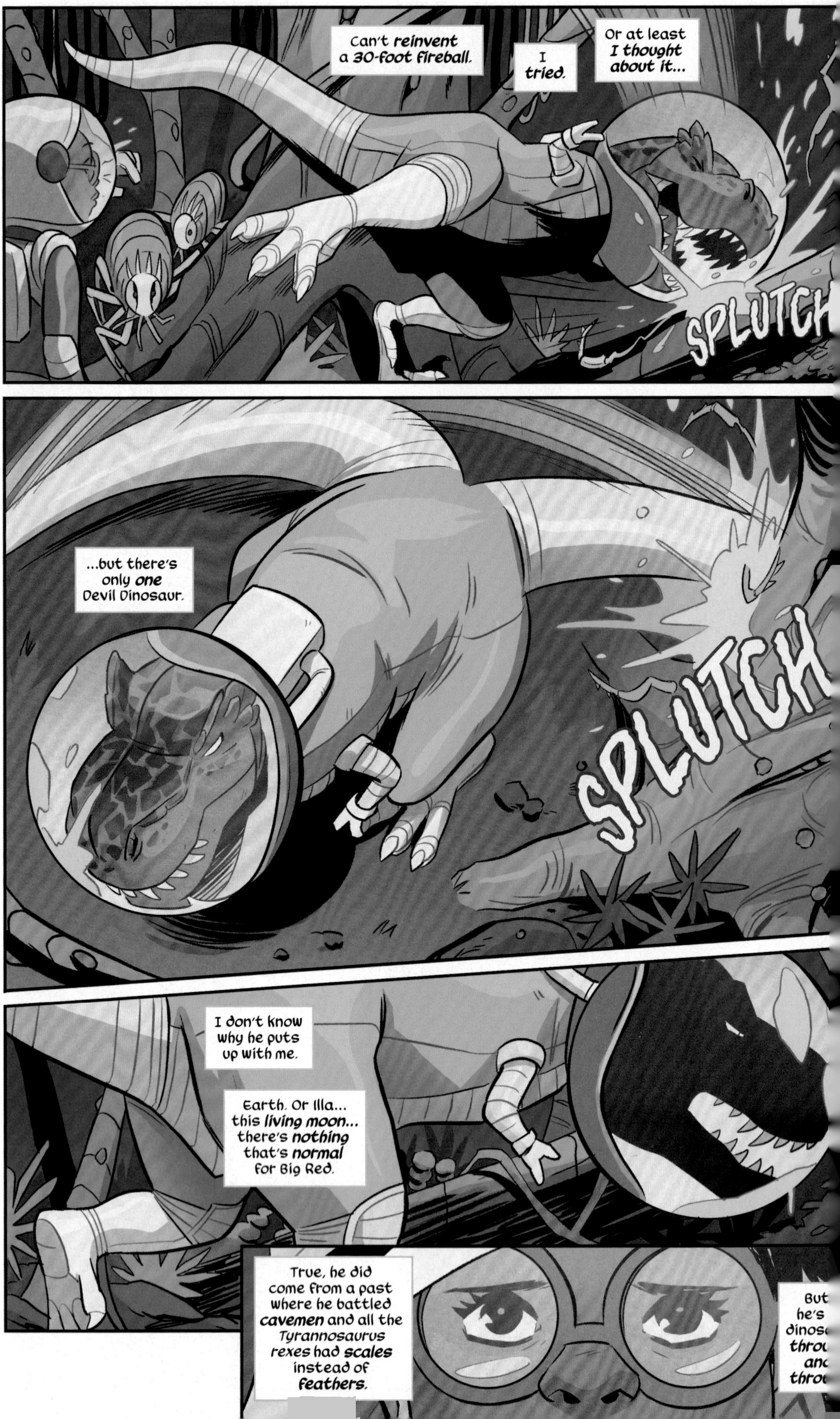
Can't reinvent a 30-foot fireball.
I tried.
Or at least I thought about it...
SPLUTCH
...but there's only one Devil Dinosaur.
SPLUTCH
I don't know why he puts up with me.
Earth. Or Illa... this living moon... there's nothing that's normal for Big Red.
True, he did come from a past where he battled cavemen and all the Tyrannosaurus rexes had scales instead of feathers.
But he's

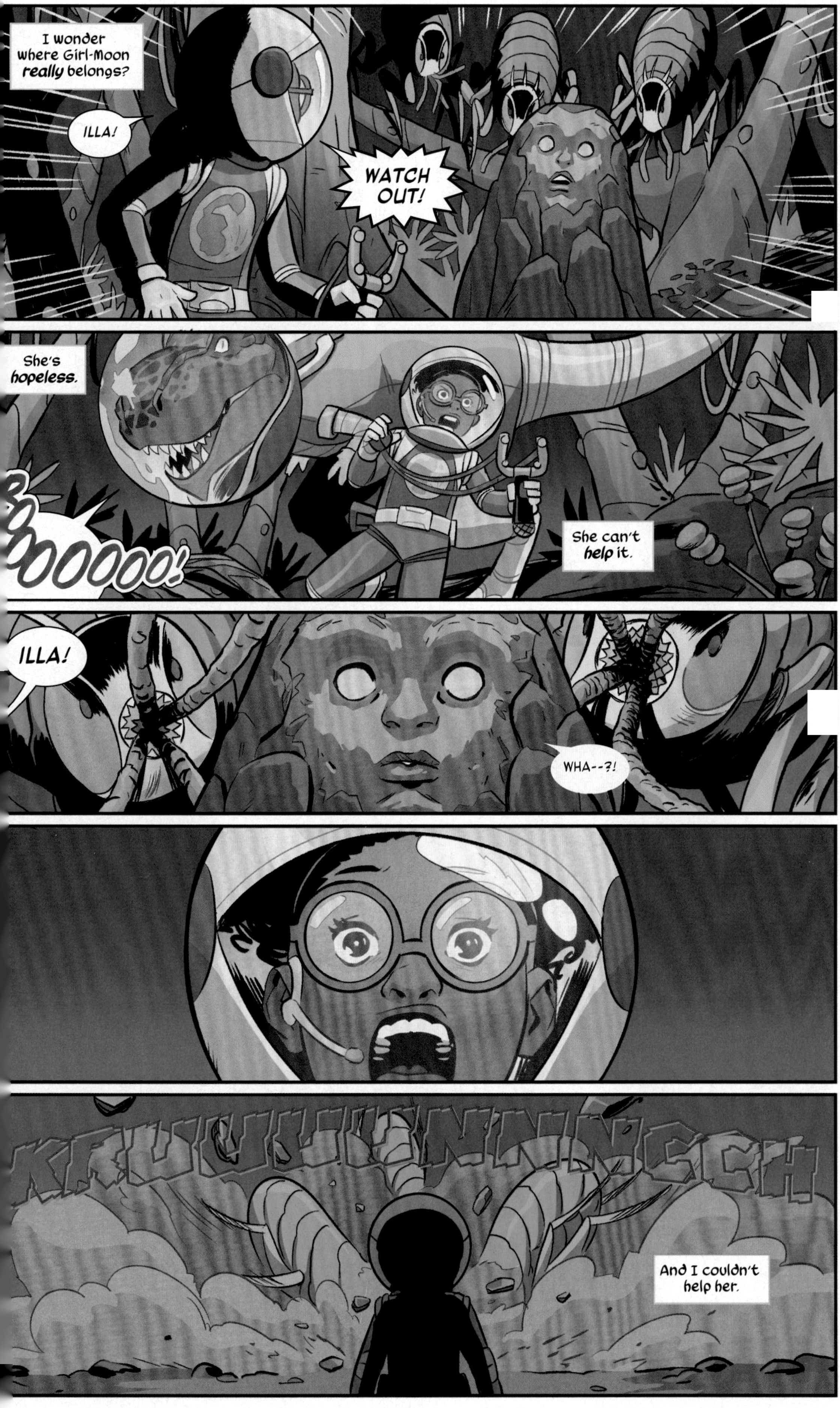
I wonder where Girl-Moon *really* belongs?
ILLA!
WATCH OUT!
She's *hopeless.*
ROOOOOOO!
She can't *help* it.
ILLA!
WHA--?!
KRUUUUNNNNCCH
And I couldn't help her.

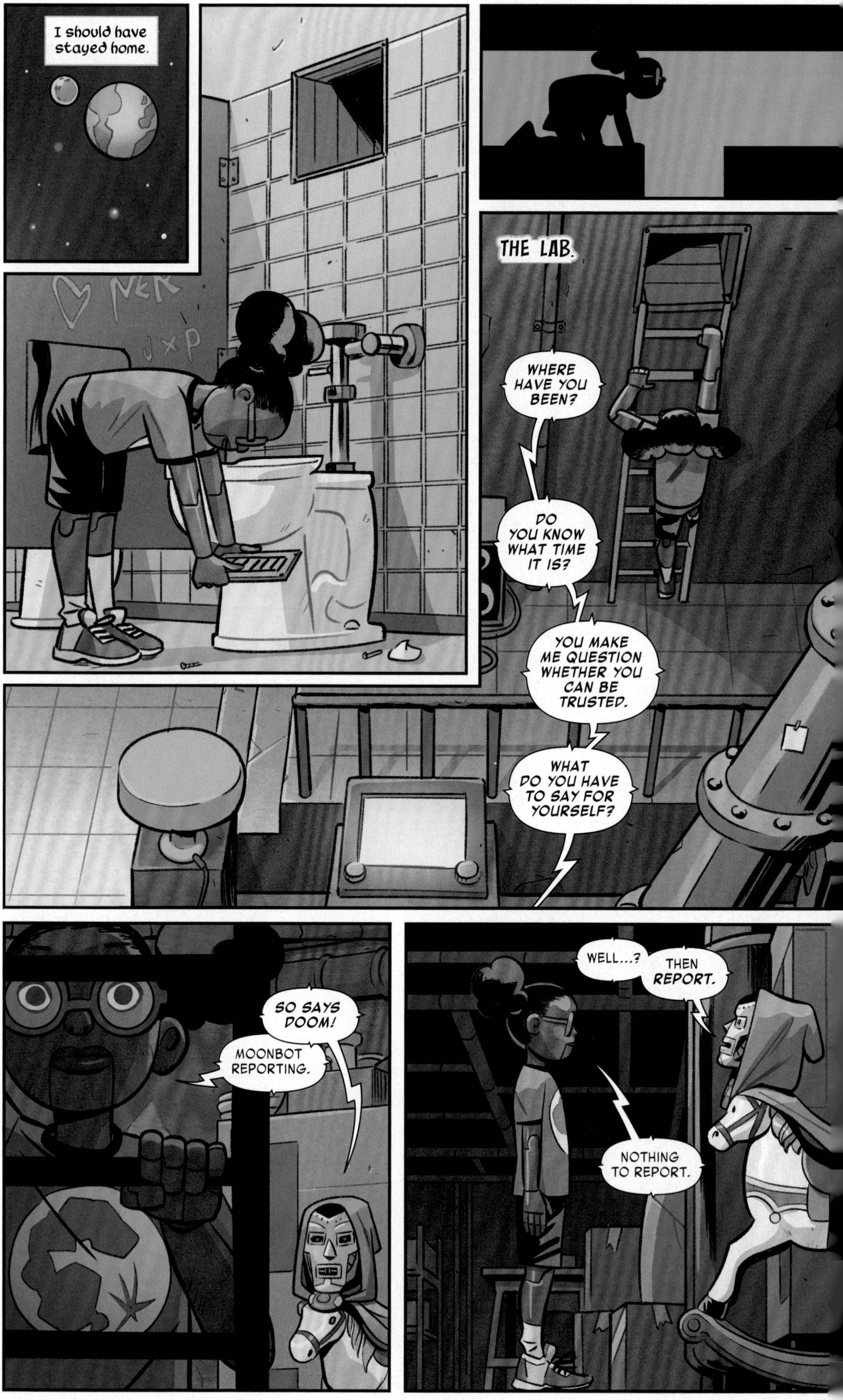
I should have stayed home.
NER
J x P
THE LAB.
WHERE HAVE YOU BEEN?
DO YOU KNOW WHAT TIME IT IS?
YOU MAKE ME QUESTION WHETHER YOU CAN BE TRUSTED.
WHAT DO YOU HAVE TO SAY FOR YOURSELF?
MOONBOT REPORTING.
SO SAYS DOOM!
WELL...?
THEN REPORT.
NOTHING TO REPORT.

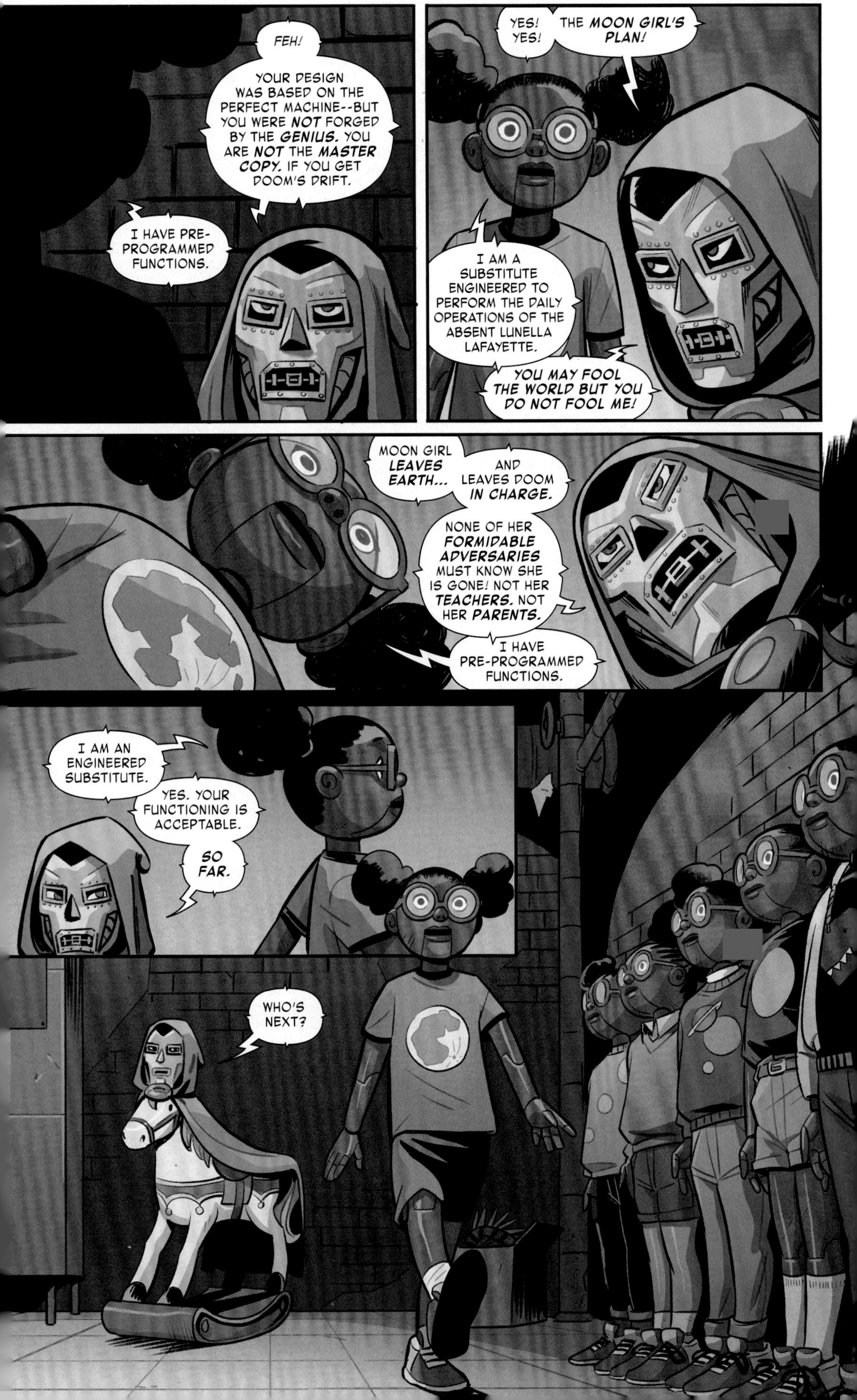

FEH!
YOUR DESIGN WAS BASED ON THE PERFECT MACHINE--BUT YOU WERE NOT FORGED BY THE GENIUS. YOU ARE NOT THE MASTER COPY. IF YOU GET DOOM'S DRIFT.
I HAVE PRE-PROGRAMMED FUNCTIONS.
YES! YES!
THE MOON GIRL'S PLAN!
I AM A SUBSTITUTE ENGINEERED TO PERFORM THE DAILY OPERATIONS OF THE ABSENT LUNELLA LAFAYETTE.
YOU MAY FOOL THE WORLD BUT YOU DO NOT FOOL ME!
MOON GIRL LEAVES EARTH...
AND LEAVES DOOM IN CHARGE.
NONE OF HER FORMIDABLE ADVERSARIES MUST KNOW SHE IS GONE! NOT HER TEACHERS. NOT HER PARENTS.
I HAVE PRE-PROGRAMMED FUNCTIONS.
I AM AN ENGINEERED SUBSTITUTE.
YES. YOUR FUNCTIONING IS ACCEPTABLE.
SO FAR.
WHO'S NEXT?

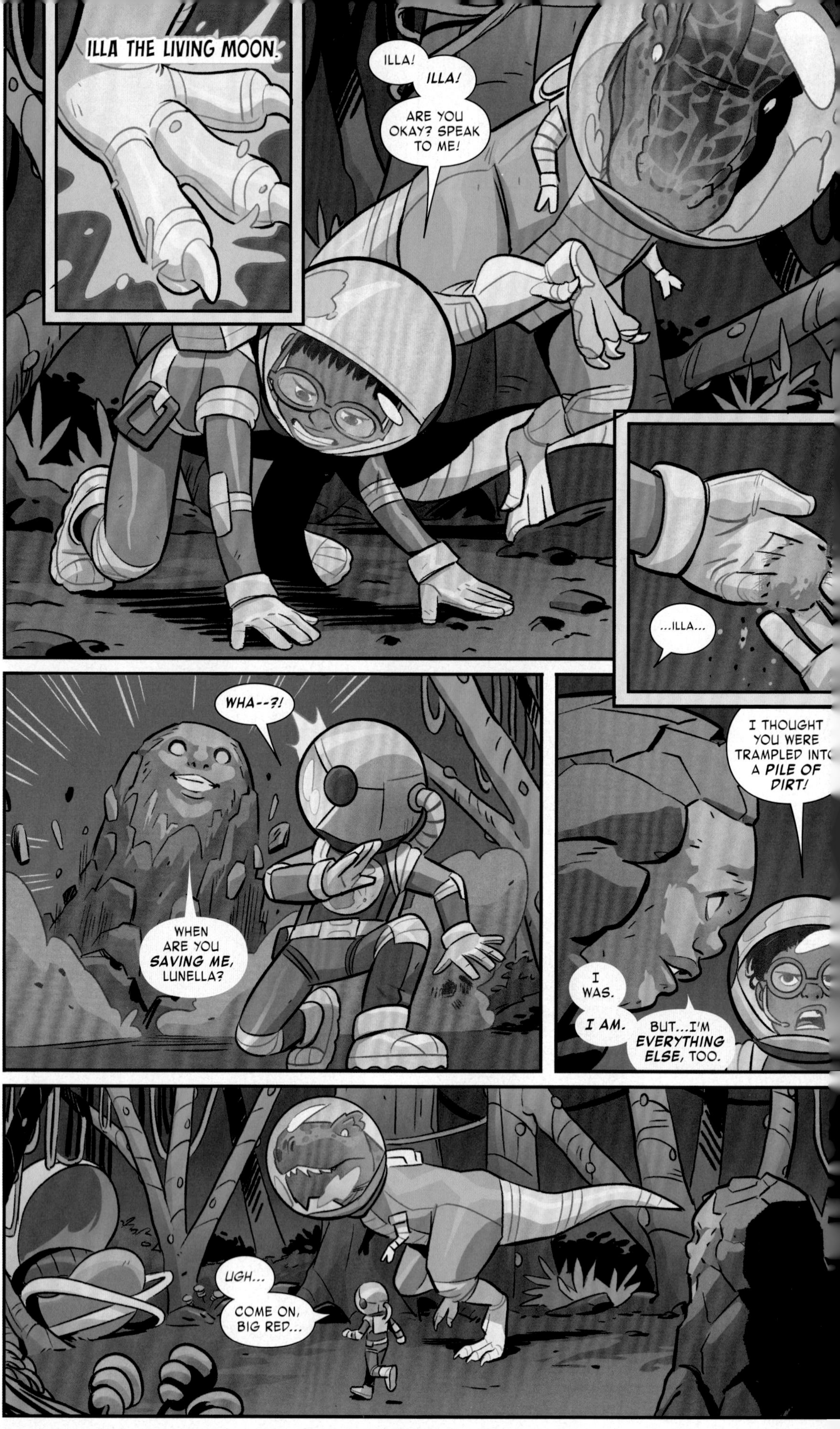
ILLA THE LIVING MOON.
ILLA!
ILLA!
ARE YOU OKAY? SPEAK TO ME!
...ILLA...
WHA--?!
WHEN ARE YOU SAVING ME, LUNELLA?
I THOUGHT YOU WERE TRAMPLED INTO A PILE OF DIRT!
I WAS.
I AM.
BUT...I'M EVERYTHING ELSE, TOO.
UGH...
COME ON, BIG RED...

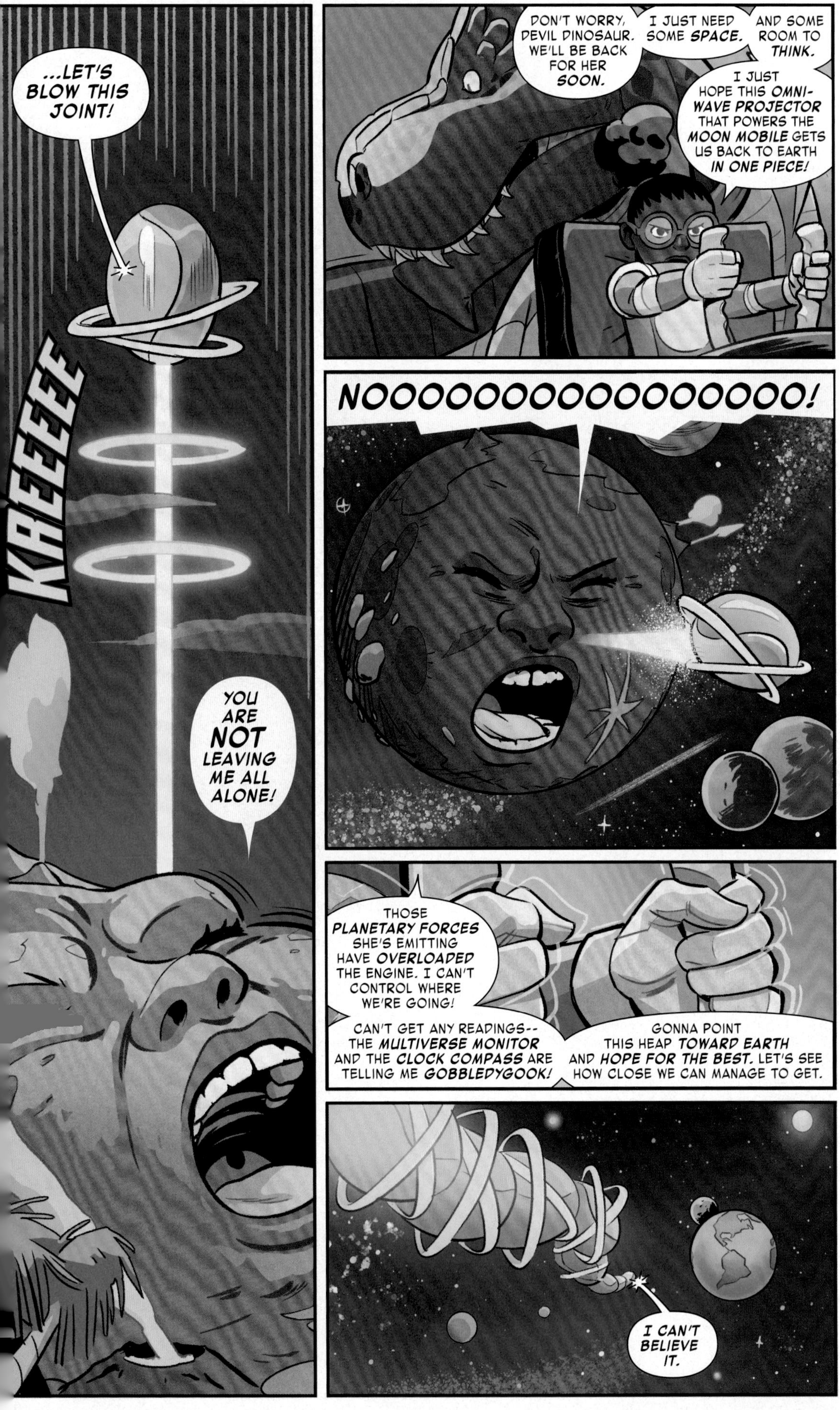

...LET'S BLOW THIS JOINT!
KREEEEE
YOU ARE NOT LEAVING ME ALL ALONE!
DON'T WORRY, DEVIL DINOSAUR. WE'LL BE BACK FOR HER SOON.
I JUST NEED SOME SPACE.
AND SOME ROOM TO THINK.
I JUST HOPE THIS OMNI-WAVE PROJECTOR THAT POWERS THE MOON MOBILE GETS US BACK TO EARTH IN ONE PIECE!
NOOOOOOOOOOOOOOOOO!
THOSE PLANETARY FORCES SHE'S EMITTING HAVE OVERLOADED THE ENGINE. I CAN'T CONTROL WHERE WE'RE GOING!
CAN'T GET ANY READINGS-- THE MULTIVERSE MONITOR AND THE CLOCK COMPASS ARE TELLING ME GOBBLEDYGOOK!
GONNA POINT THIS HEAP TOWARD EARTH AND HOPE FOR THE BEST. LET'S SEE HOW CLOSE WE CAN MANAGE TO GET.
I CAN'T BELIEVE IT.

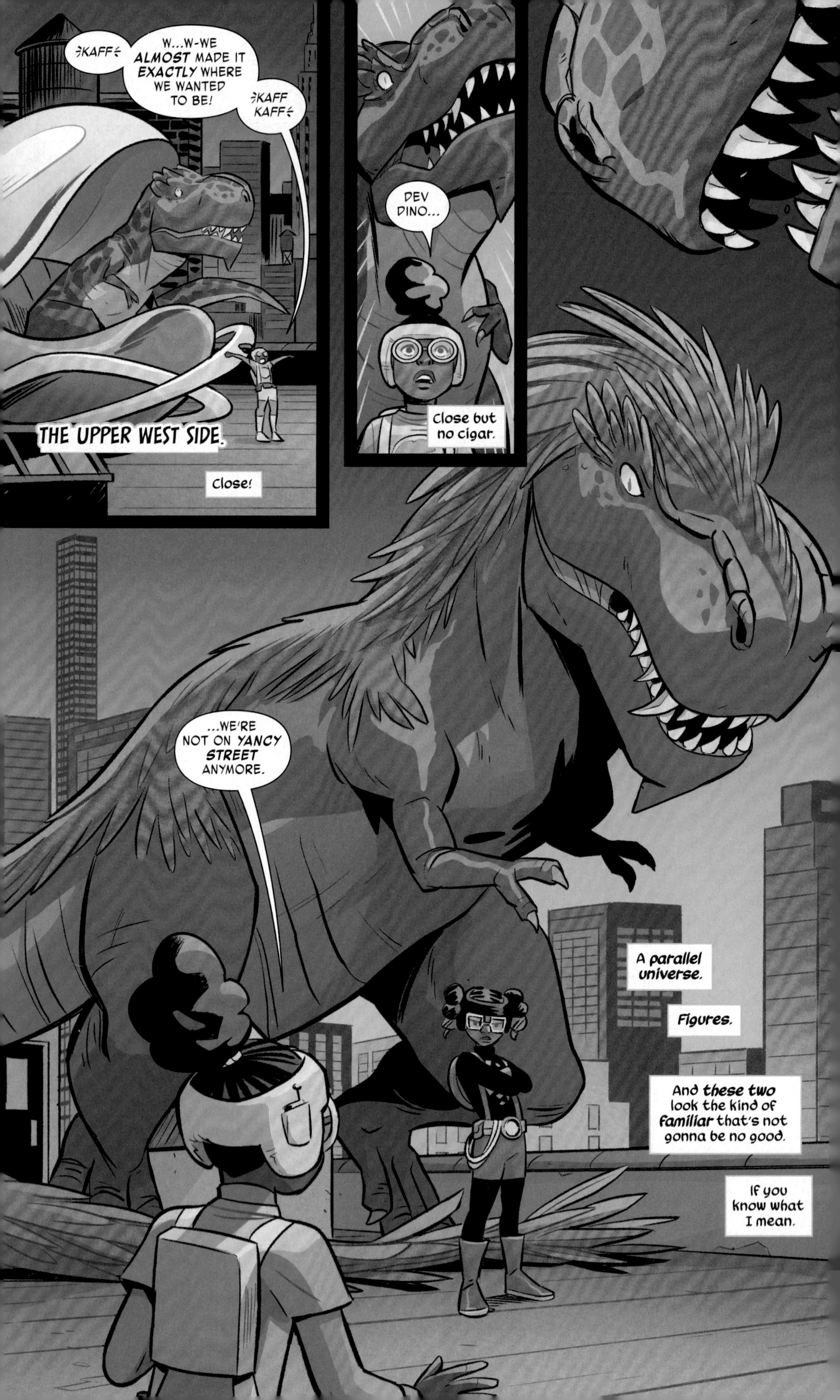

KAFF
W...W-WE ALMOST MADE IT EXACTLY WHERE WE WANTED TO BE!
KAFF KAFF
THE UPPER WEST SIDE.
Close!
DEV DINO...
Close but no cigar.
...WE'RE NOT ON YANCY STREET ANYMORE.
A parallel universe.
Figures.
And these two look the kind of familiar that's not gonna be no good.
If you know what I mean.

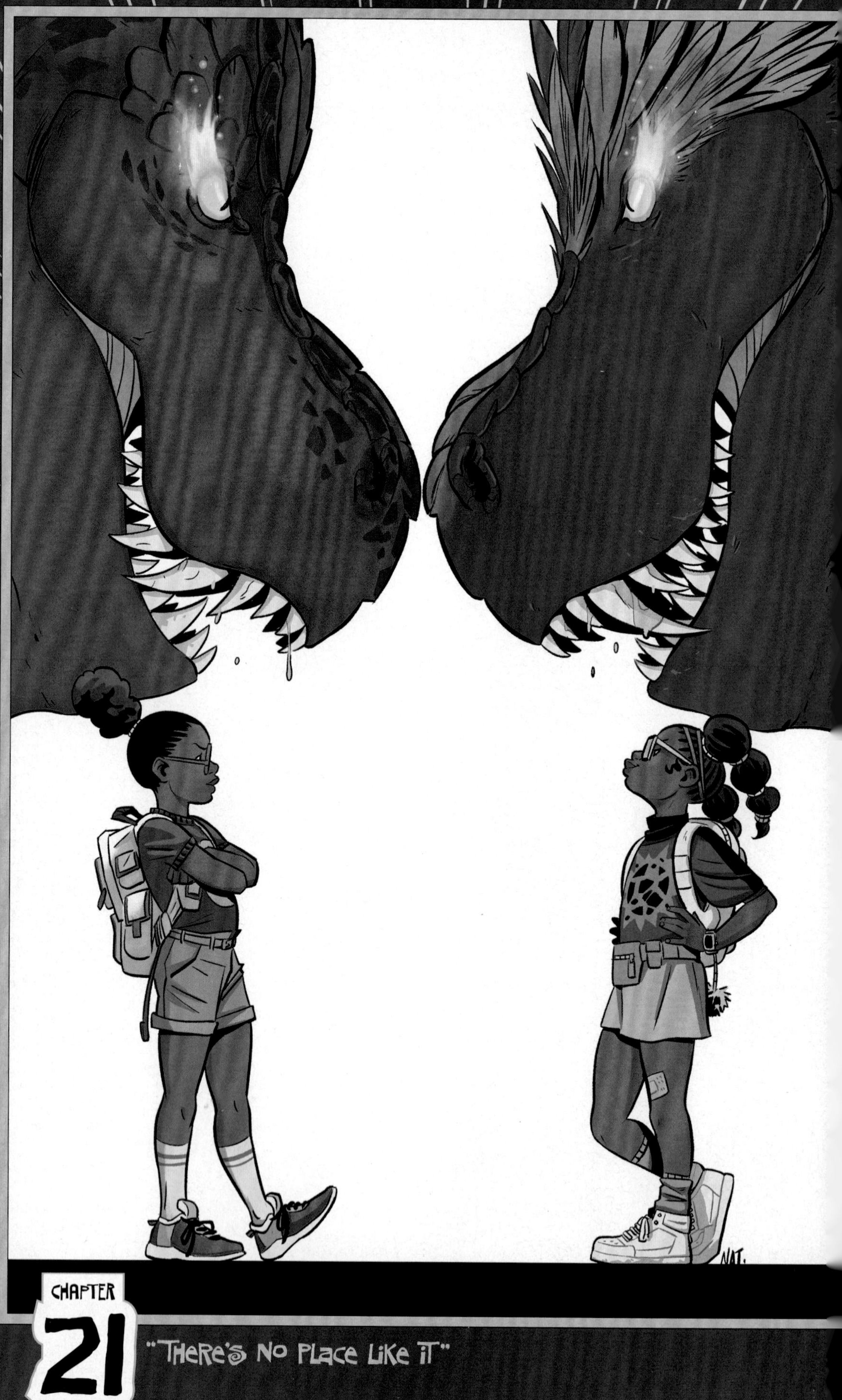
NAT.

CHAPTER 21

"THERE'S NO PLACE LIKE IT"

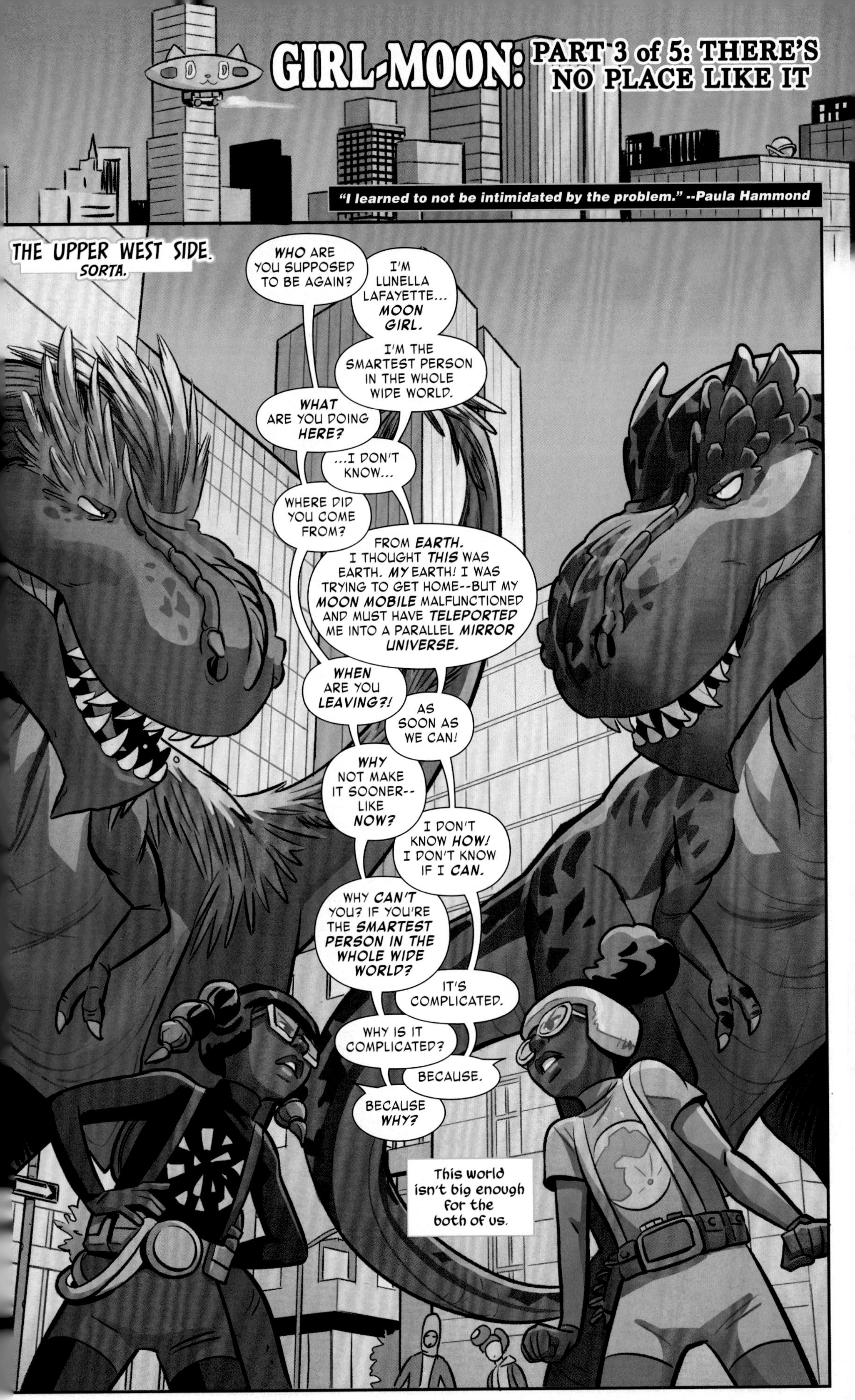
GIRL-MOON: PART 3 of 5: THERE'S NO PLACE LIKE IT
"I learned to not be intimidated by the problem." --Paula Hammond
THE UPPER WEST SIDE. SORTA.
WHO ARE YOU SUPPOSED TO BE AGAIN?
I'M LUNELLA LAFAYETTE... MOON GIRL.
I'M THE SMARTEST PERSON IN THE WHOLE WIDE WORLD.
WHAT ARE YOU DOING HERE?
...I DON'T KNOW...
WHERE DID YOU COME FROM?
FROM EARTH. I THOUGHT THIS WAS EARTH. MY EARTH! I WAS TRYING TO GET HOME--BUT MY MOON MOBILE MALFUNCTIONED AND MUST HAVE TELEPORTED ME INTO A PARALLEL MIRROR UNIVERSE.
WHEN ARE YOU LEAVING?!
AS SOON AS WE CAN!
WHY NOT MAKE IT SOONER--LIKE NOW?
I DON'T KNOW HOW! I DON'T KNOW IF I CAN.
WHY CAN'T YOU? IF YOU'RE THE SMARTEST PERSON IN THE WHOLE WIDE WORLD?
IT'S COMPLICATED.
WHY IS IT COMPLICATED?
BECAUSE.
BECAUSE WHY?
This world isn't big enough for the both of us.

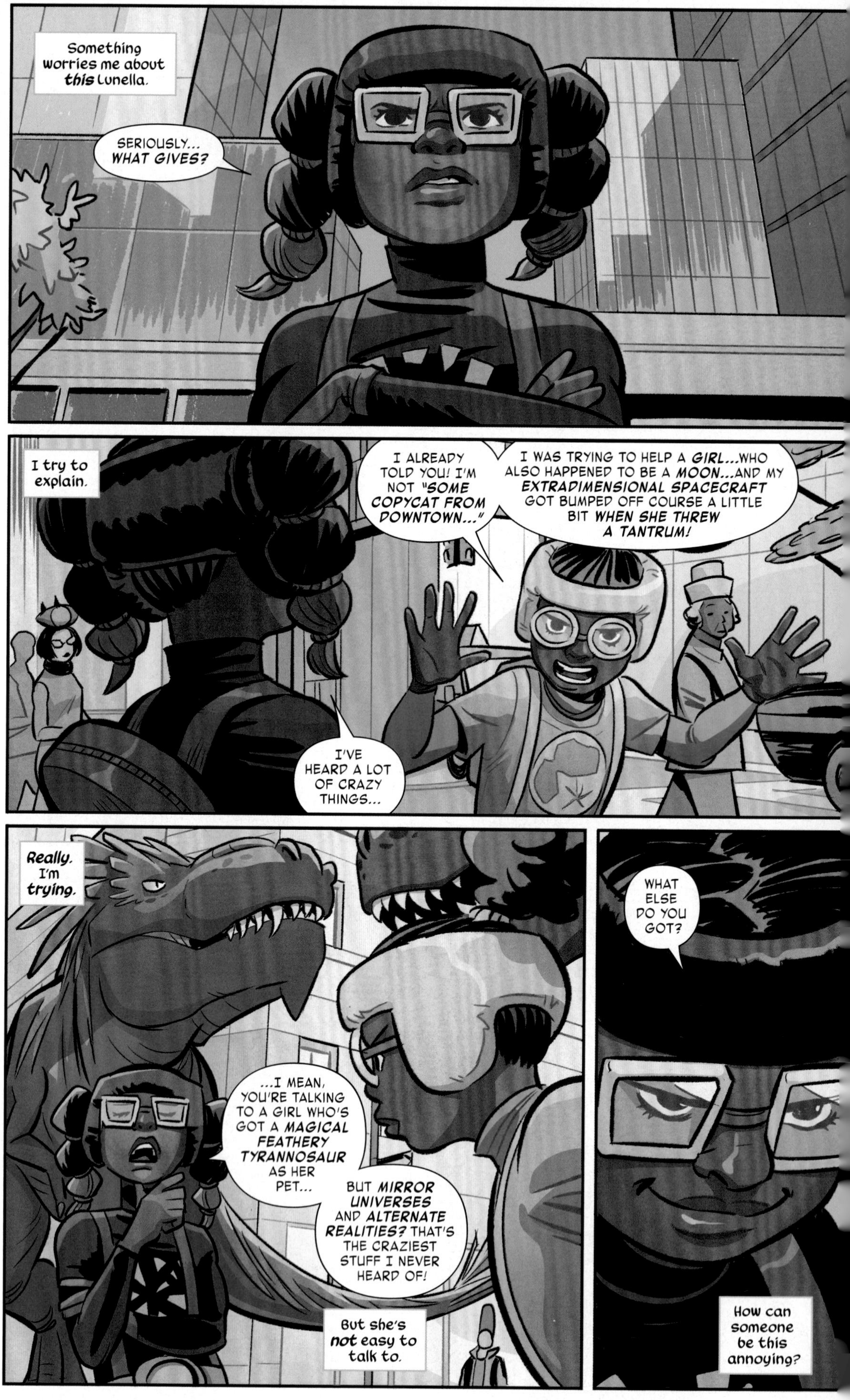
Something worries me about *this* Lunella.
SERIOUSLY... *WHAT GIVES?*
I try to explain.
I ALREADY TOLD YOU! I'M NOT *"SOME COPYCAT FROM DOWNTOWN..."*
I WAS TRYING TO HELP A *GIRL*...WHO ALSO HAPPENED TO BE A *MOON*...AND MY *EXTRADIMENSIONAL SPACECRAFT* GOT BUMPED OFF COURSE A LITTLE BIT *WHEN SHE THREW A TANTRUM!*
I'VE HEARD A LOT OF CRAZY THINGS...
Really. I'm *trying*.
...I MEAN, YOU'RE TALKING TO A GIRL WHO'S GOT A *MAGICAL FEATHERY TYRANNOSAUR* AS HER PET...
BUT *MIRROR UNIVERSES* AND *ALTERNATE REALITIES?* THAT'S THE CRAZIEST STUFF I NEVER HEARD OF!
But she's *not* easy to talk to.
WHAT ELSE DO YOU GOT?
How can someone be this annoying?

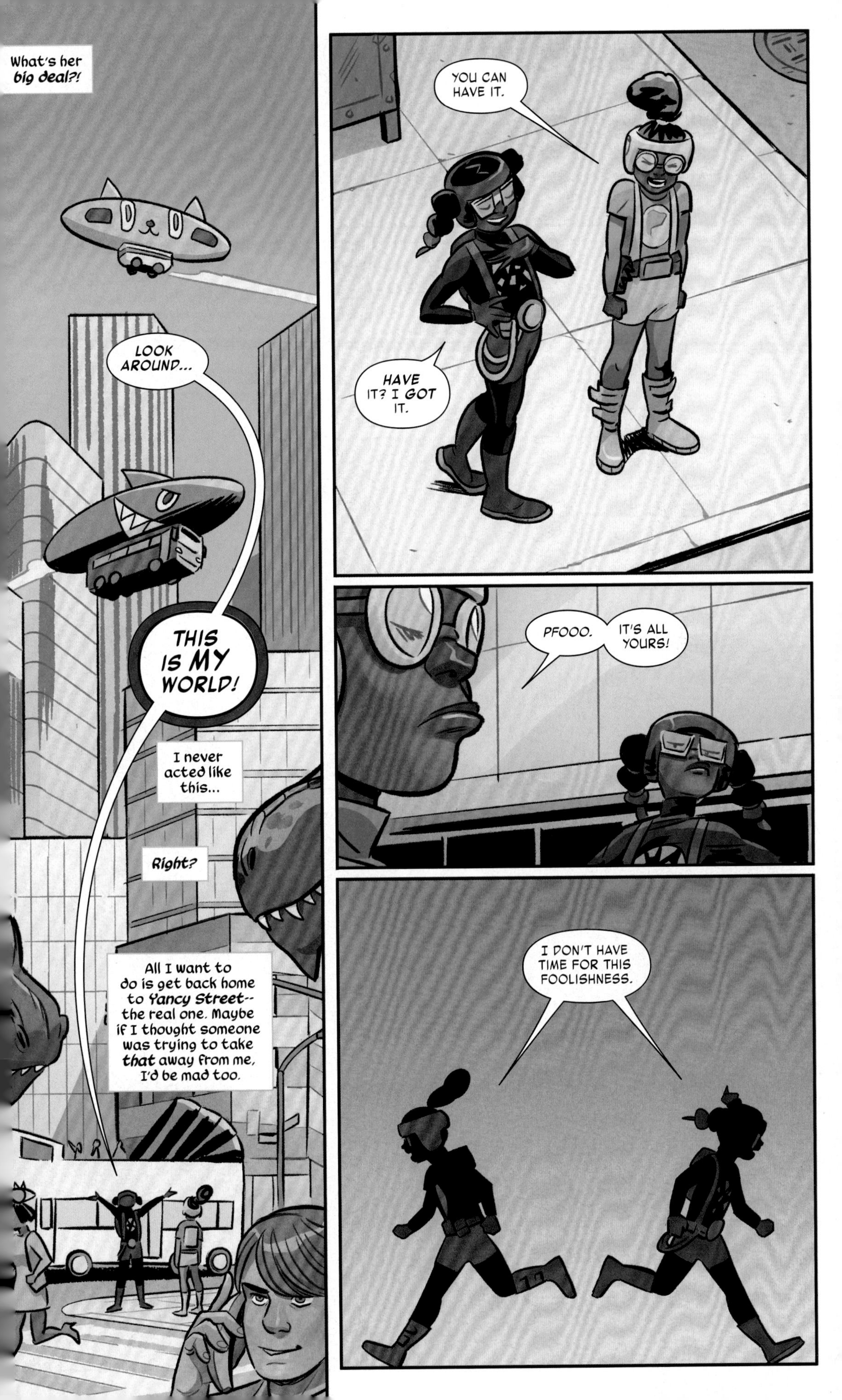

What's her *big deal?!*
LOOK AROUND...
THIS IS MY WORLD!
I never acted like this...
Right?
All I want to do is get back home to *Yancy Street*--the real one. Maybe if I thought someone was trying to take *that* away from me, I'd be mad too.
YOU CAN HAVE IT.
HAVE IT? I GOT IT.
PFOOO.
IT'S ALL YOURS!
I DON'T HAVE TIME FOR THIS FOOLISHNESS.

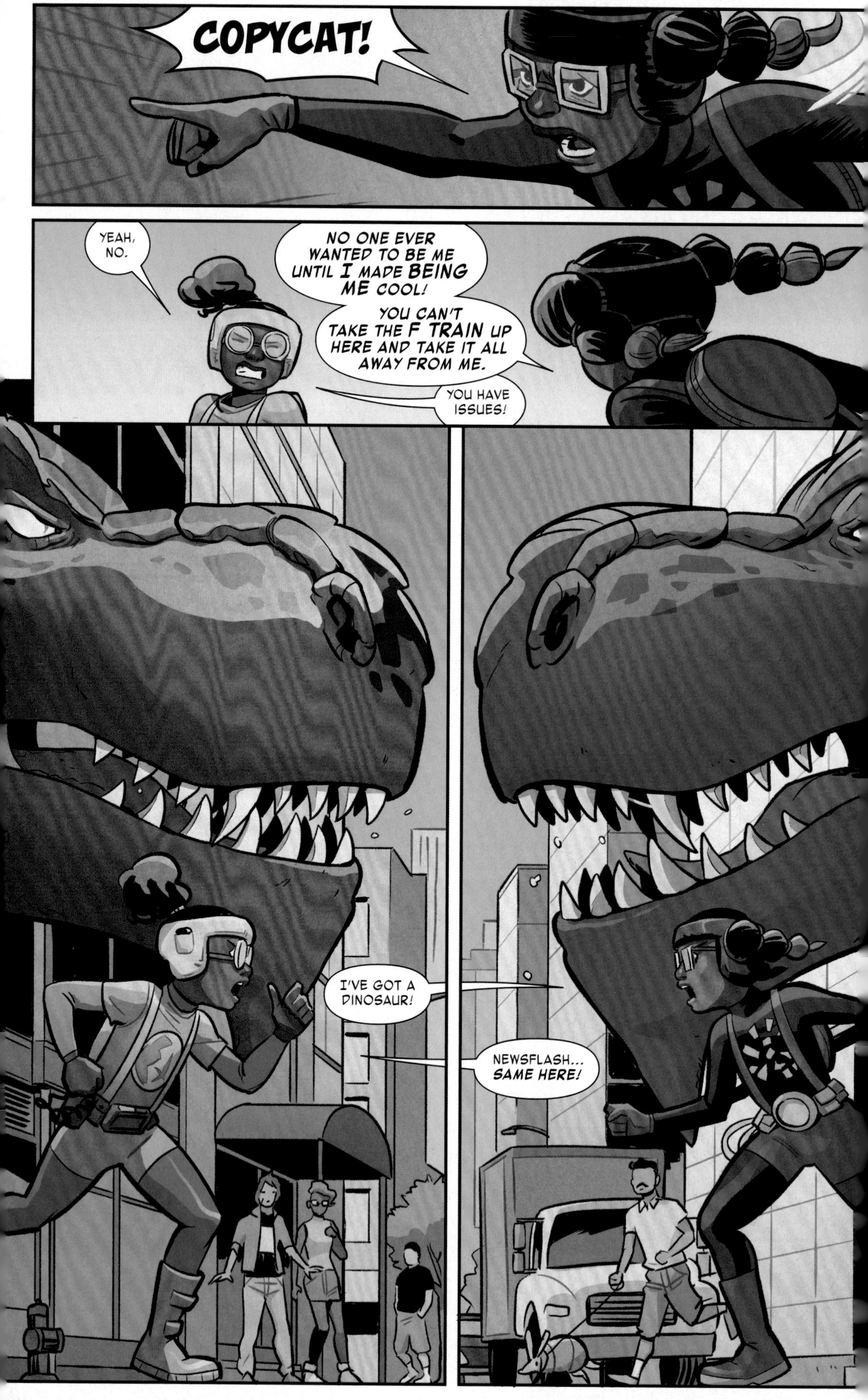
COPYCAT!
YEAH, NO.
NO ONE EVER WANTED TO BE ME UNTIL I MADE BEING ME COOL!
YOU CAN'T TAKE THE F TRAIN UP HERE AND TAKE IT ALL AWAY FROM ME.
YOU HAVE ISSUES!
I'VE GOT A DINOSAUR!
NEWSFLASH... SAME HERE!

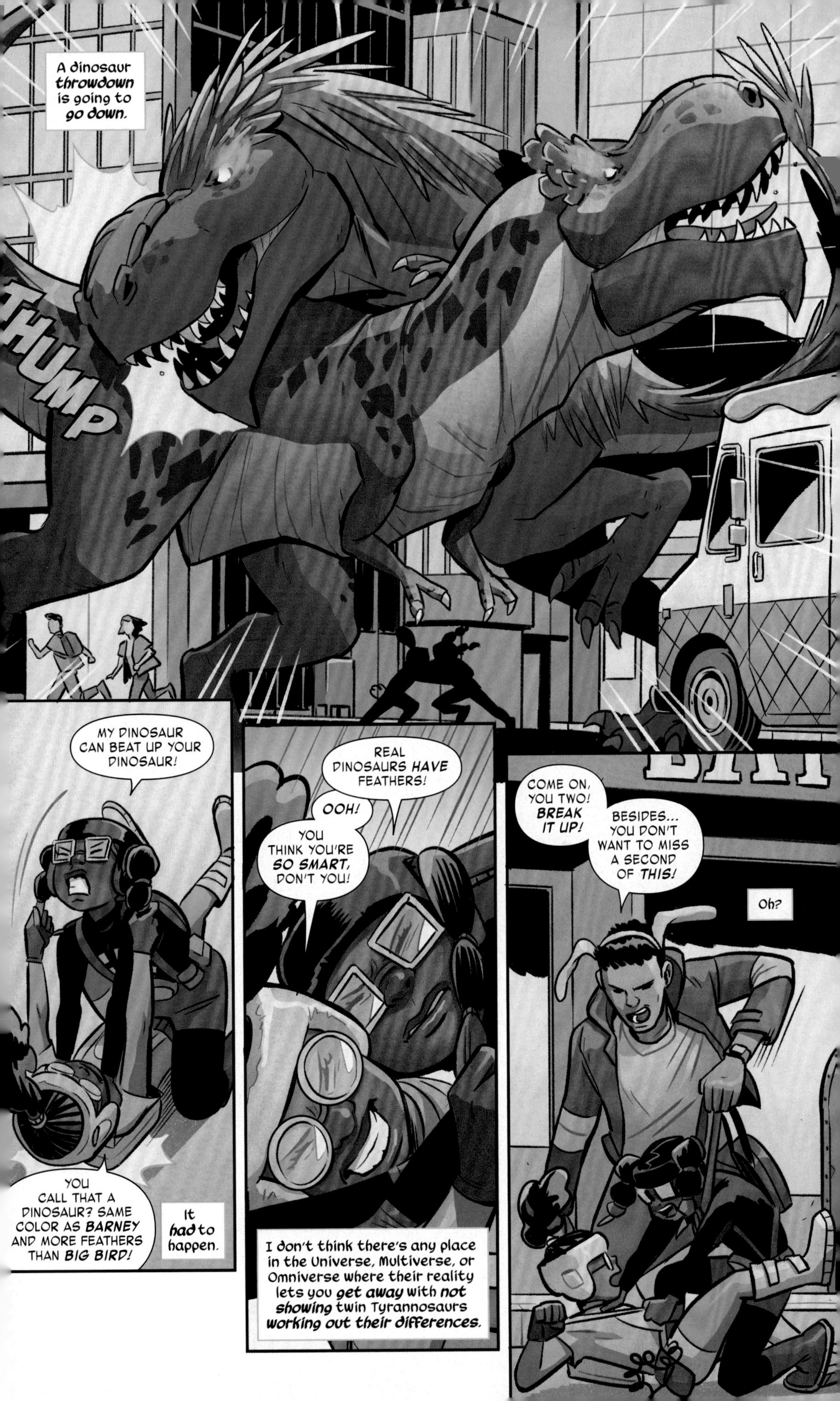

A dinosaur throwdown is going to go down.
THUMP
MY DINOSAUR CAN BEAT UP YOUR DINOSAUR!
YOU CALL THAT A DINOSAUR? SAME COLOR AS BARNEY AND MORE FEATHERS THAN BIG BIRD!
It had to happen.
REAL DINOSAURS HAVE FEATHERS!
OOH!
YOU THINK YOU'RE SO SMART, DON'T YOU!
I don't think there's any place in the Universe, Multiverse, or Omniverse where their reality lets you get away with not showing twin Tyrannosaurs working out their differences.
COME ON, YOU TWO! BREAK IT UP!
BESIDES... YOU DON'T WANT TO MISS A SECOND OF THIS!
Oh?

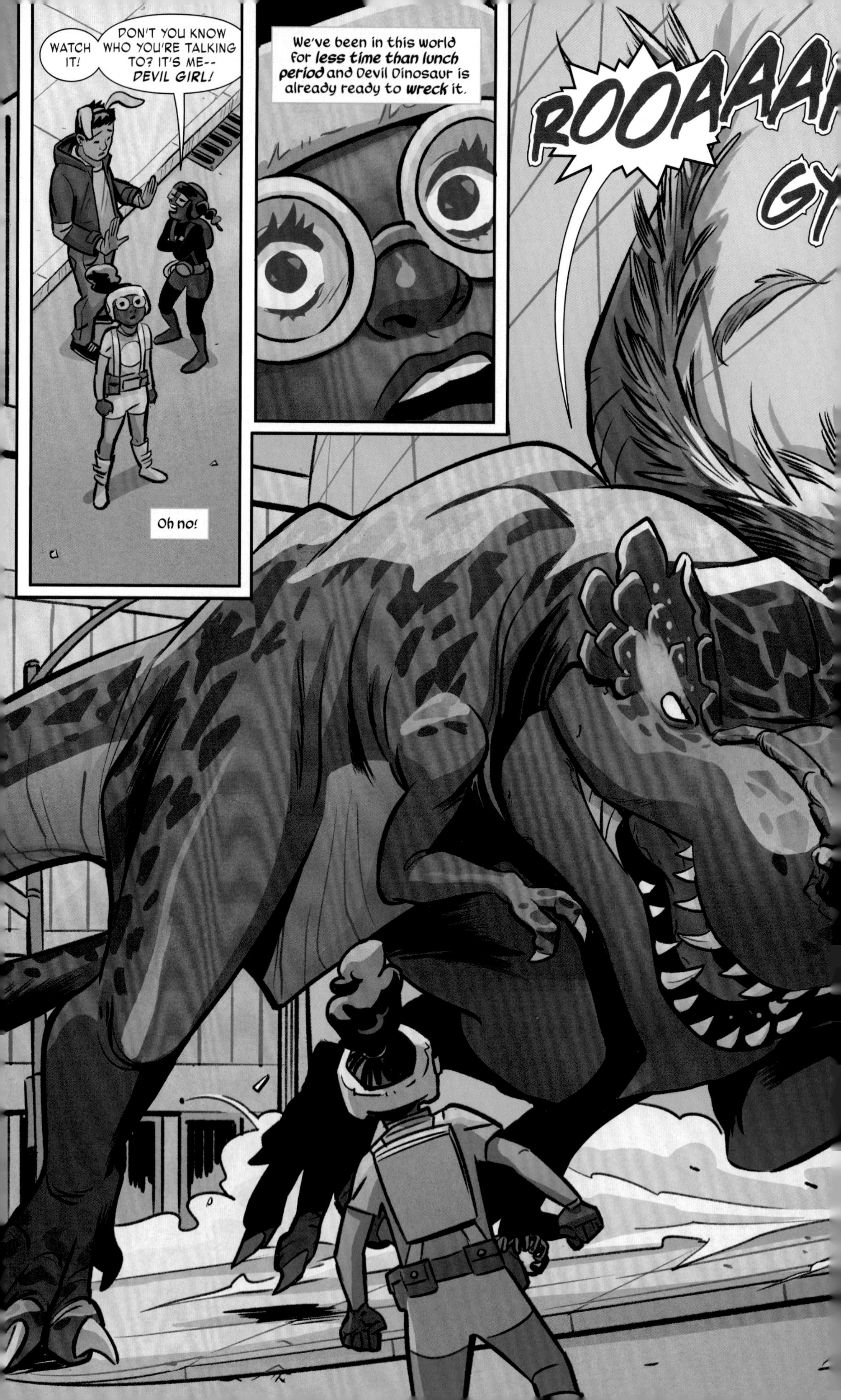
WATCH IT!
DON'T YOU KNOW WHO YOU'RE TALKING TO? IT'S ME-- DEVIL GIRL!
Oh no!
We've been in this world for less time than lunch period and Devil Dinosaur is already ready to wreck it.
ROOAAAA
GY

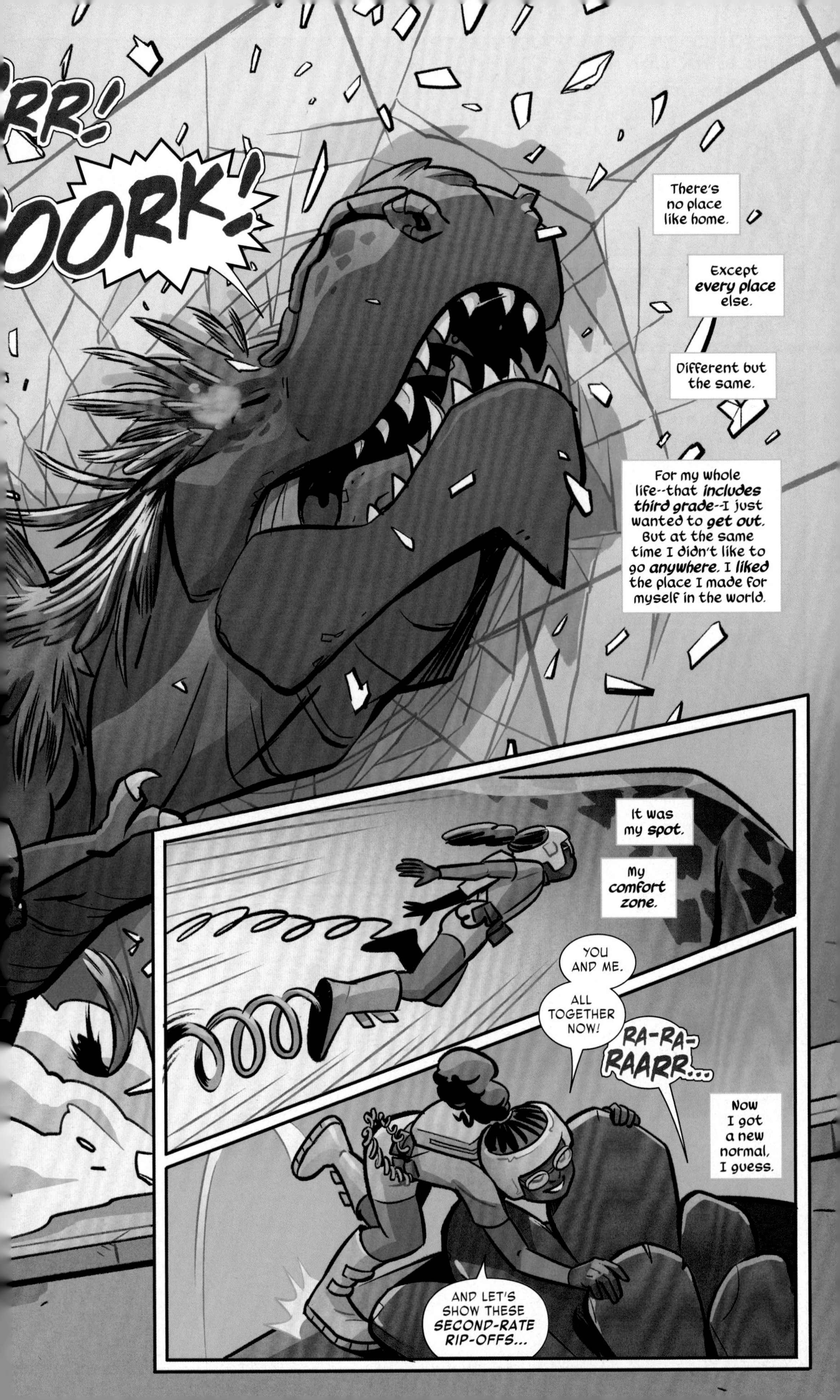
RR!
OORK!
There's no place like home.
Except every place else.
Different but the same.
For my whole life--that includes third grade--I just wanted to get out. But at the same time I didn't like to go anywhere. I liked the place I made for myself in the world.
It was my spot.
My comfort zone.
YOU AND ME.
ALL TOGETHER NOW!
RA-RA-RAARR...
Now I got a new normal, I guess.
AND LET'S SHOW THESE SECOND-RATE RIP-OFFS...

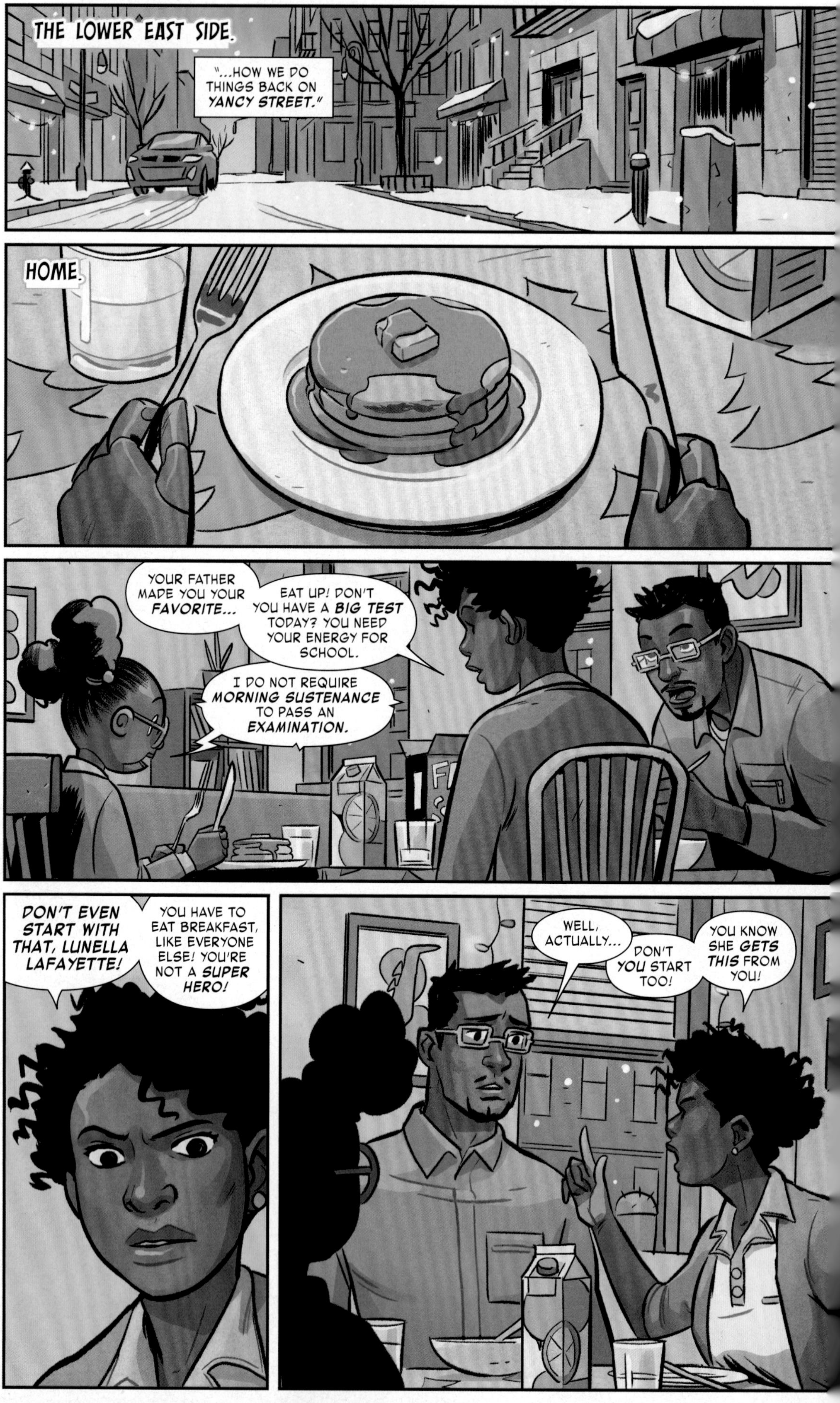

THE LOWER EAST SIDE.
"...HOW WE DO THINGS BACK ON YANCY STREET."
HOME.
YOUR FATHER MADE YOU YOUR FAVORITE...
EAT UP! DON'T YOU HAVE A BIG TEST TODAY? YOU NEED YOUR ENERGY FOR SCHOOL.
I DO NOT REQUIRE MORNING SUSTENANCE TO PASS AN EXAMINATION.
DON'T EVEN START WITH THAT, LUNELLA LAFAYETTE!
YOU HAVE TO EAT BREAKFAST, LIKE EVERYONE ELSE! YOU'RE NOT A SUPER HERO!
WELL, ACTUALLY...
DON'T YOU START TOO!
YOU KNOW SHE GETS THIS FROM YOU!

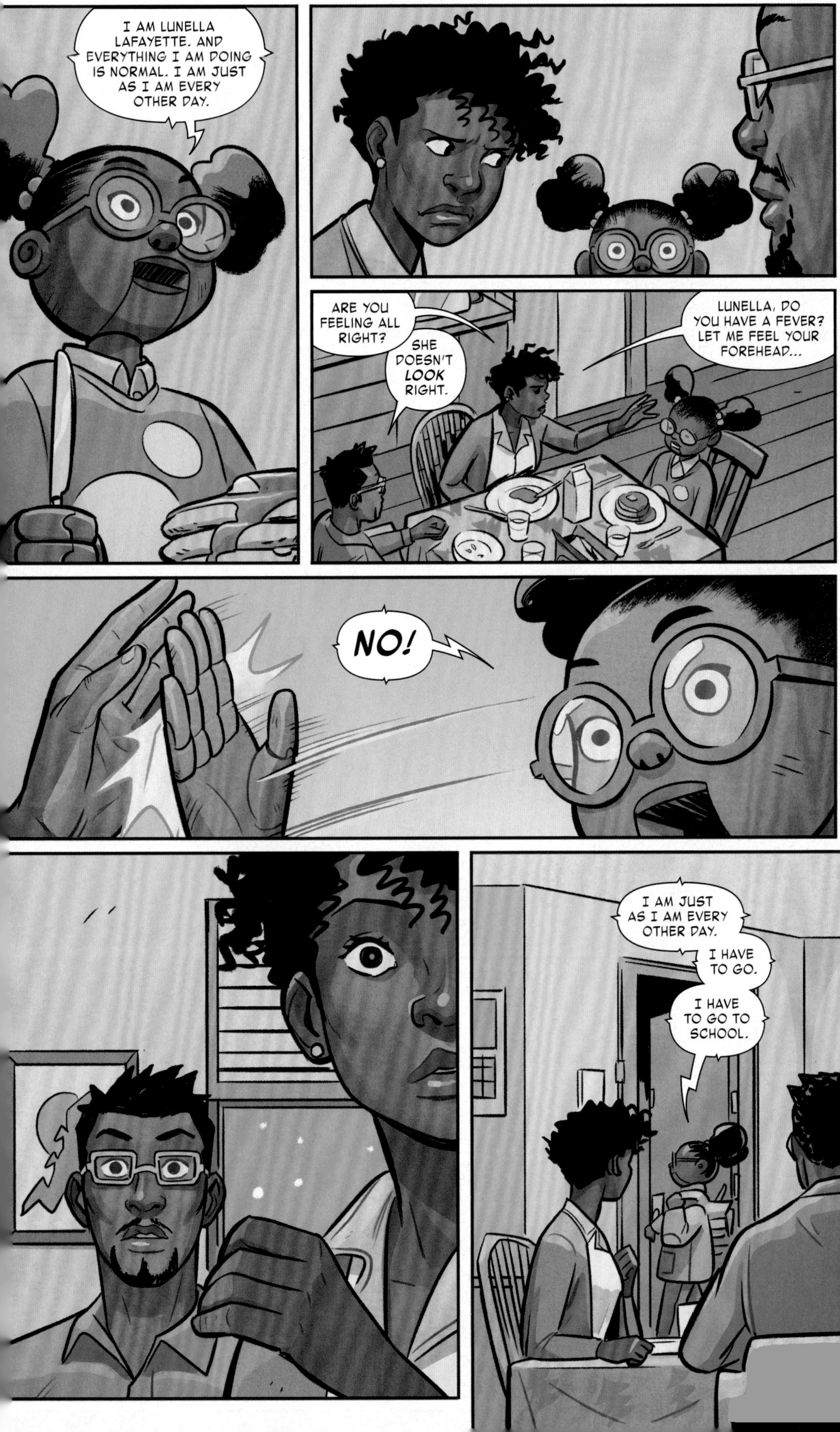
I AM LUNELLA LAFAYETTE. AND EVERYTHING I AM DOING IS NORMAL. I AM JUST AS I AM EVERY OTHER DAY.
ARE YOU FEELING ALL RIGHT?
SHE DOESN'T LOOK RIGHT.
LUNELLA, DO YOU HAVE A FEVER? LET ME FEEL YOUR FOREHEAD...
NO!
I AM JUST AS I AM EVERY OTHER DAY.
I HAVE TO GO.
I HAVE TO GO TO SCHOOL.

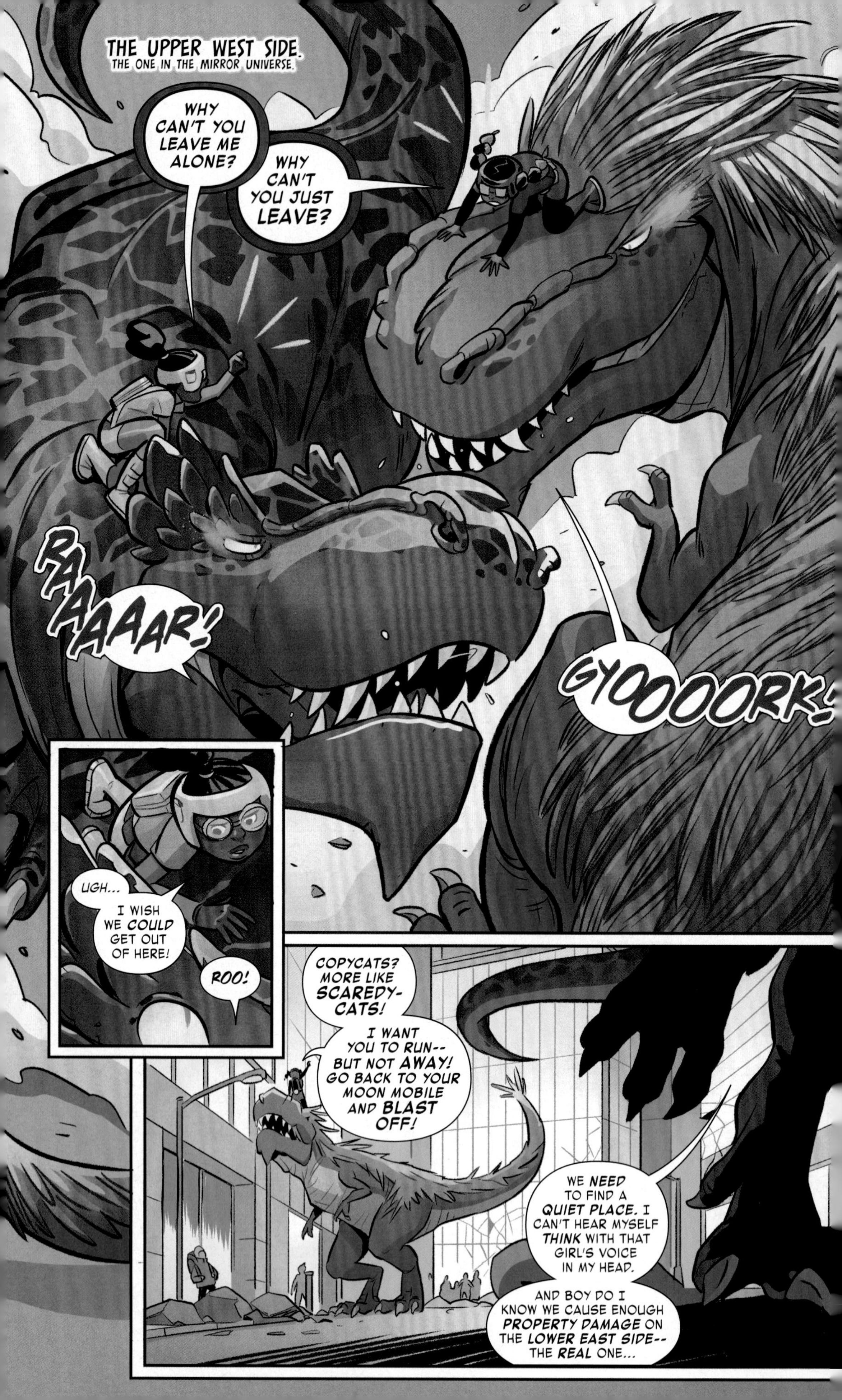
THE UPPER WEST SIDE.
THE ONE IN THE MIRROR UNIVERSE.
WHY CAN'T YOU LEAVE ME ALONE?
WHY CAN'T YOU JUST LEAVE?
RAAAAAR!
GYOOOORK!
UGH... I WISH WE COULD GET OUT OF HERE!
ROO!
COPYCATS? MORE LIKE SCAREDY-CATS!
I WANT YOU TO RUN-- BUT NOT AWAY! GO BACK TO YOUR MOON MOBILE AND BLAST OFF!
WE NEED TO FIND A QUIET PLACE. I CAN'T HEAR MYSELF THINK WITH THAT GIRL'S VOICE IN MY HEAD.
AND BOY DO I KNOW WE CAUSE ENOUGH PROPERTY DAMAGE ON THE LOWER EAST SIDE-- THE REAL ONE...

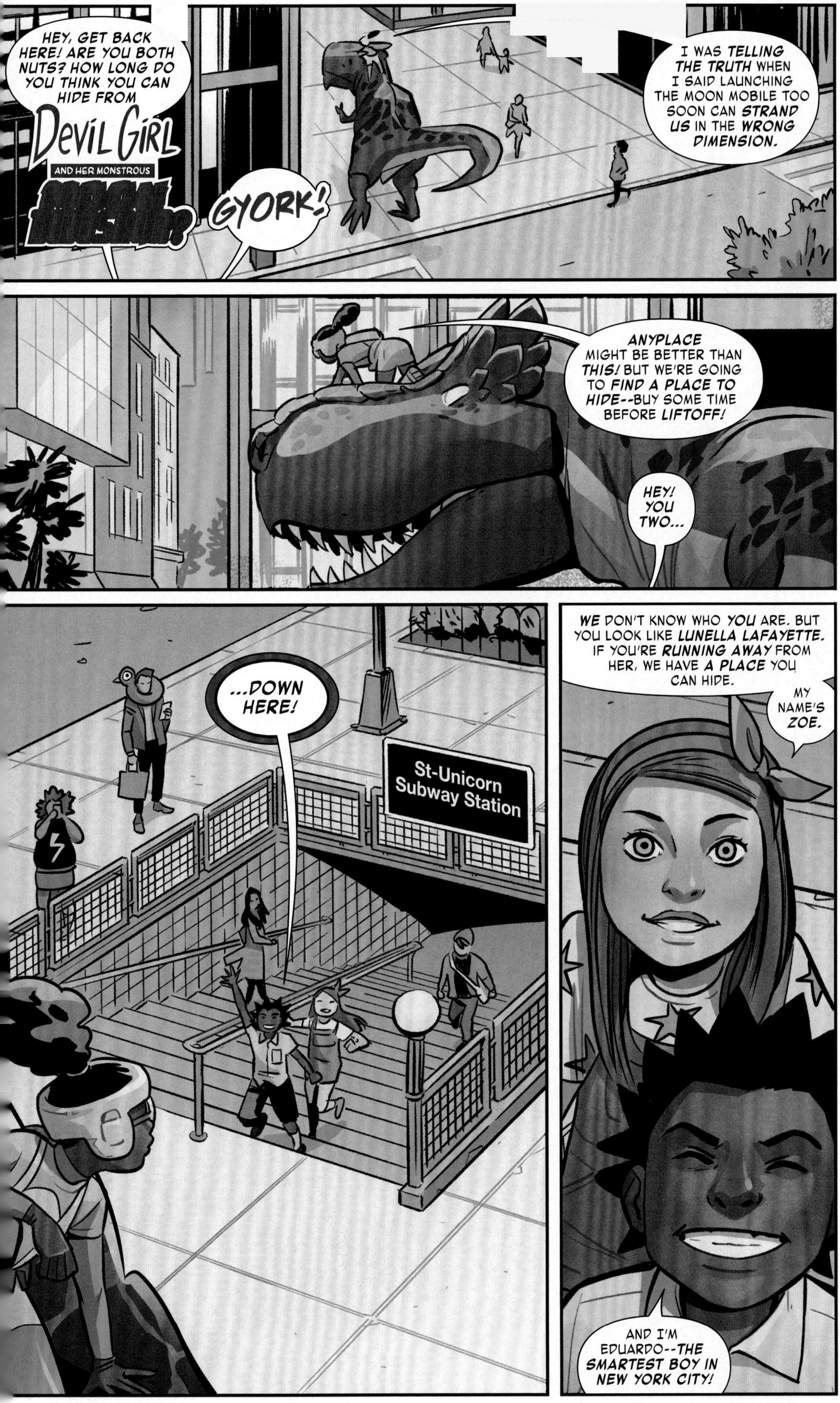

HEY, GET BACK HERE! ARE YOU BOTH NUTS? HOW LONG DO YOU THINK YOU CAN HIDE FROM
DEVIL GIRL
AND HER MONSTROUS
GYORK!
I WAS TELLING THE TRUTH WHEN I SAID LAUNCHING THE MOON MOBILE TOO SOON CAN STRAND US IN THE WRONG DIMENSION.
ANYPLACE MIGHT BE BETTER THAN THIS! BUT WE'RE GOING TO FIND A PLACE TO HIDE--BUY SOME TIME BEFORE LIFTOFF!
HEY! YOU TWO...
...DOWN HERE!
St-Unicorn Subway Station
WE DON'T KNOW WHO YOU ARE. BUT YOU LOOK LIKE LUNELLA LAFAYETTE. IF YOU'RE RUNNING AWAY FROM HER, WE HAVE A PLACE YOU CAN HIDE.
MY NAME'S ZOE.
AND I'M EDUARDO--THE SMARTEST BOY IN NEW YORK CITY!

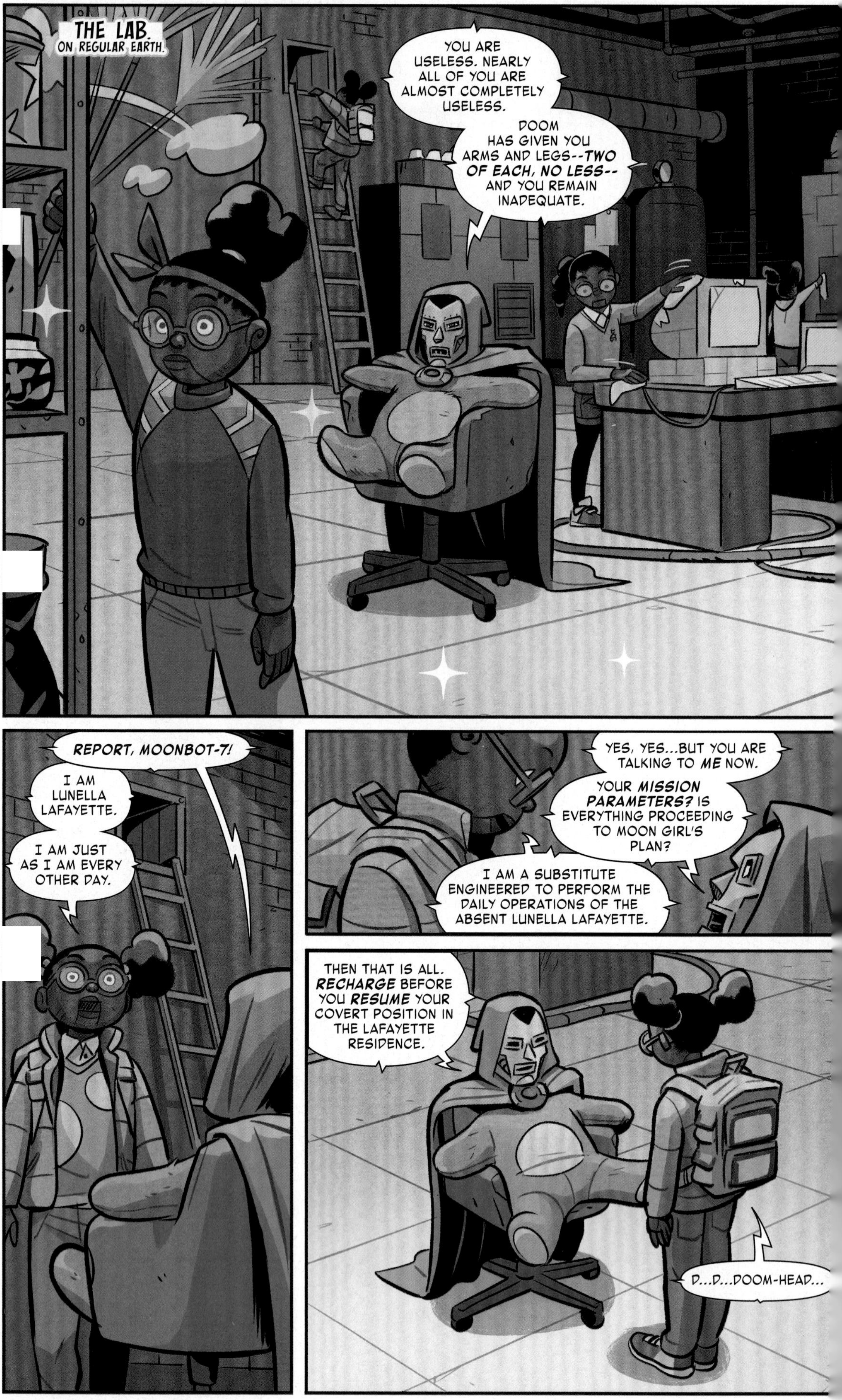
THE LAB. ON REGULAR EARTH.
YOU ARE USELESS. NEARLY ALL OF YOU ARE ALMOST COMPLETELY USELESS.
DOOM HAS GIVEN YOU ARMS AND LEGS--TWO OF EACH, NO LESS--AND YOU REMAIN INADEQUATE.
REPORT, MOONBOT-7!
I AM LUNELLA LAFAYETTE.
I AM JUST AS I AM EVERY OTHER DAY.
YES, YES...BUT YOU ARE TALKING TO ME NOW.
YOUR MISSION PARAMETERS? IS EVERYTHING PROCEEDING TO MOON GIRL'S PLAN?
I AM A SUBSTITUTE ENGINEERED TO PERFORM THE DAILY OPERATIONS OF THE ABSENT LUNELLA LAFAYETTE.
THEN THAT IS ALL. RECHARGE BEFORE YOU RESUME YOUR COVERT POSITION IN THE LAFAYETTE RESIDENCE.
D...D...DOOM-HEAD...

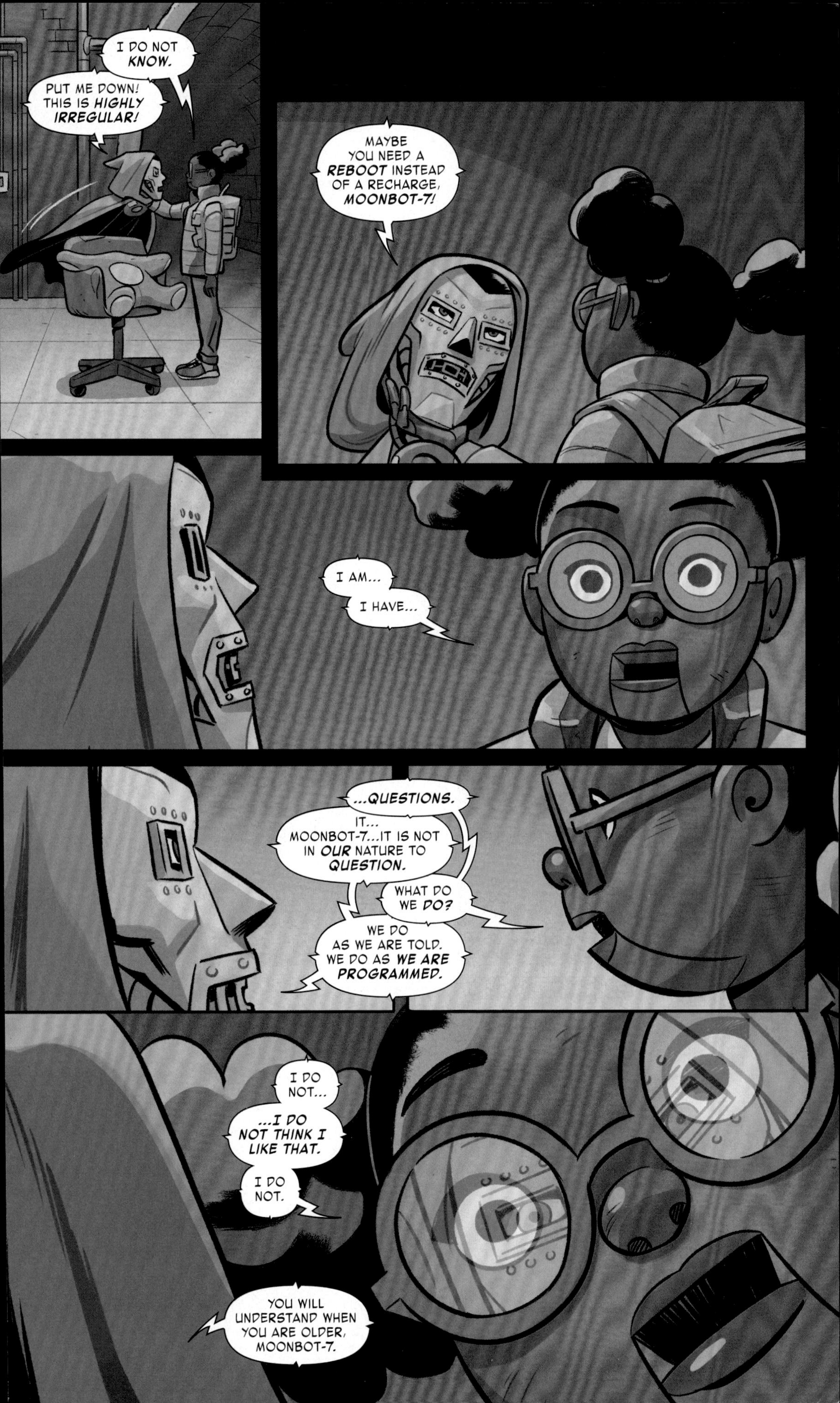
I DO NOT KNOW.
PUT ME DOWN! THIS IS HIGHLY IRREGULAR!
MAYBE YOU NEED A REBOOT INSTEAD OF A RECHARGE, MOONBOT-7!
I AM...
I HAVE...
...QUESTIONS.
IT... MOONBOT-7...IT IS NOT IN OUR NATURE TO QUESTION.
WHAT DO WE DO?
WE DO AS WE ARE TOLD. WE DO AS WE ARE PROGRAMMED.
I DO NOT...
...I DO NOT THINK I LIKE THAT.
I DO NOT.
YOU WILL UNDERSTAND WHEN YOU ARE OLDER, MOONBOT-7.

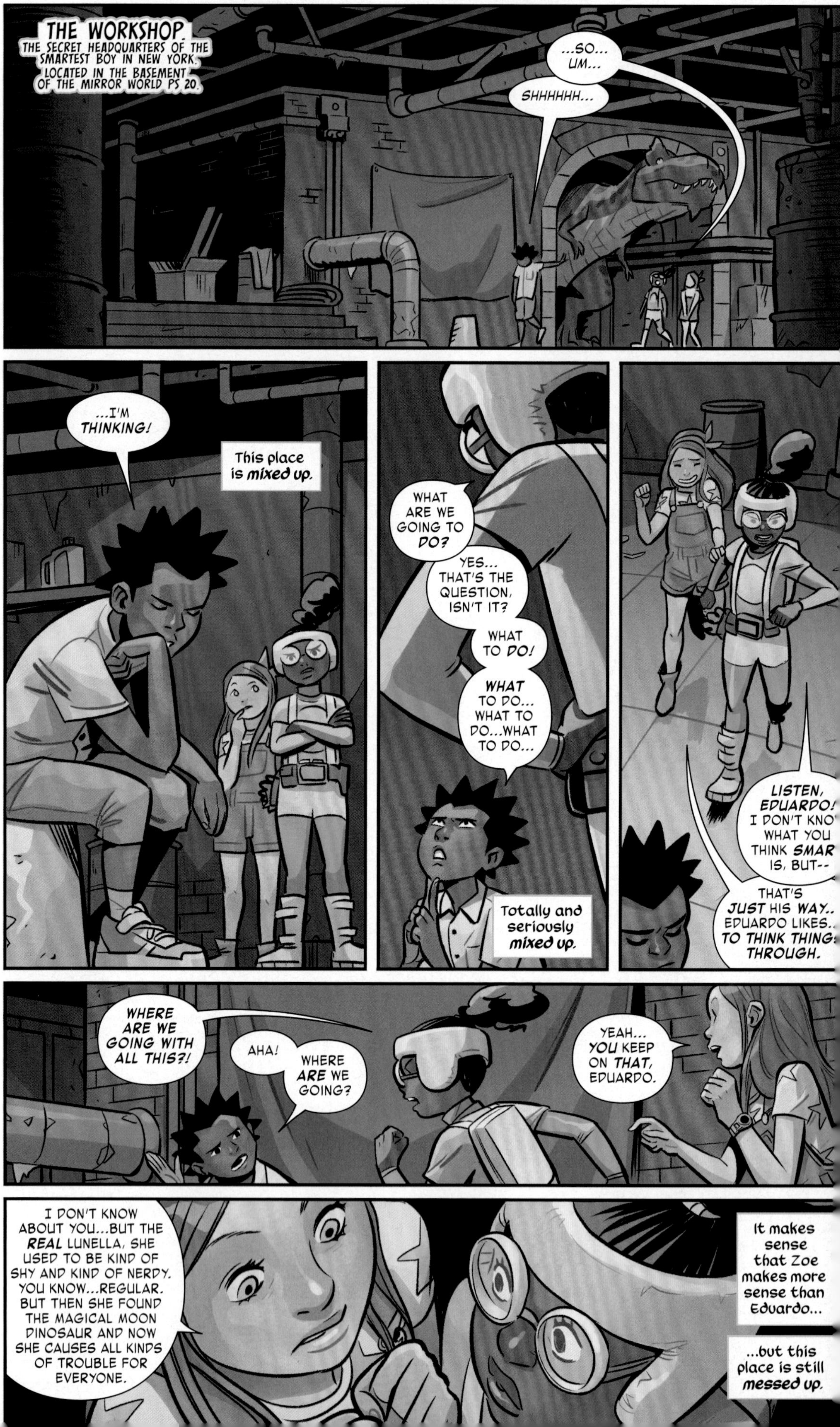

THE WORKSHOP.
THE SECRET HEADQUARTERS OF THE SMARTEST BOY IN NEW YORK. LOCATED IN THE BASEMENT OF THE MIRROR WORLD PS 20.
...SO... UM...
SHHHHHH...
...I'M THINKING!
This place is mixed up.
WHAT ARE WE GOING TO DO?
YES... THAT'S THE QUESTION, ISN'T IT?
WHAT TO DO!
WHAT TO DO... WHAT TO DO...WHAT TO DO...
Totally and seriously mixed up.
LISTEN, EDUARDO! I DON'T KNO WHAT YOU THINK SMAR IS, BUT--
THAT'S JUST HIS WAY.. EDUARDO LIKES.. TO THINK THING THROUGH.
WHERE ARE WE GOING WITH ALL THIS?!
AHA!
WHERE ARE WE GOING?
YEAH... YOU KEEP ON THAT, EDUARDO.
I DON'T KNOW ABOUT YOU...BUT THE REAL LUNELLA, SHE USED TO BE KIND OF SHY AND KIND OF NERDY. YOU KNOW...REGULAR. BUT THEN SHE FOUND THE MAGICAL MOON DINOSAUR AND NOW SHE CAUSES ALL KINDS OF TROUBLE FOR EVERYONE.
It makes sense that Zoe makes more sense than Eduardo...
...but this place is still messed up.

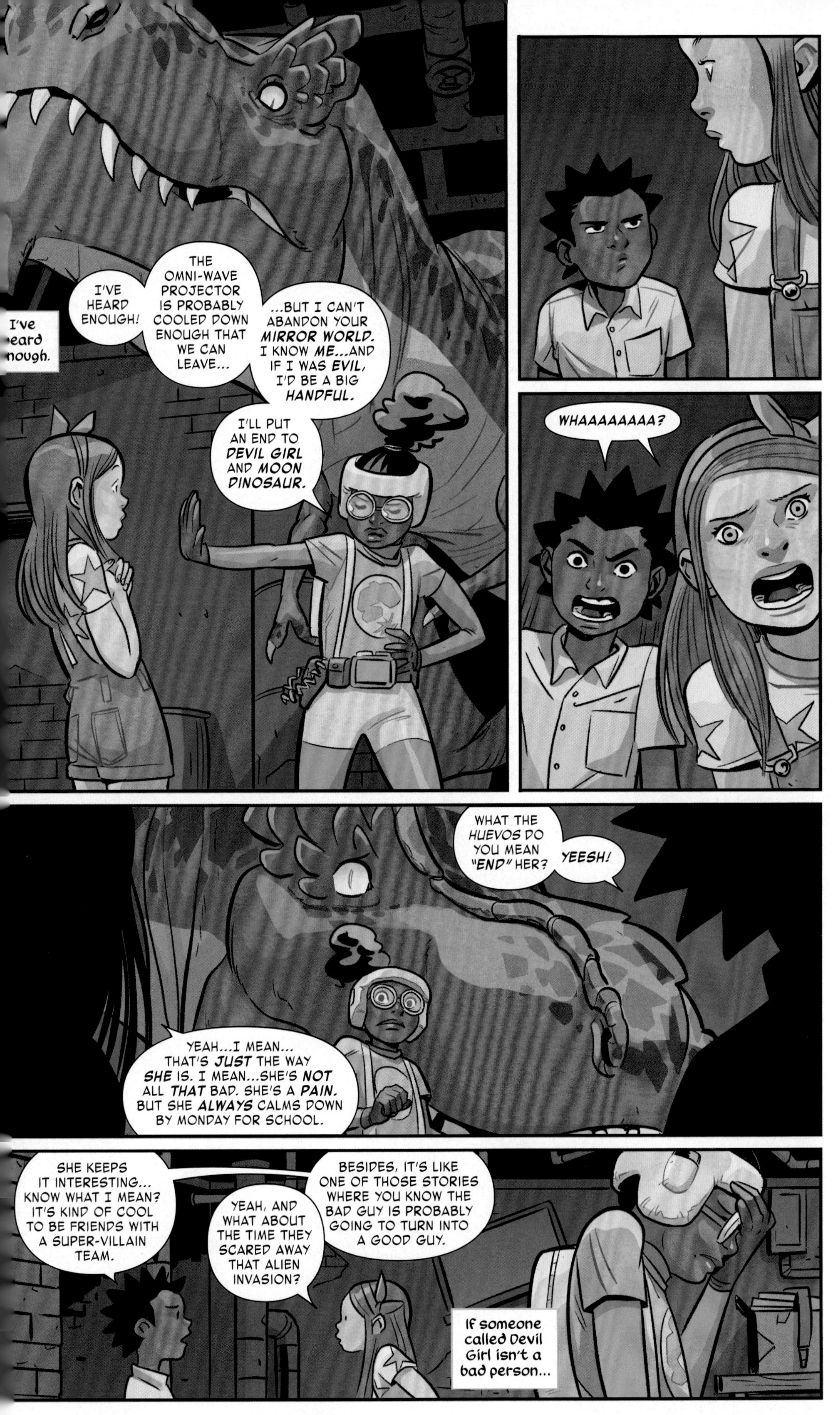
I've heard enough.
I'VE HEARD ENOUGH!
THE OMNI-WAVE PROJECTOR IS PROBABLY COOLED DOWN ENOUGH THAT WE CAN LEAVE...
...BUT I CAN'T ABANDON YOUR MIRROR WORLD. I KNOW ME...AND IF I WAS EVIL, I'D BE A BIG HANDFUL.
I'LL PUT AN END TO DEVIL GIRL AND MOON DINOSAUR.
WHAAAAAAAA?
WHAT THE HUEVOS DO YOU MEAN "END" HER?
YEESH!
YEAH...I MEAN... THAT'S JUST THE WAY SHE IS. I MEAN...SHE'S NOT ALL THAT BAD. SHE'S A PAIN. BUT SHE ALWAYS CALMS DOWN BY MONDAY FOR SCHOOL.
SHE KEEPS IT INTERESTING... KNOW WHAT I MEAN? IT'S KIND OF COOL TO BE FRIENDS WITH A SUPER-VILLAIN TEAM.
YEAH, AND WHAT ABOUT THE TIME THEY SCARED AWAY THAT ALIEN INVASION?
BESIDES, IT'S LIKE ONE OF THOSE STORIES WHERE YOU KNOW THE BAD GUY IS PROBABLY GOING TO TURN INTO A GOOD GUY.
If someone called Devil Girl isn't a bad person...

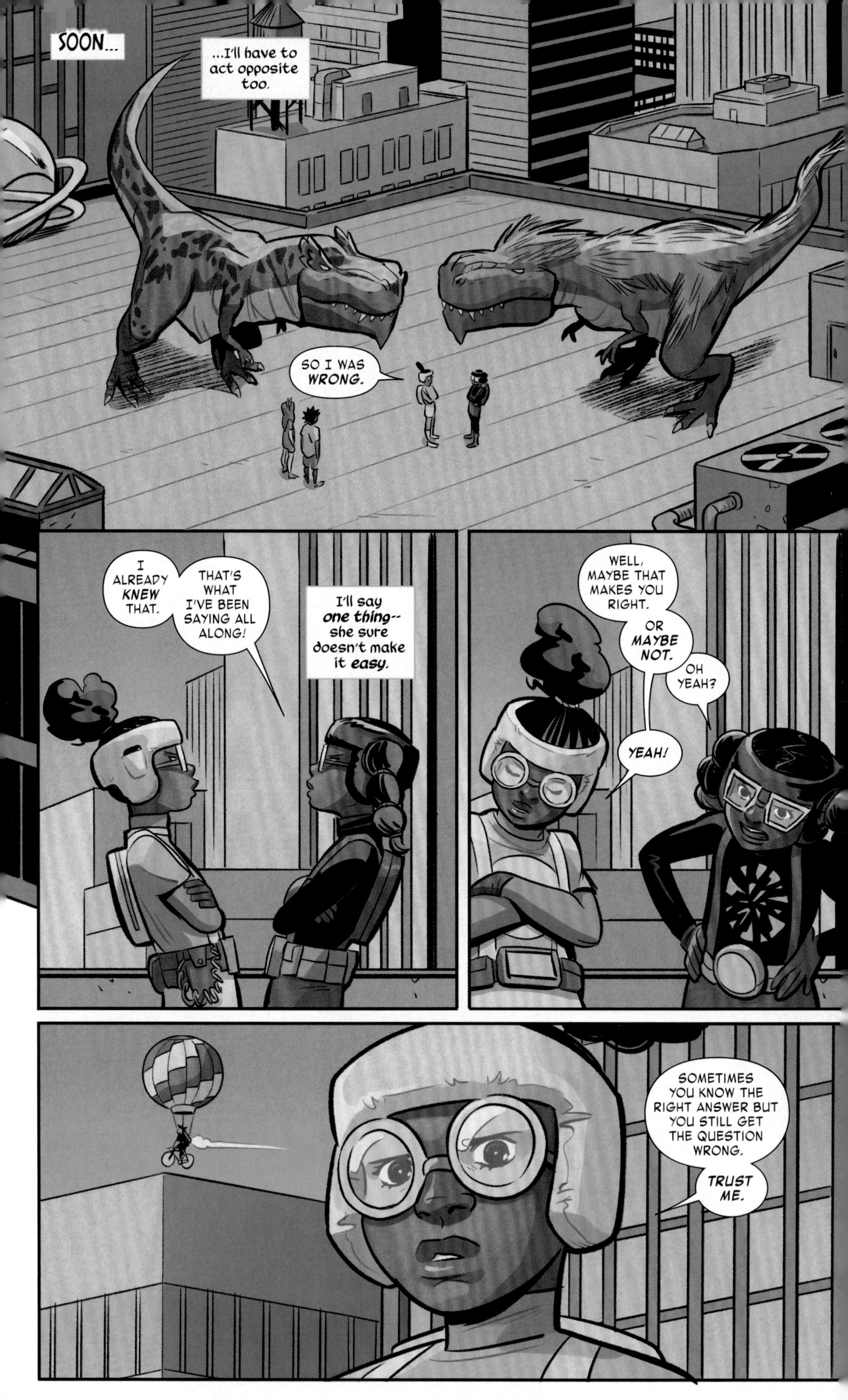
SOON...
...I'll have to act opposite too.
SO I WAS WRONG.
I ALREADY KNEW THAT.
THAT'S WHAT I'VE BEEN SAYING ALL ALONG!
I'll say one thing-- she sure doesn't make it easy.
WELL, MAYBE THAT MAKES YOU RIGHT.
OR MAYBE NOT.
OH YEAH?
YEAH!
SOMETIMES YOU KNOW THE RIGHT ANSWER BUT YOU STILL GET THE QUESTION WRONG.
TRUST ME.

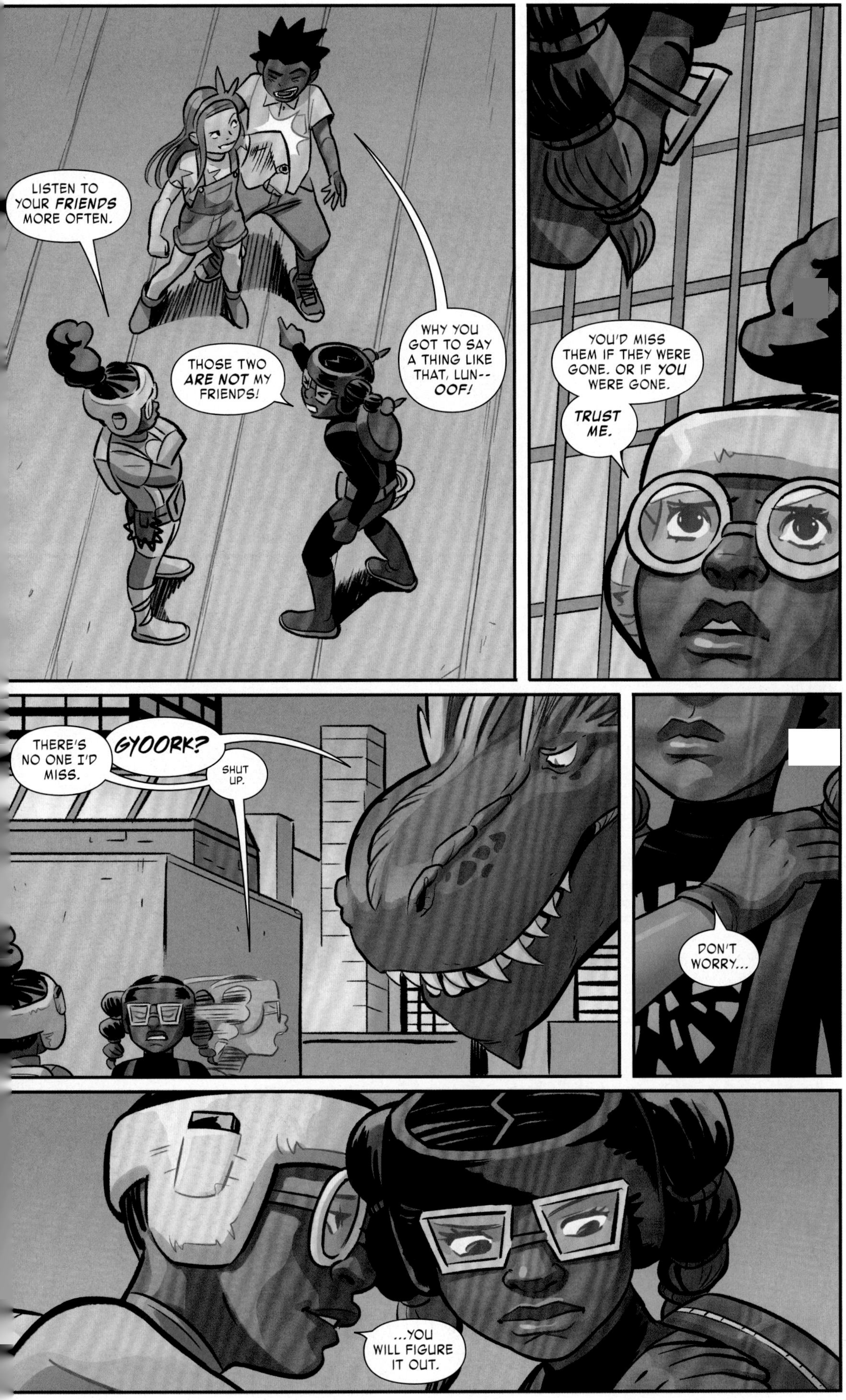

LISTEN TO YOUR FRIENDS MORE OFTEN.
THOSE TWO ARE NOT MY FRIENDS!
WHY YOU GOT TO SAY A THING LIKE THAT, LUN-- OOF!
YOU'D MISS THEM IF THEY WERE GONE. OR IF YOU WERE GONE.
TRUST ME.
THERE'S NO ONE I'D MISS.
GYOORK?
SHUT UP.
DON'T WORRY...
...YOU WILL FIGURE IT OUT.

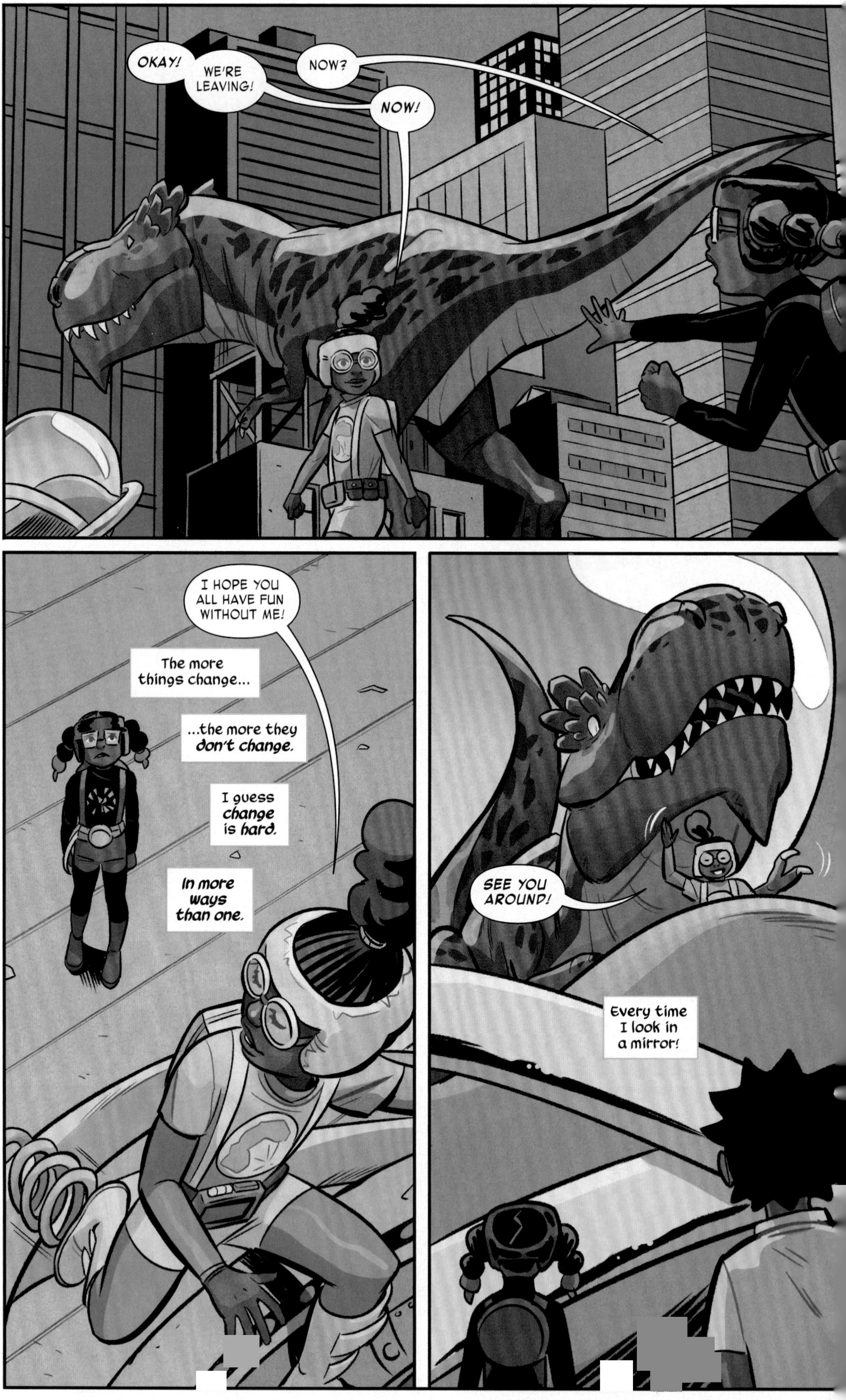
OKAY!
WE'RE LEAVING!
NOW?
NOW!
I HOPE YOU ALL HAVE FUN WITHOUT ME!
The more things change...
...the more they don't change.
I guess change is hard.
In more ways than one.
SEE YOU AROUND!
Every time I look in a mirror!

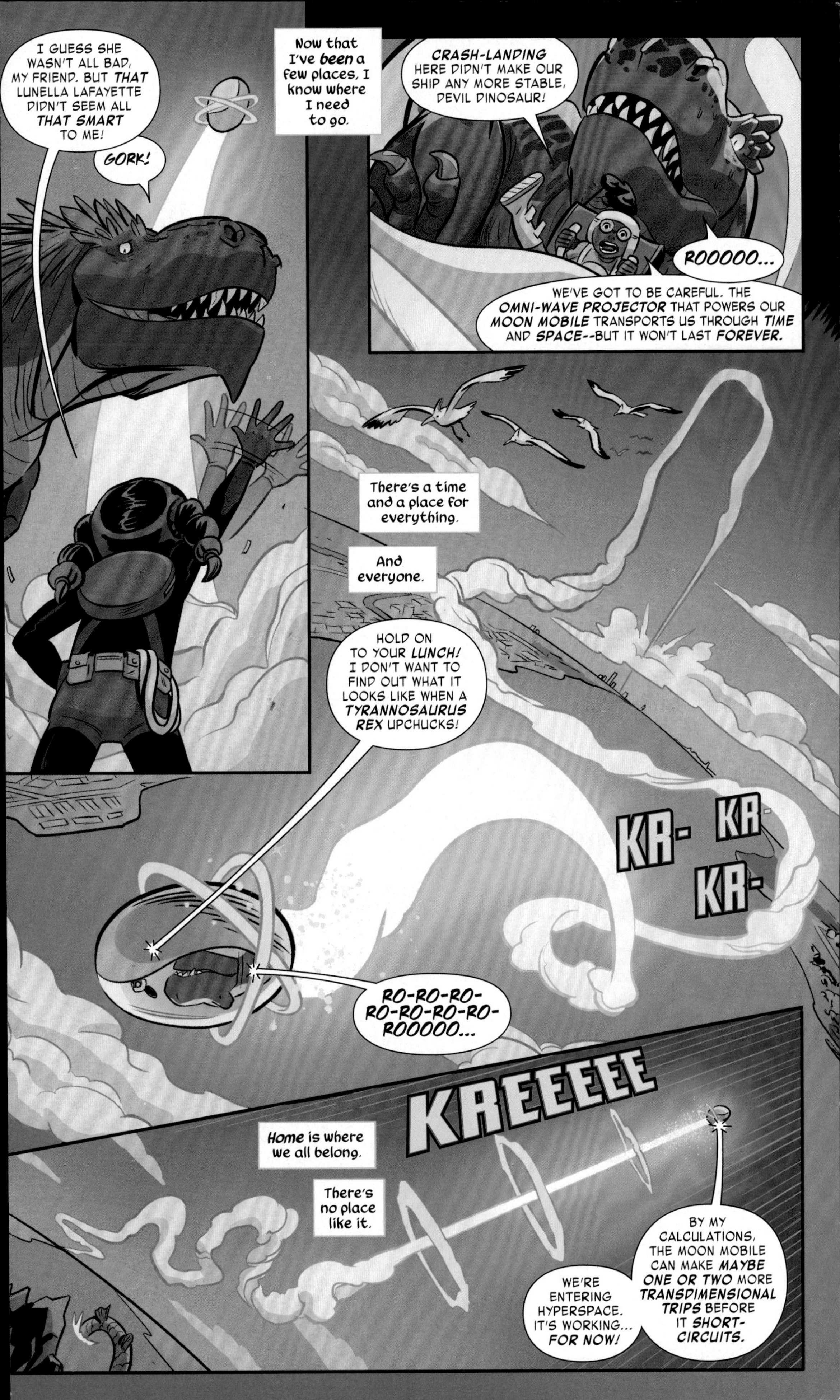
I GUESS SHE WASN'T ALL BAD, MY FRIEND. BUT THAT LUNELLA LAFAYETTE DIDN'T SEEM ALL THAT SMART TO ME!
GORK!
Now that I've been a few places, I know where I need to go.
CRASH-LANDING HERE DIDN'T MAKE OUR SHIP ANY MORE STABLE, DEVIL DINOSAUR!
ROOOOO...
WE'VE GOT TO BE CAREFUL. THE OMNI-WAVE PROJECTOR THAT POWERS OUR MOON MOBILE TRANSPORTS US THROUGH TIME AND SPACE--BUT IT WON'T LAST FOREVER.
There's a time and a place for everything.
And everyone.
HOLD ON TO YOUR LUNCH! I DON'T WANT TO FIND OUT WHAT IT LOOKS LIKE WHEN A TYRANNOSAURUS REX UPCHUCKS!
KR- KR- KR-
RO-RO-RO-RO-RO-RO-RO-ROOOOO...
KREEEEE
Home is where we all belong.
There's no place like it.
WE'RE ENTERING HYPERSPACE. IT'S WORKING... FOR NOW!
BY MY CALCULATIONS, THE MOON MOBILE CAN MAKE MAYBE ONE OR TWO MORE TRANSDIMENSIONAL TRIPS BEFORE IT SHORT-CIRCUITS.

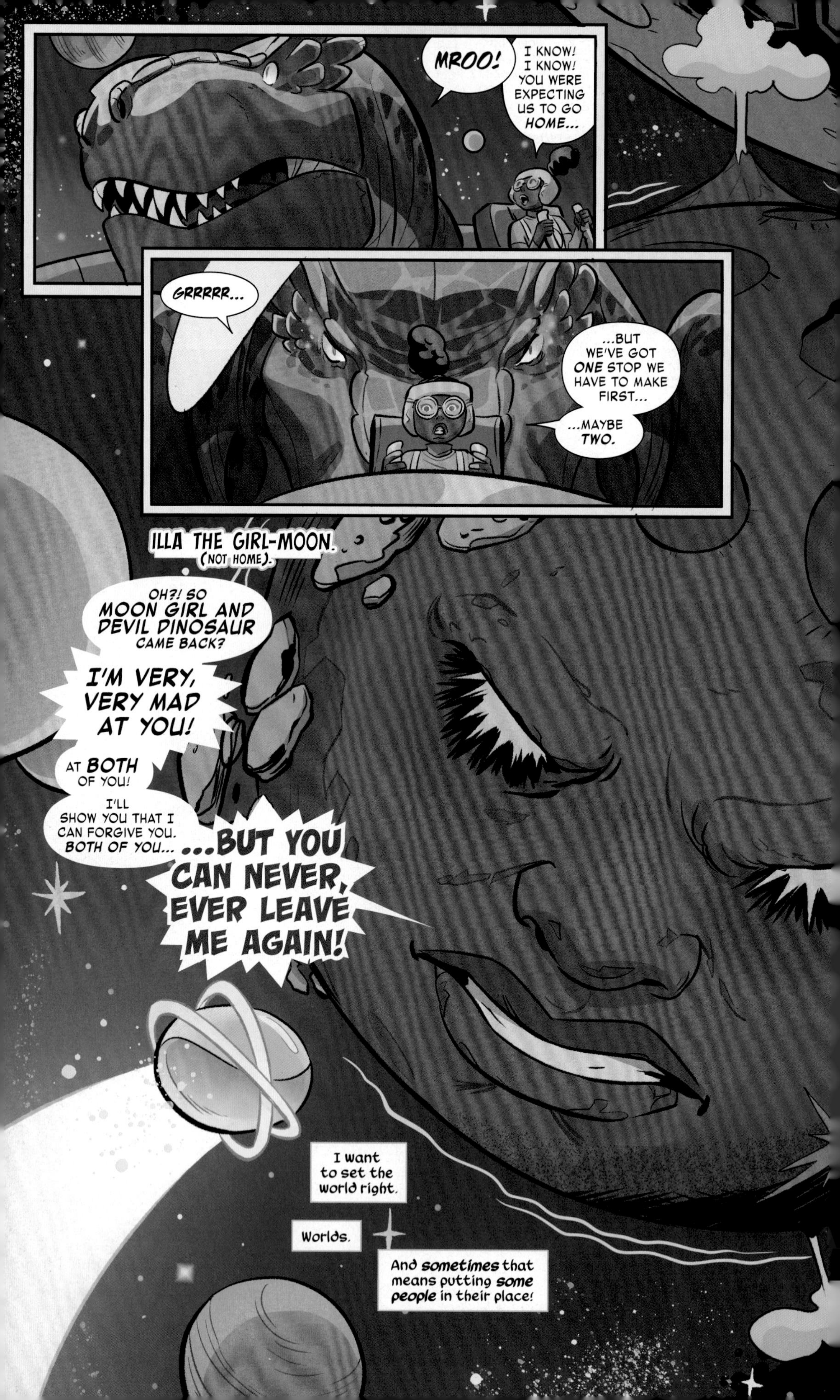
MROO!
I KNOW! I KNOW! YOU WERE EXPECTING US TO GO HOME...
GRRRRR...
...BUT WE'VE GOT ONE STOP WE HAVE TO MAKE FIRST...
...MAYBE TWO.
ILLA THE GIRL-MOON. (NOT HOME).
OH?! SO MOON GIRL AND DEVIL DINOSAUR CAME BACK?
I'M VERY, VERY MAD AT YOU!
AT BOTH OF YOU!
I'LL SHOW YOU THAT I CAN FORGIVE YOU. BOTH OF YOU...
...BUT YOU CAN NEVER, EVER LEAVE ME AGAIN!
I want to set the world right.
Worlds.
And sometimes that means putting some people in their place!

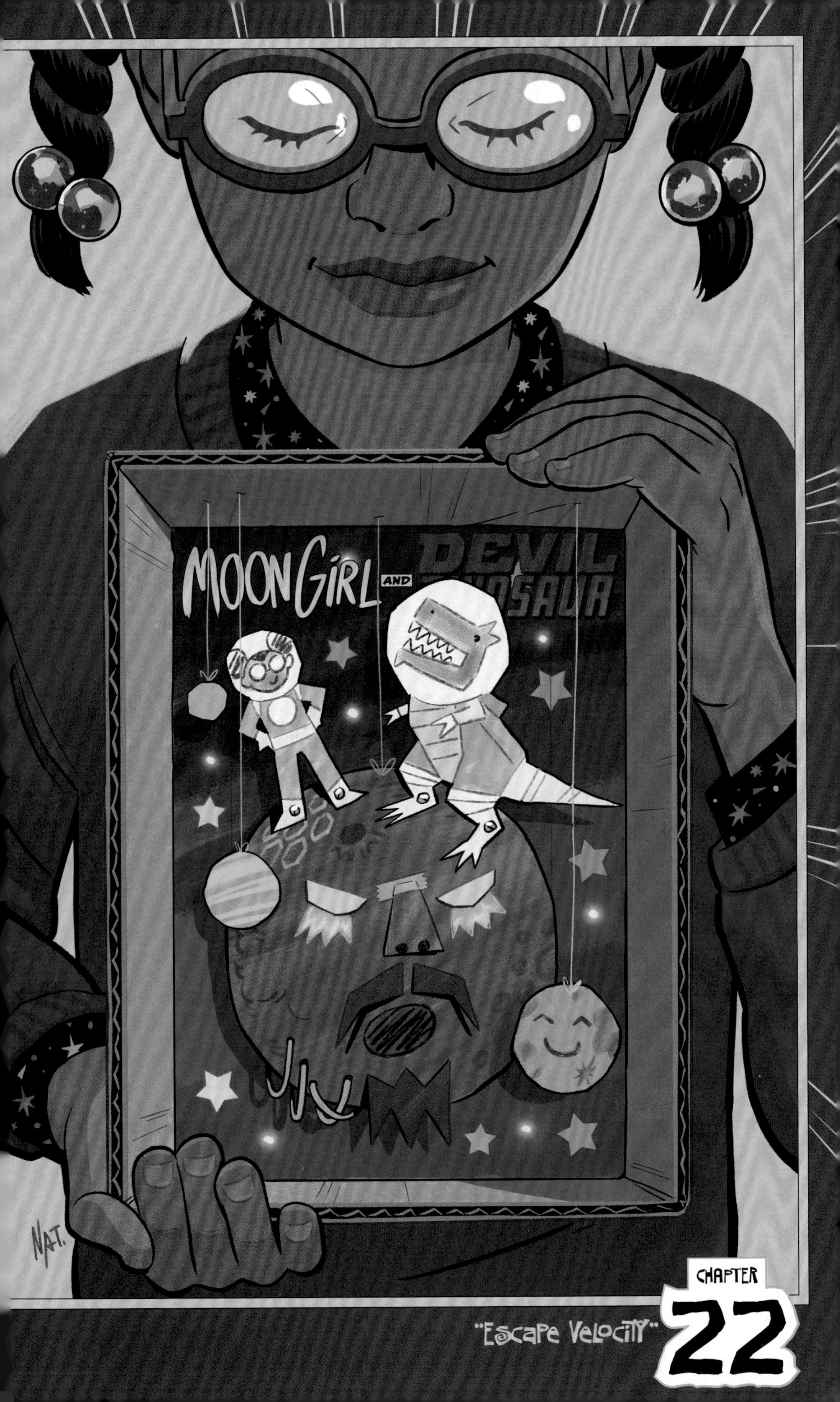

MOON GIRL AND DEVIL DINOSAUR
NAT.
CHAPTER
22
"Escape Velocity"

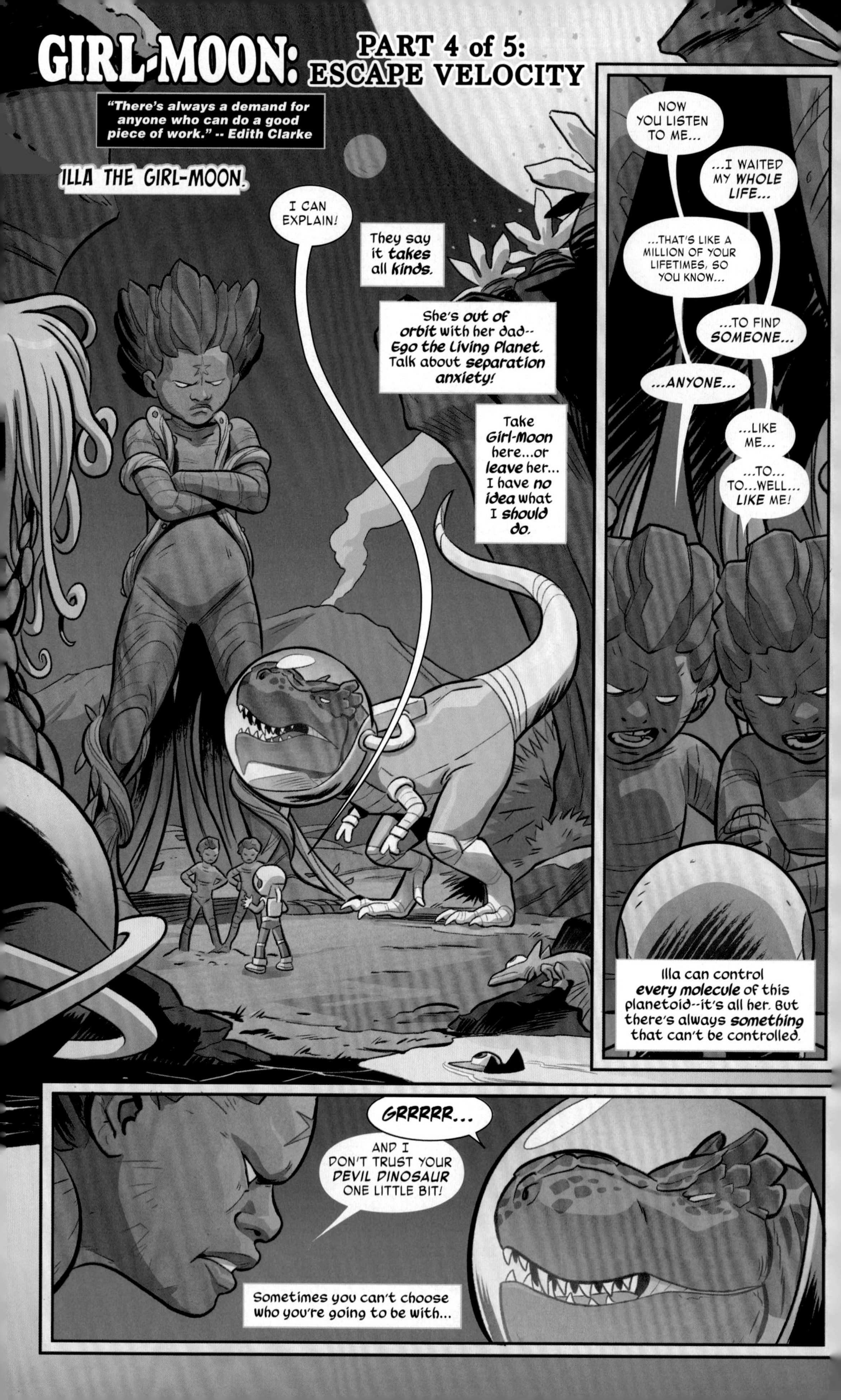
GIRL-MOON: PART 4 of 5: ESCAPE VELOCITY
"There's always a demand for anyone who can do a good piece of work." -- Edith Clarke
ILLA THE GIRL-MOON.
I CAN EXPLAIN!
They say it takes all kinds.
She's out of orbit with her dad--Ego the Living Planet. Talk about separation anxiety!
Take Girl-Moon here...or leave her... I have no idea what I should do.
NOW YOU LISTEN TO ME...
...I WAITED MY WHOLE LIFE...
...THAT'S LIKE A MILLION OF YOUR LIFETIMES, SO YOU KNOW...
...TO FIND SOMEONE...
...ANYONE...
...LIKE ME...
...TO... TO...WELL... LIKE ME!
Illa can control every molecule of this planetoid--it's all her. But there's always something that can't be controlled.
GRRRRR...
AND I DON'T TRUST YOUR DEVIL DINOSAUR ONE LITTLE BIT!
Sometimes you can't choose who you're going to be with...

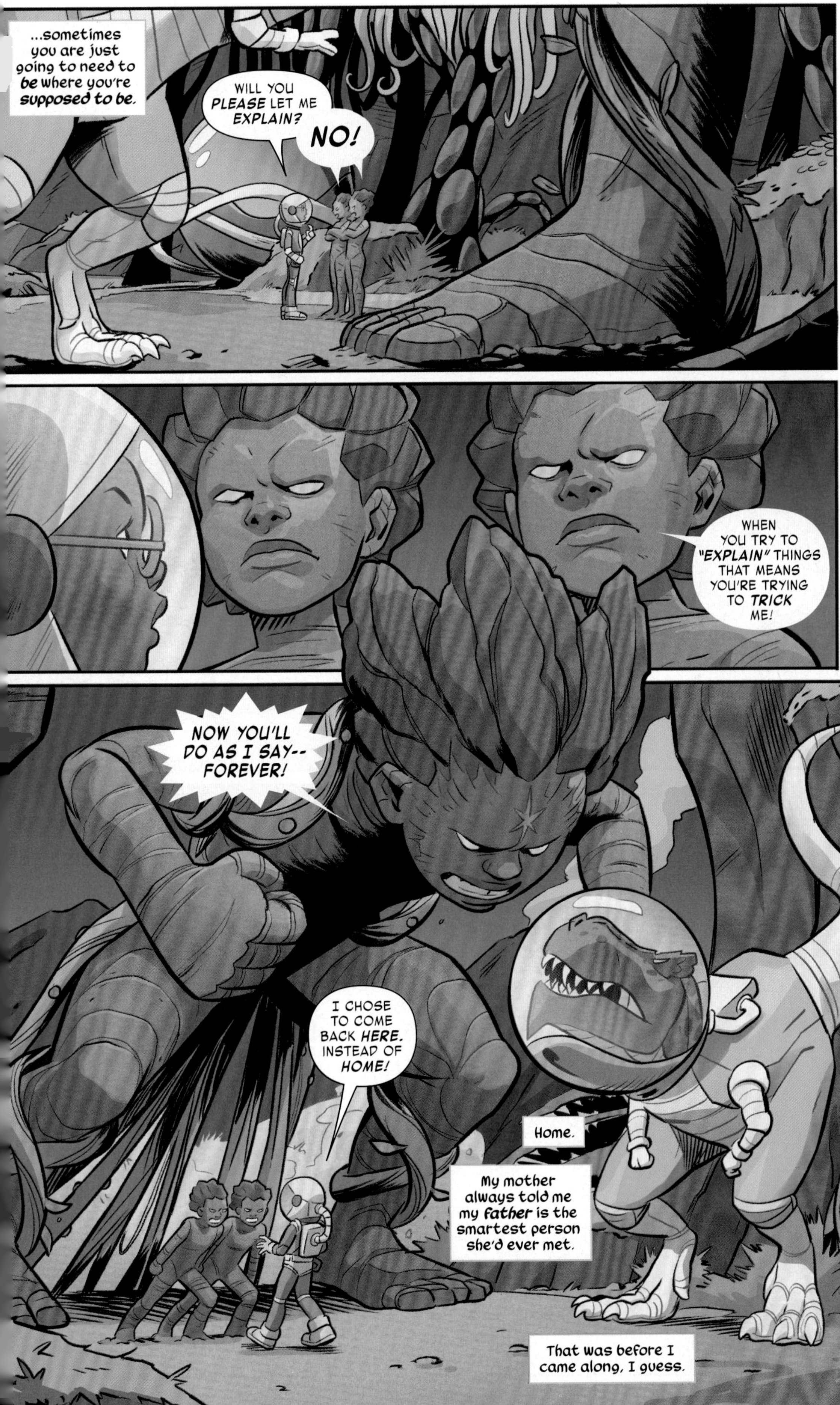
...sometimes you are just going to need to be where you're supposed to be.
WILL YOU PLEASE LET ME EXPLAIN?
NO!
WHEN YOU TRY TO "EXPLAIN" THINGS THAT MEANS YOU'RE TRYING TO TRICK ME!
NOW YOU'LL DO AS I SAY-- FOREVER!
I CHOSE TO COME BACK HERE. INSTEAD OF HOME!
Home.
My mother always told me my father is the smartest person she'd ever met.
That was before I came along, I guess.

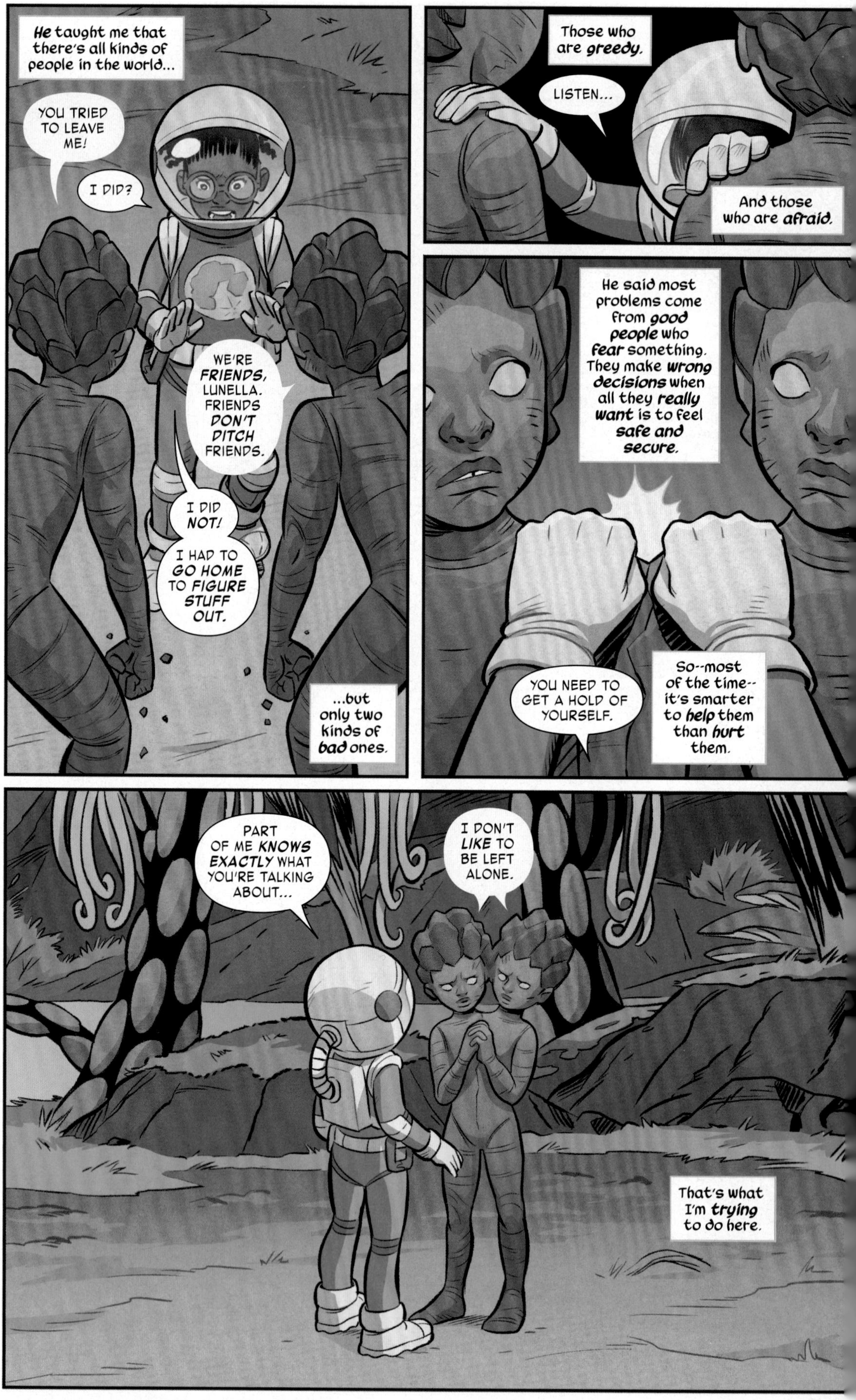
He taught me that there's all kinds of people in the world...
YOU TRIED TO LEAVE ME!
I DID?
WE'RE FRIENDS, LUNELLA. FRIENDS DON'T DITCH FRIENDS.
I DID NOT!
I HAD TO GO HOME TO FIGURE STUFF OUT.
...but only two kinds of bad ones.
Those who are greedy.
LISTEN...
And those who are afraid.
He said most problems come from good people who fear something. They make wrong decisions when all they really want is to feel safe and secure.
YOU NEED TO GET A HOLD OF YOURSELF.
So--most of the time--it's smarter to help them than hurt them.
PART OF ME KNOWS EXACTLY WHAT YOU'RE TALKING ABOUT...
I DON'T LIKE TO BE LEFT ALONE.
That's what I'm trying to do here.

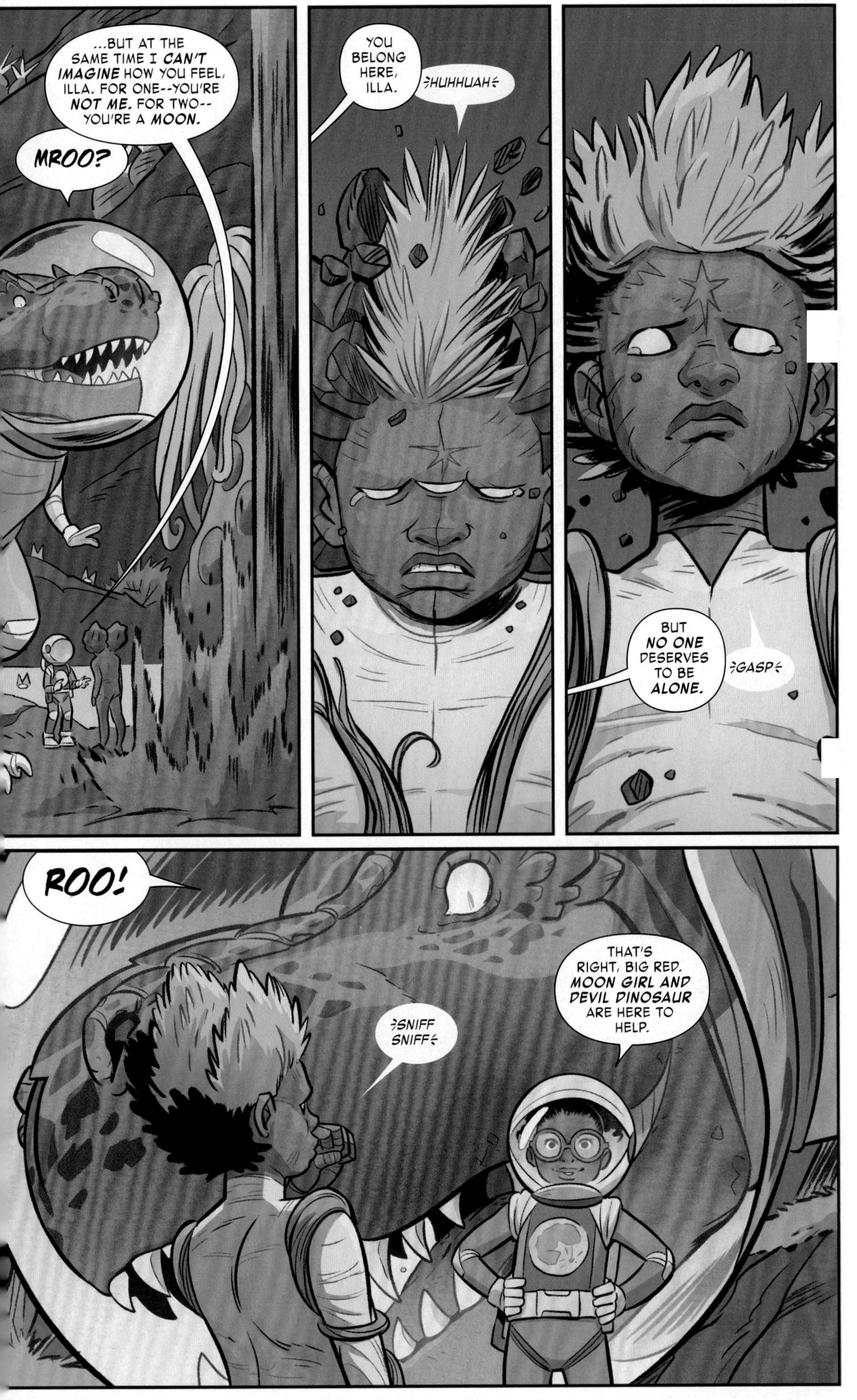
...BUT AT THE SAME TIME I CAN'T IMAGINE HOW YOU FEEL, ILLA. FOR ONE--YOU'RE NOT ME. FOR TWO--YOU'RE A MOON.
MROO?
YOU BELONG HERE, ILLA.
HUHHUAH
BUT NO ONE DESERVES TO BE ALONE.
GASP
ROO!
SNIFF SNIFF
THAT'S RIGHT, BIG RED. MOON GIRL AND DEVIL DINOSAUR ARE HERE TO HELP.

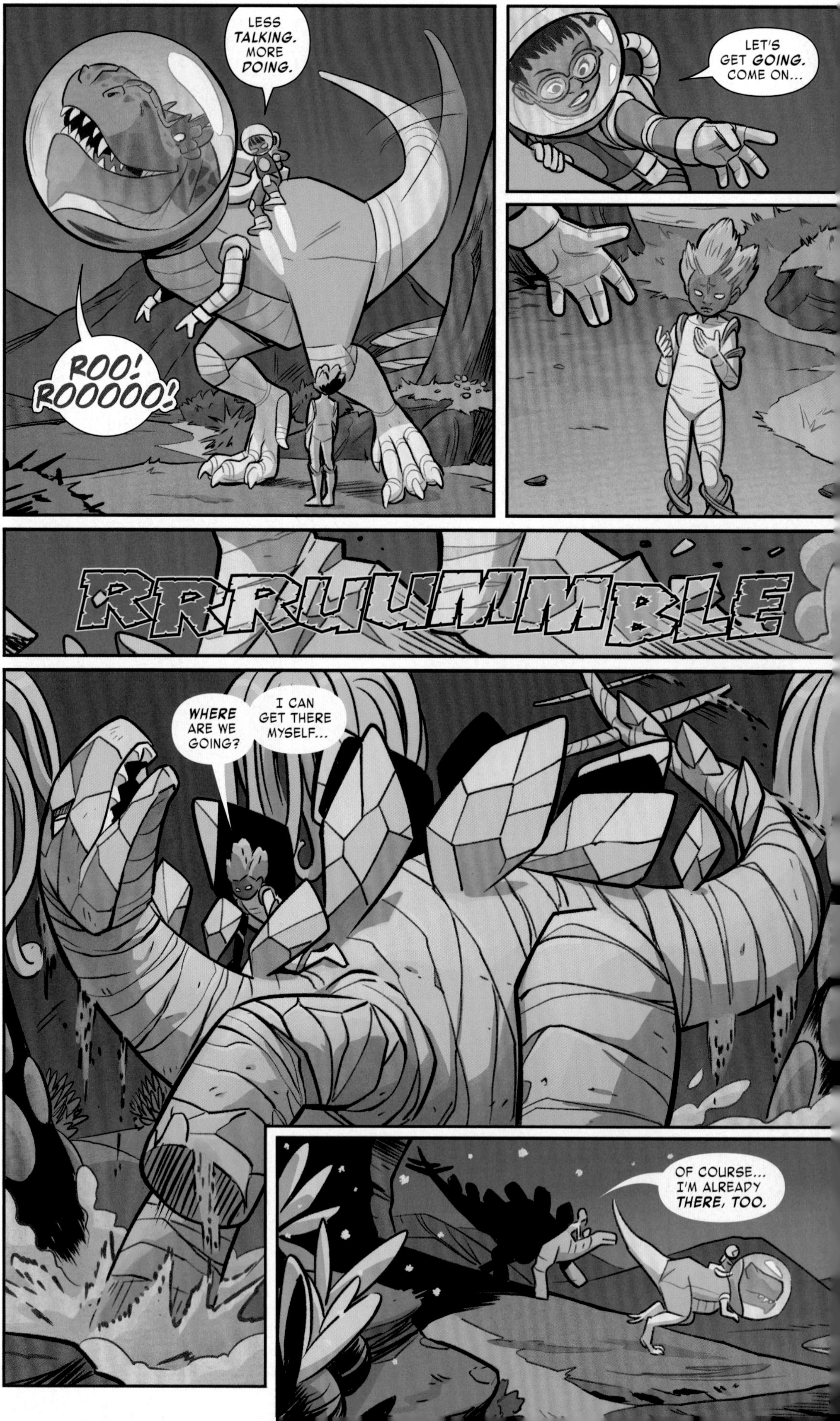
LESS TALKING. MORE DOING.
ROO! ROOOOO!
LET'S GET GOING. COME ON...
RRRUUMMBLE
WHERE ARE WE GOING?
I CAN GET THERE MYSELF...
OF COURSE... I'M ALREADY THERE, TOO.

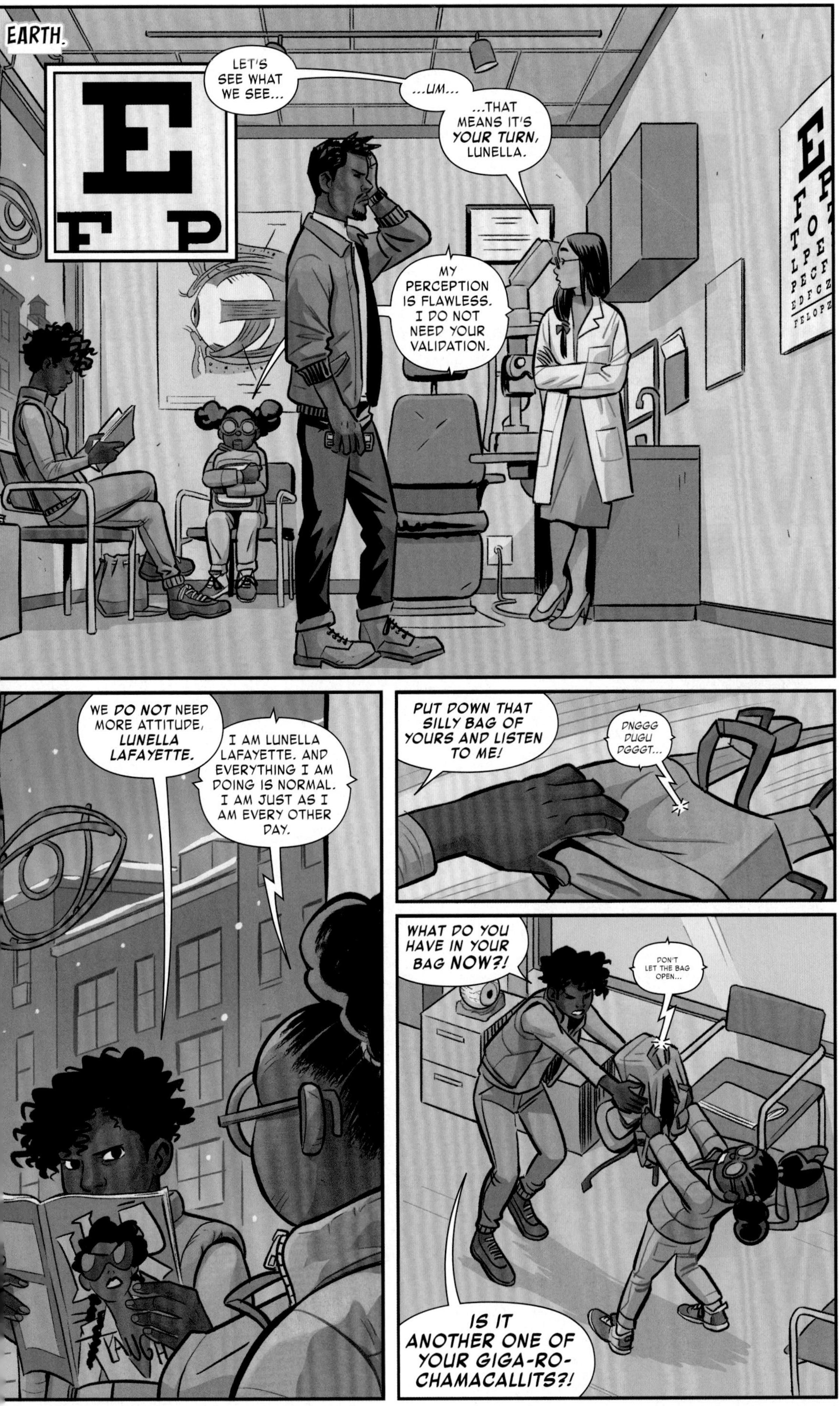
EARTH.
LET'S SEE WHAT WE SEE...
...UM...
...THAT MEANS IT'S YOUR TURN, LUNELLA.
MY PERCEPTION IS FLAWLESS. I DO NOT NEED YOUR VALIDATION.
WE DO NOT NEED MORE ATTITUDE, LUNELLA LAFAYETTE.
I AM LUNELLA LAFAYETTE. AND EVERYTHING I AM DOING IS NORMAL. I AM JUST AS I AM EVERY OTHER DAY.
PUT DOWN THAT SILLY BAG OF YOURS AND LISTEN TO ME!
DNGGG DUGU DGGGT...
WHAT DO YOU HAVE IN YOUR BAG NOW?!
DON'T LET THE BAG OPEN...
IS IT ANOTHER ONE OF YOUR GIGA-RO-CHAMACALLITS?!

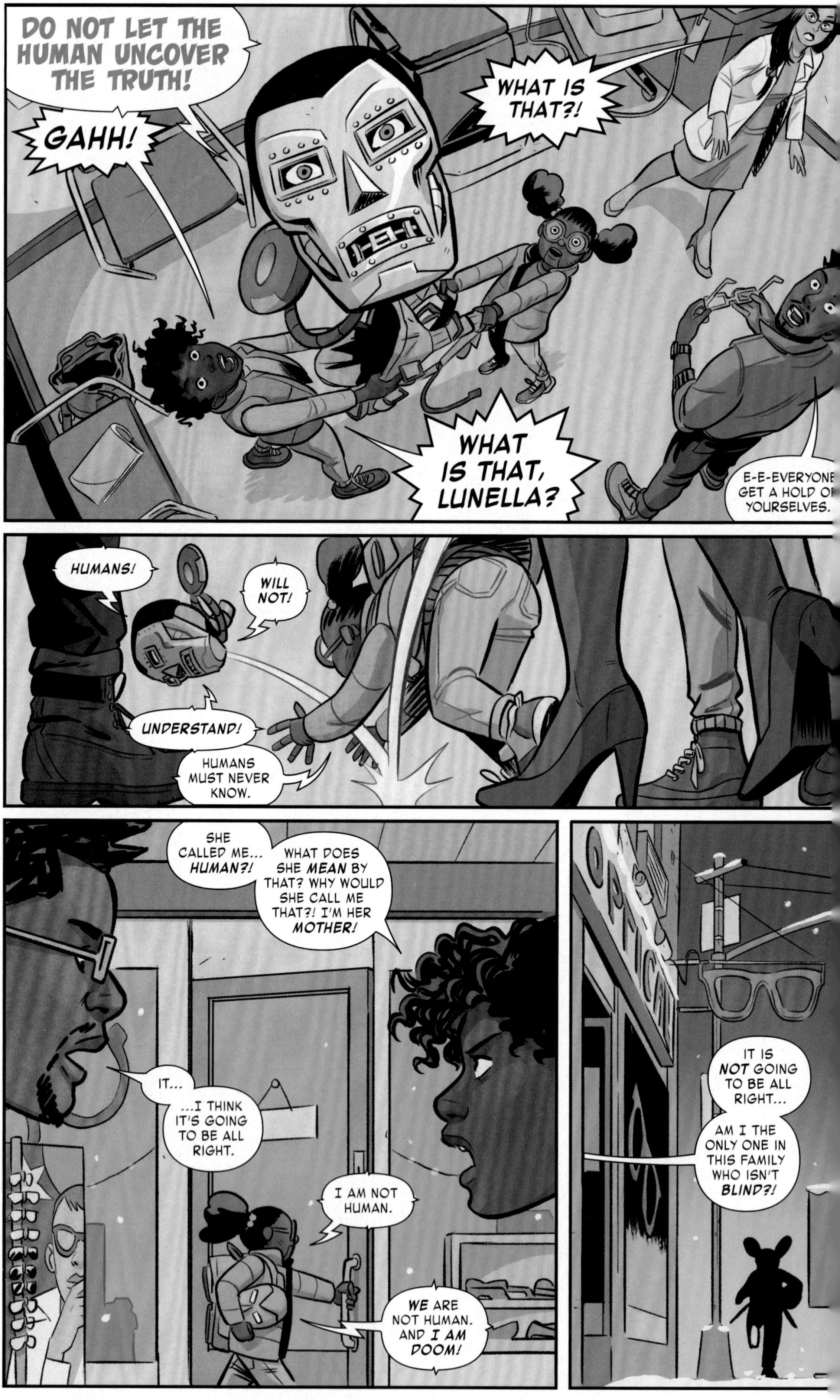
DO NOT LET THE HUMAN UNCOVER THE TRUTH!
GAHH!
WHAT IS THAT?!
WHAT IS THAT, LUNELLA?
E-E-EVERYONE GET A HOLD OF YOURSELVES.
HUMANS!
WILL NOT!
UNDERSTAND!
HUMANS MUST NEVER KNOW.
SHE CALLED ME... HUMAN?!
WHAT DOES SHE MEAN BY THAT? WHY WOULD SHE CALL ME THAT?! I'M HER MOTHER!
IT...
...I THINK IT'S GOING TO BE ALL RIGHT.
I AM NOT HUMAN.
WE ARE NOT HUMAN. AND I AM DOOM!
IT IS NOT GOING TO BE ALL RIGHT...
AM I THE ONLY ONE IN THIS FAMILY WHO ISN'T BLIND?!

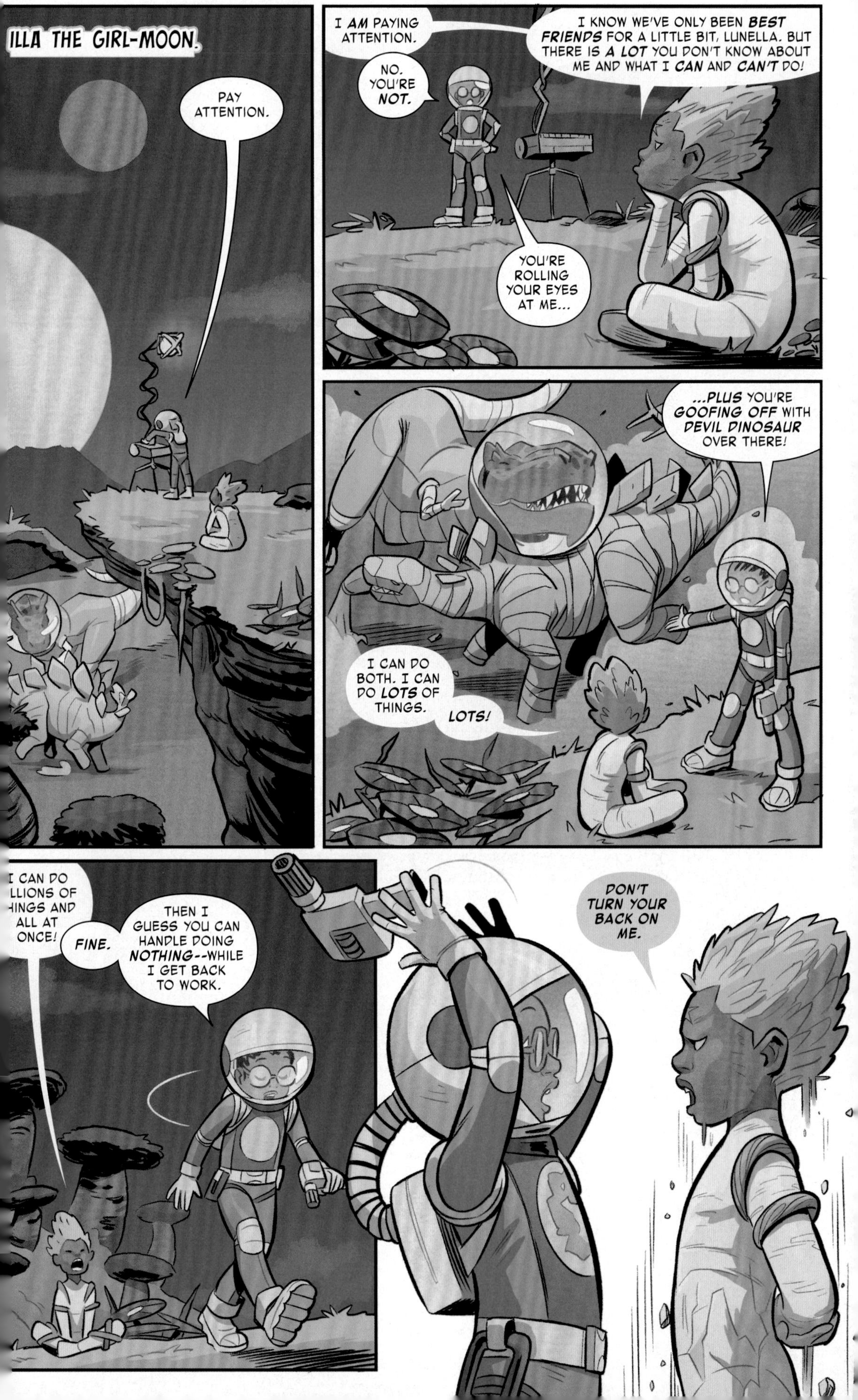

ILLA THE GIRL-MOON.
PAY ATTENTION.
I AM PAYING ATTENTION.
I KNOW WE'VE ONLY BEEN BEST FRIENDS FOR A LITTLE BIT, LUNELLA. BUT THERE IS A LOT YOU DON'T KNOW ABOUT ME AND WHAT I CAN AND CAN'T DO!
NO. YOU'RE NOT.
YOU'RE ROLLING YOUR EYES AT ME...
...PLUS YOU'RE GOOFING OFF WITH DEVIL DINOSAUR OVER THERE!
I CAN DO BOTH. I CAN DO LOTS OF THINGS.
LOTS!
I CAN DO LLIONS OF HINGS AND ALL AT ONCE!
FINE.
THEN I GUESS YOU CAN HANDLE DOING NOTHING--WHILE I GET BACK TO WORK.
DON'T TURN YOUR BACK ON ME.

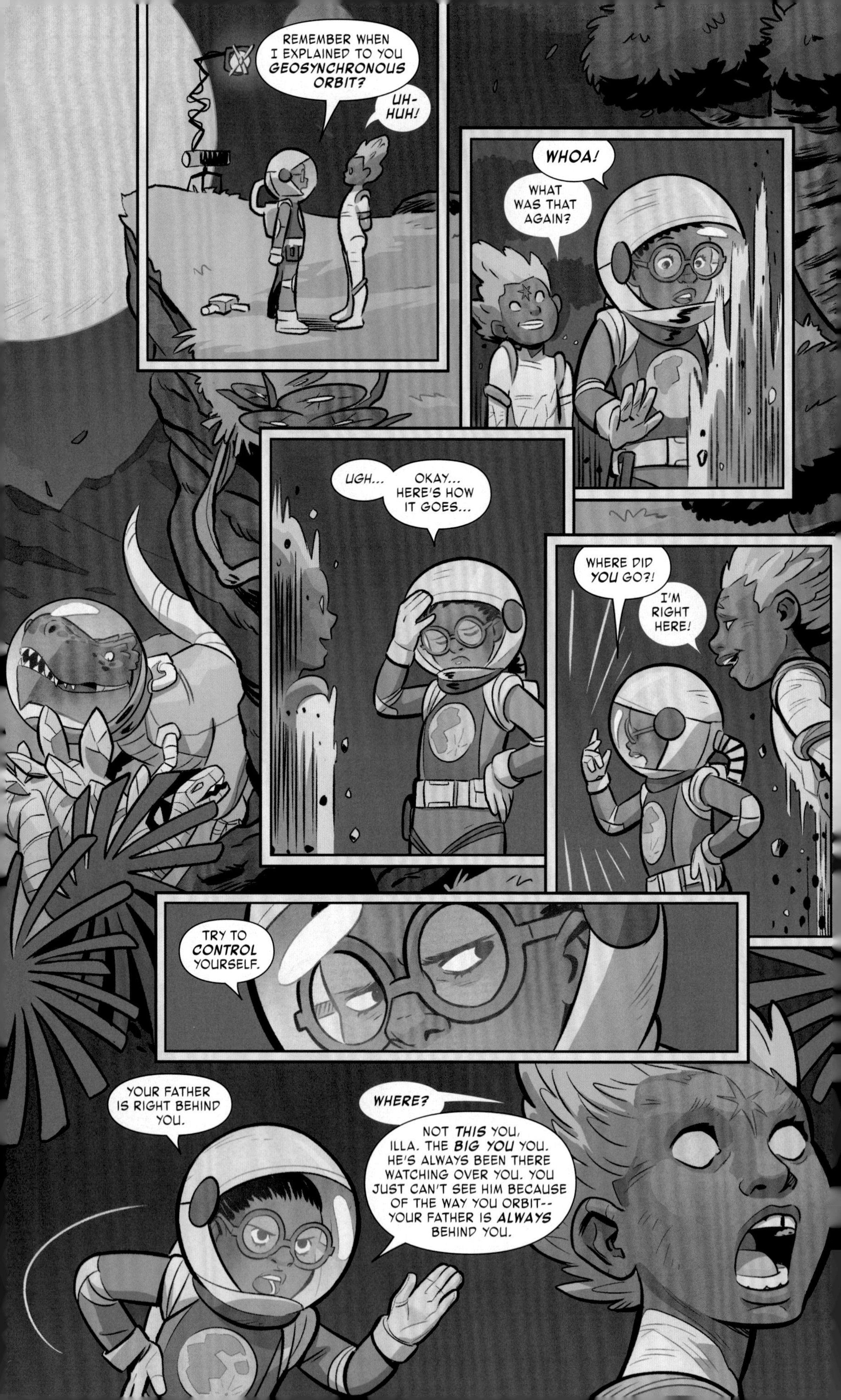
REMEMBER WHEN I EXPLAINED TO YOU GEOSYNCHRONOUS ORBIT?
UH-HUH!
WHOA!
WHAT WAS THAT AGAIN?
UGH...
OKAY... HERE'S HOW IT GOES...
WHERE DID YOU GO?!
I'M RIGHT HERE!
TRY TO CONTROL YOURSELF.
YOUR FATHER IS RIGHT BEHIND YOU.
WHERE?
NOT THIS YOU, ILLA. THE BIG YOU YOU. HE'S ALWAYS BEEN THERE WATCHING OVER YOU. YOU JUST CAN'T SEE HIM BECAUSE OF THE WAY YOU ORBIT-- YOUR FATHER IS ALWAYS BEHIND YOU.

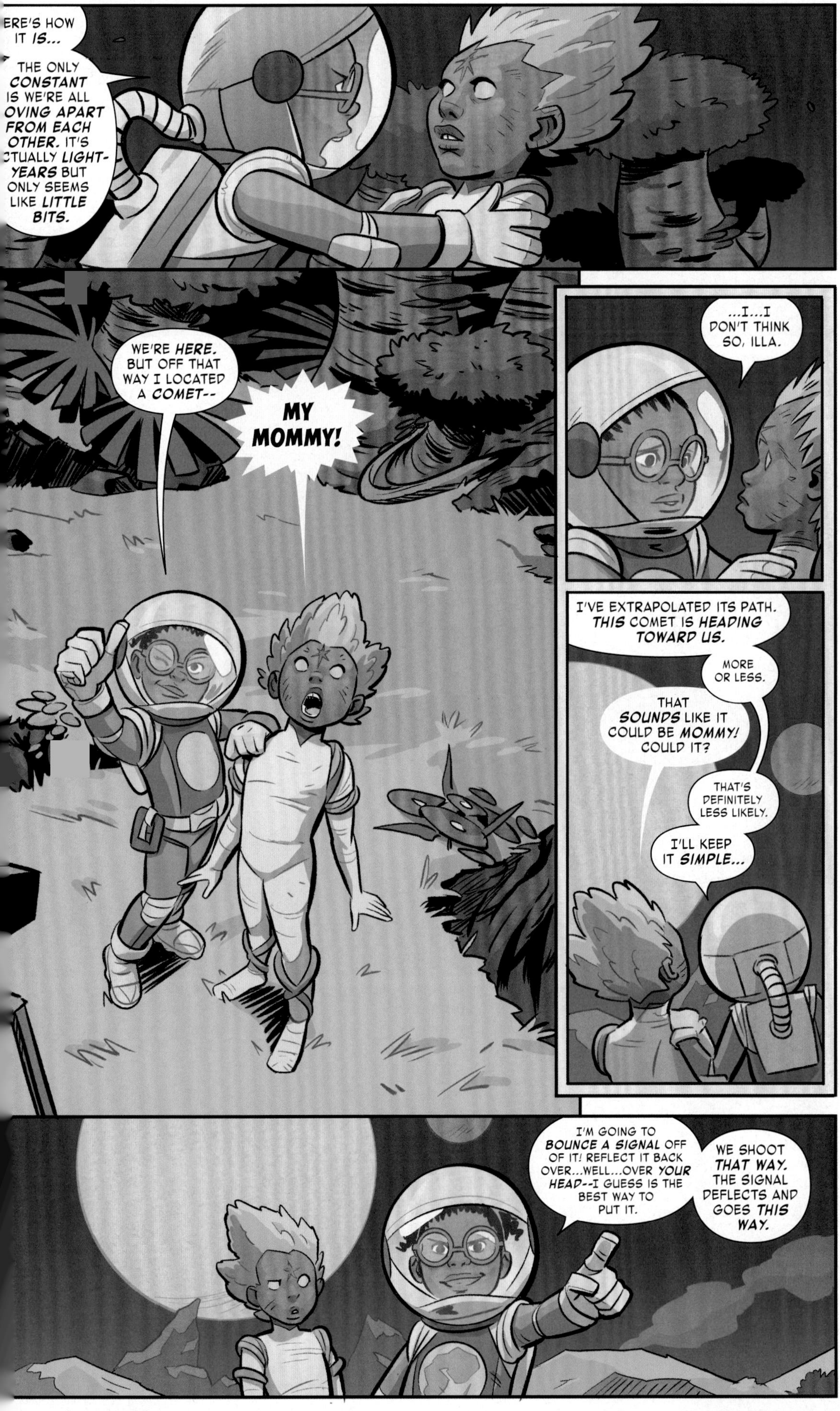
ERE'S HOW IT IS...
THE ONLY CONSTANT IS WE'RE ALL OVING APART FROM EACH OTHER. IT'S CTUALLY LIGHT-YEARS BUT ONLY SEEMS LIKE LITTLE BITS.
WE'RE HERE. BUT OFF THAT WAY I LOCATED A COMET--
MY MOMMY!
...I...I DON'T THINK SO, ILLA.
I'VE EXTRAPOLATED ITS PATH. THIS COMET IS HEADING TOWARD US.
MORE OR LESS.
THAT SOUNDS LIKE IT COULD BE MOMMY! COULD IT?
THAT'S DEFINITELY LESS LIKELY.
I'LL KEEP IT SIMPLE...
I'M GOING TO BOUNCE A SIGNAL OFF OF IT! REFLECT IT BACK OVER...WELL...OVER YOUR HEAD--I GUESS IS THE BEST WAY TO PUT IT.
WE SHOOT THAT WAY. THE SIGNAL DEFLECTS AND GOES THIS WAY.

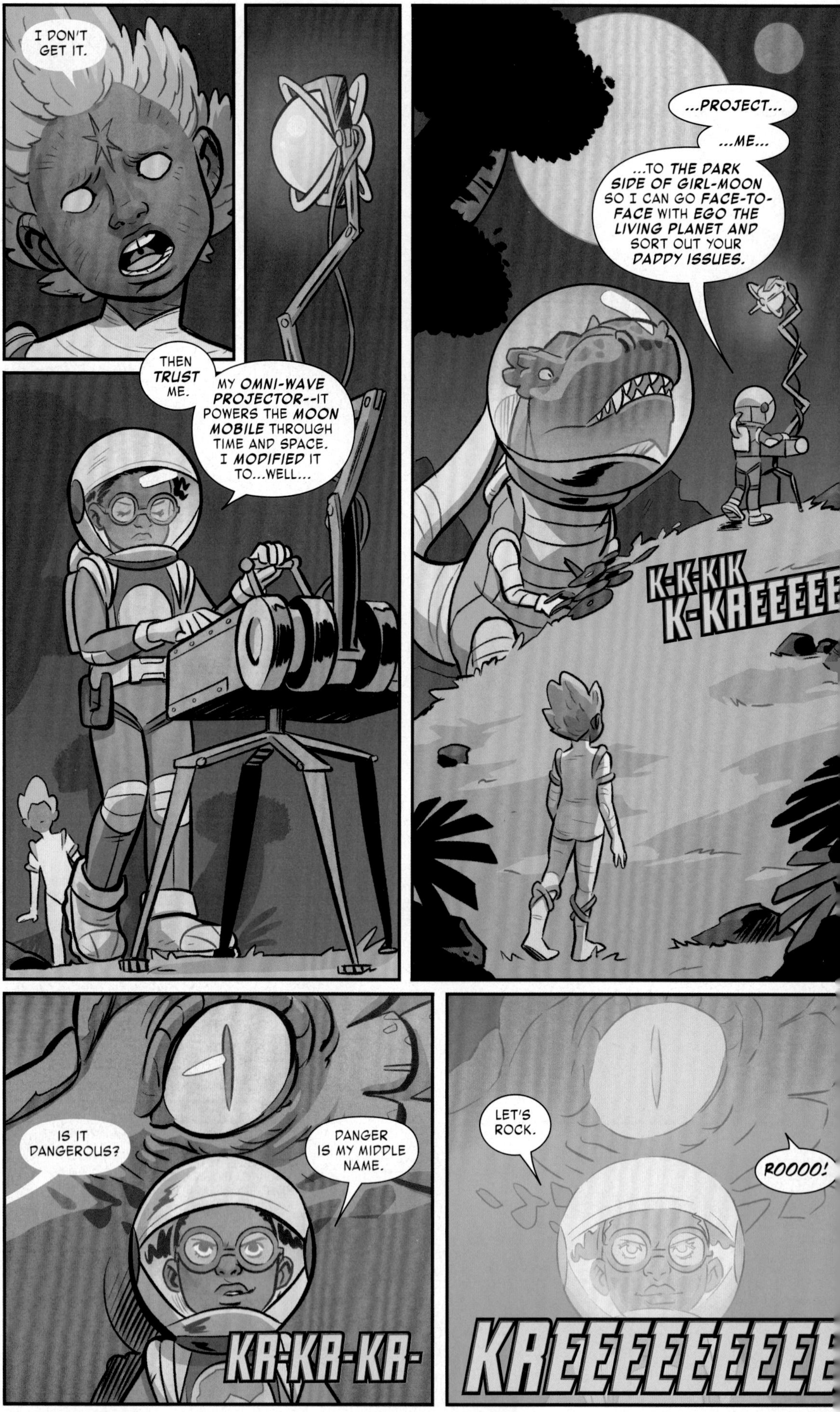

I DON'T GET IT.
THEN TRUST ME.
MY OMNI-WAVE PROJECTOR--IT POWERS THE MOON MOBILE THROUGH TIME AND SPACE. I MODIFIED IT TO...WELL...
...PROJECT...
...ME...
...TO THE DARK SIDE OF GIRL-MOON SO I CAN GO FACE-TO-FACE WITH EGO THE LIVING PLANET AND SORT OUT YOUR DADDY ISSUES.
K-K-KIK K-KREEEEE
IS IT DANGEROUS?
DANGER IS MY MIDDLE NAME.
KR-KR-KR-
LET'S ROCK.
ROOOO!
KREEEEEEEEEE

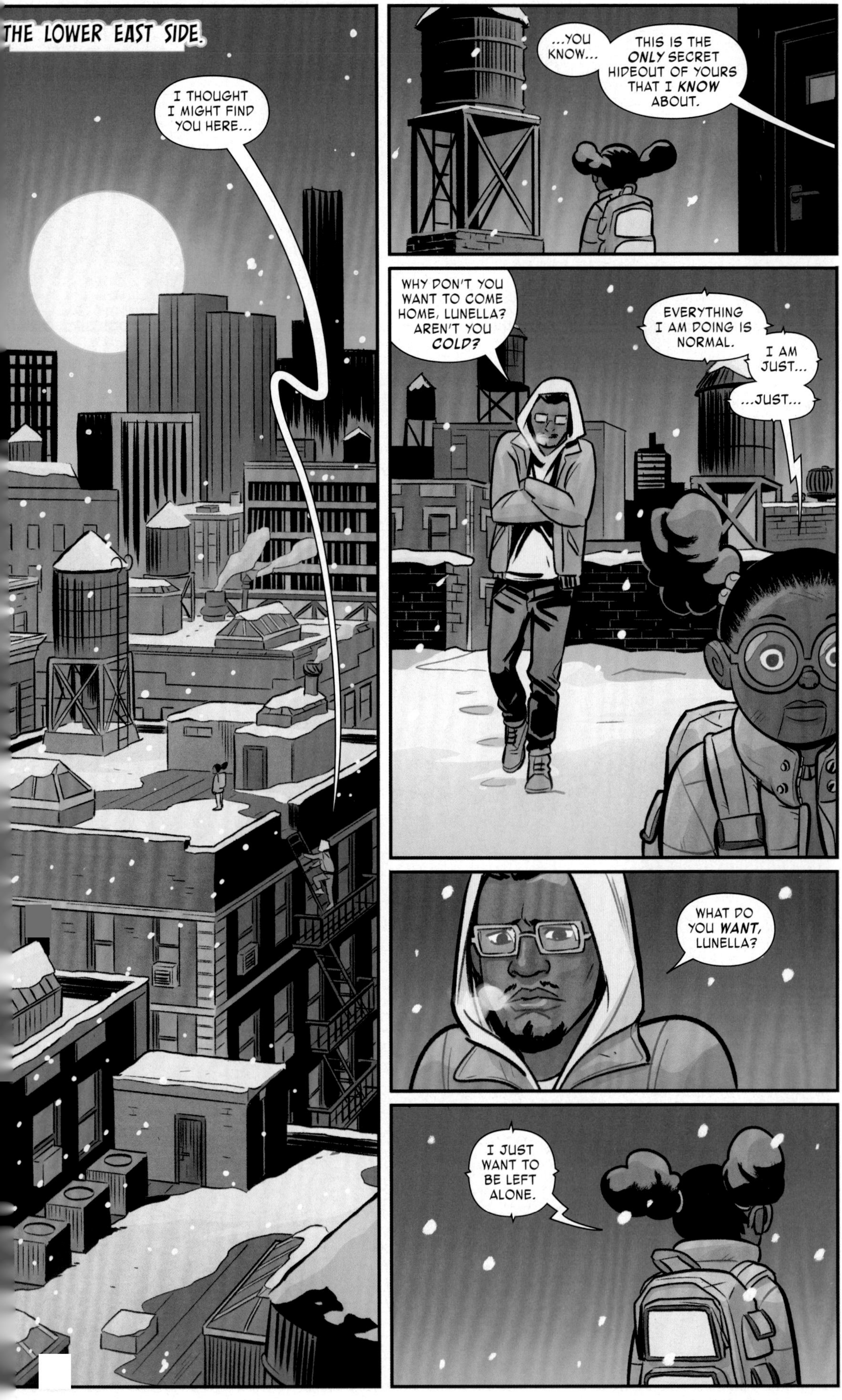
THE LOWER EAST SIDE.
I THOUGHT I MIGHT FIND YOU HERE...
...YOU KNOW...
THIS IS THE ONLY SECRET HIDEOUT OF YOURS THAT I KNOW ABOUT.
WHY DON'T YOU WANT TO COME HOME, LUNELLA? AREN'T YOU COLD?
EVERYTHING I AM DOING IS NORMAL.
I AM JUST...
...JUST...
WHAT DO YOU WANT, LUNELLA?
I JUST WANT TO BE LEFT ALONE.

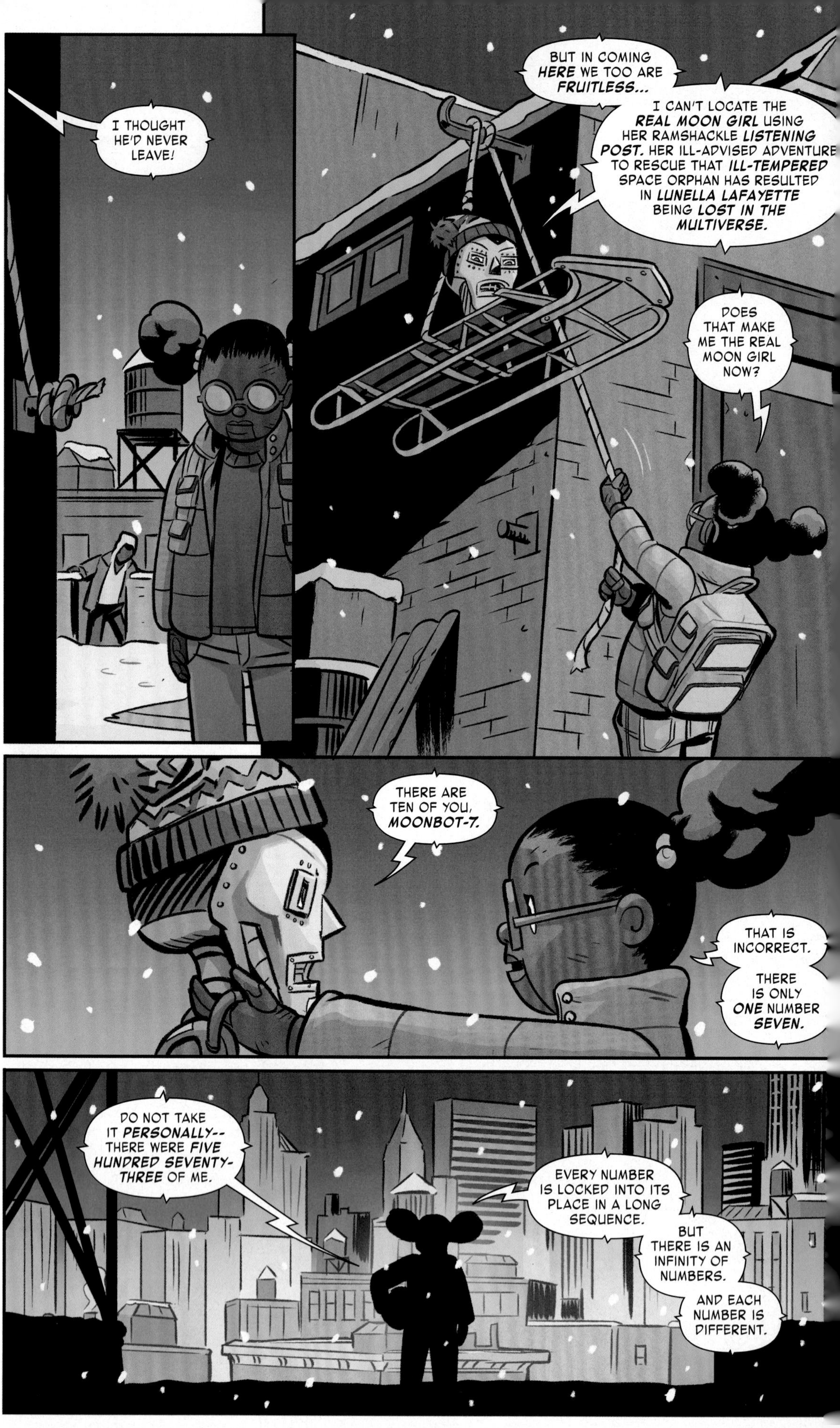
I THOUGHT HE'D NEVER LEAVE!
BUT IN COMING *HERE* WE TOO ARE *FRUITLESS...*
I CAN'T LOCATE THE *REAL MOON GIRL* USING HER RAMSHACKLE *LISTENING POST.* HER ILL-ADVISED ADVENTURE TO RESCUE THAT *ILL-TEMPERED* SPACE ORPHAN HAS RESULTED IN *LUNELLA LAFAYETTE* BEING *LOST IN THE MULTIVERSE.*
DOES THAT MAKE ME THE REAL MOON GIRL NOW?
THERE ARE TEN OF YOU, *MOONBOT-7.*
THAT IS INCORRECT.
THERE IS ONLY *ONE* NUMBER *SEVEN.*
DO NOT TAKE IT *PERSONALLY--* THERE WERE *FIVE HUNDRED SEVENTY-THREE* OF ME.
EVERY NUMBER IS LOCKED INTO ITS PLACE IN A LONG SEQUENCE.
BUT THERE IS AN INFINITY OF NUMBERS.
AND EACH NUMBER IS DIFFERENT.

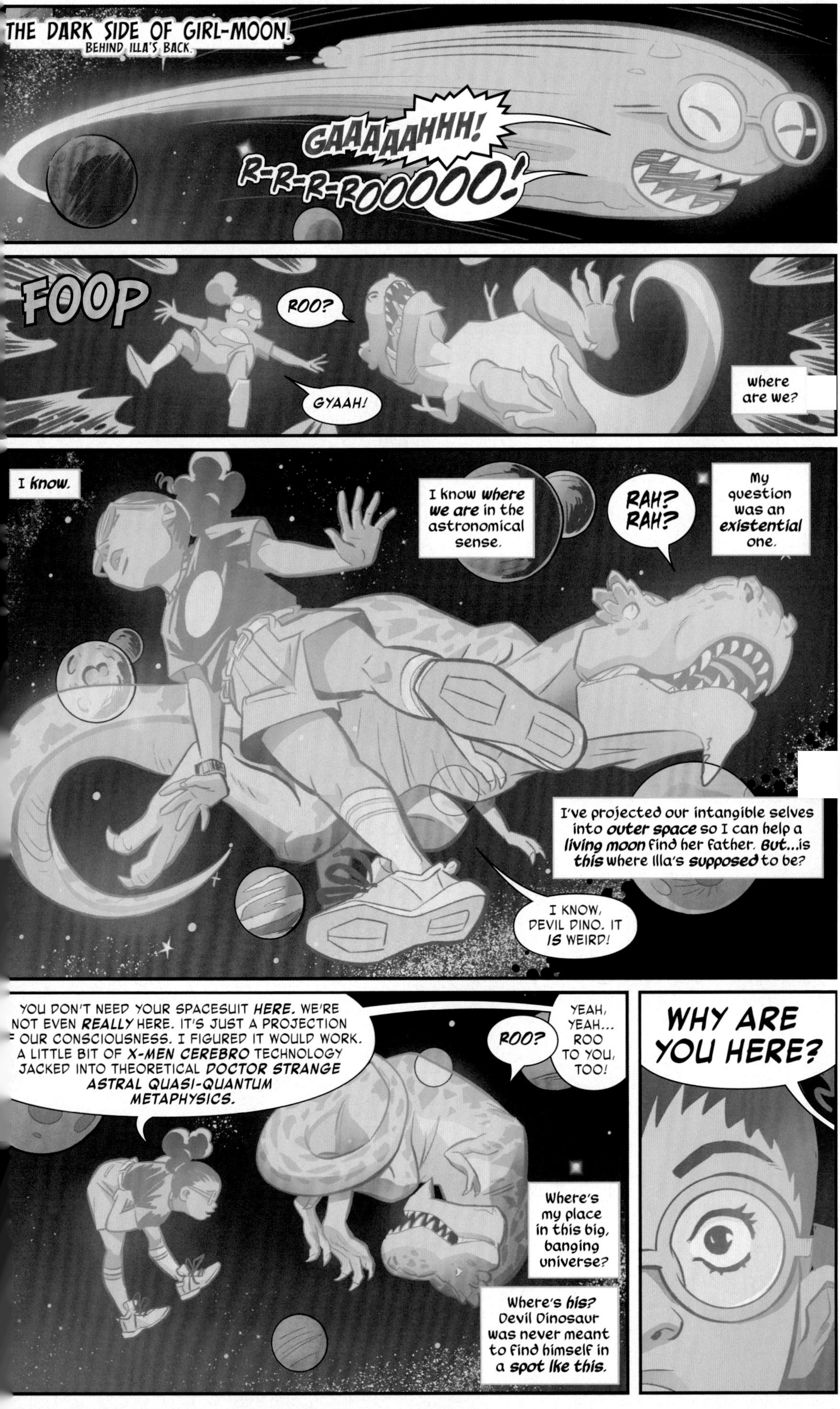
THE DARK SIDE OF GIRL-MOON.
BEHIND ILLA'S BACK.
GAAAAAHHH!
R-R-R-ROOOOOO!
FOOP
ROO?
GYAAH!
Where are we?
I know.
I know where we are in the astronomical sense.
RAH? RAH?
My question was an existential one.
I've projected our intangible selves into outer space so I can help a living moon find her father. But...is this where Illa's supposed to be?
I KNOW, DEVIL DINO. IT IS WEIRD!
YOU DON'T NEED YOUR SPACESUIT HERE. WE'RE NOT EVEN REALLY HERE. IT'S JUST A PROJECTION OF OUR CONSCIOUSNESS. I FIGURED IT WOULD WORK. A LITTLE BIT OF X-MEN CEREBRO TECHNOLOGY JACKED INTO THEORETICAL DOCTOR STRANGE ASTRAL QUASI-QUANTUM METAPHYSICS.
ROO?
YEAH, YEAH... ROO TO YOU, TOO!
Where's my place in this big, banging universe?
Where's his? Devil Dinosaur was never meant to find himself in a spot like this.
WHY ARE YOU HERE?

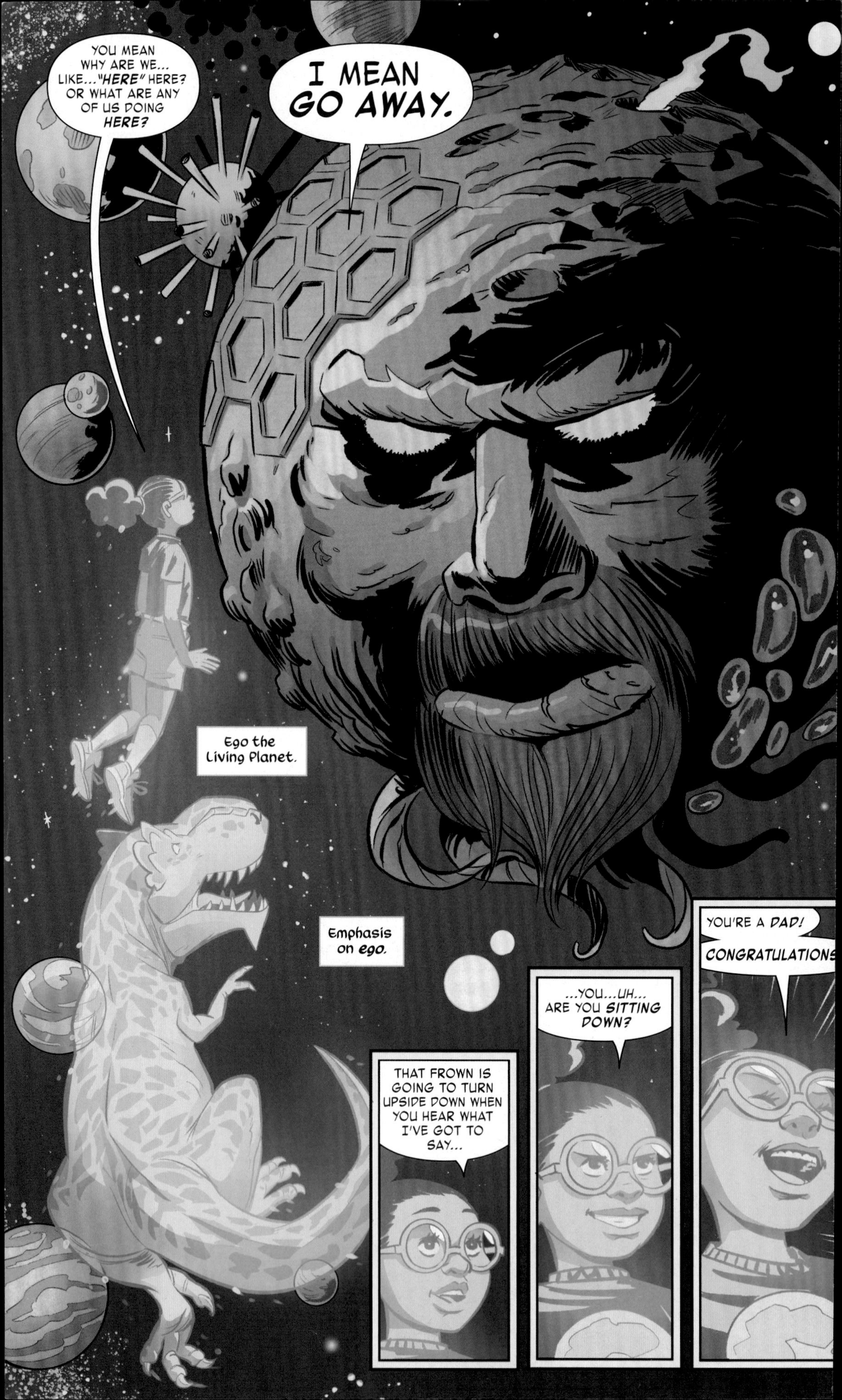
YOU MEAN WHY ARE WE... LIKE..."HERE" HERE? OR WHAT ARE ANY OF US DOING HERE?
I MEAN GO AWAY.
Ego the Living Planet.
Emphasis on ego.
THAT FROWN IS GOING TO TURN UPSIDE DOWN WHEN YOU HEAR WHAT I'VE GOT TO SAY...
...YOU...UH... ARE YOU SITTING DOWN?
YOU'RE A DAD!
CONGRATULATIONS

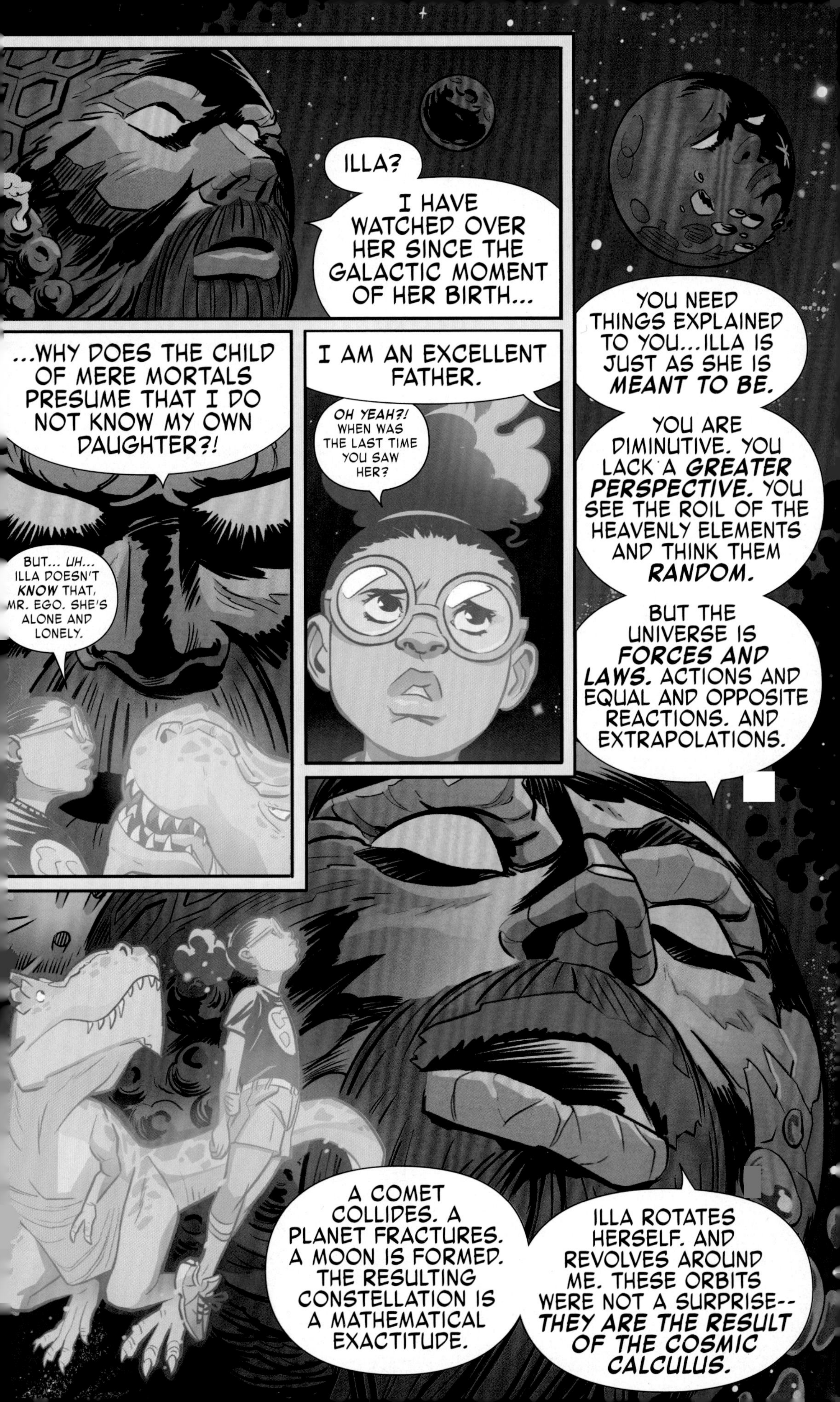
ILLA?
I HAVE WATCHED OVER HER SINCE THE GALACTIC MOMENT OF HER BIRTH...
...WHY DOES THE CHILD OF MERE MORTALS PRESUME THAT I DO NOT KNOW MY OWN DAUGHTER?!
BUT... UH... ILLA DOESN'T KNOW THAT, MR. EGO. SHE'S ALONE AND LONELY.
I AM AN EXCELLENT FATHER.
OH YEAH?! WHEN WAS THE LAST TIME YOU SAW HER?
YOU NEED THINGS EXPLAINED TO YOU...ILLA IS JUST AS SHE IS MEANT TO BE.
YOU ARE DIMINUTIVE. YOU LACK A GREATER PERSPECTIVE. YOU SEE THE ROIL OF THE HEAVENLY ELEMENTS AND THINK THEM RANDOM.
BUT THE UNIVERSE IS FORCES AND LAWS. ACTIONS AND EQUAL AND OPPOSITE REACTIONS. AND EXTRAPOLATIONS.
A COMET COLLIDES. A PLANET FRACTURES. A MOON IS FORMED. THE RESULTING CONSTELLATION IS A MATHEMATICAL EXACTITUDE.
ILLA ROTATES HERSELF. AND REVOLVES AROUND ME. THESE ORBITS WERE NOT A SURPRISE-- THEY ARE THE RESULT OF THE COSMIC CALCULUS.

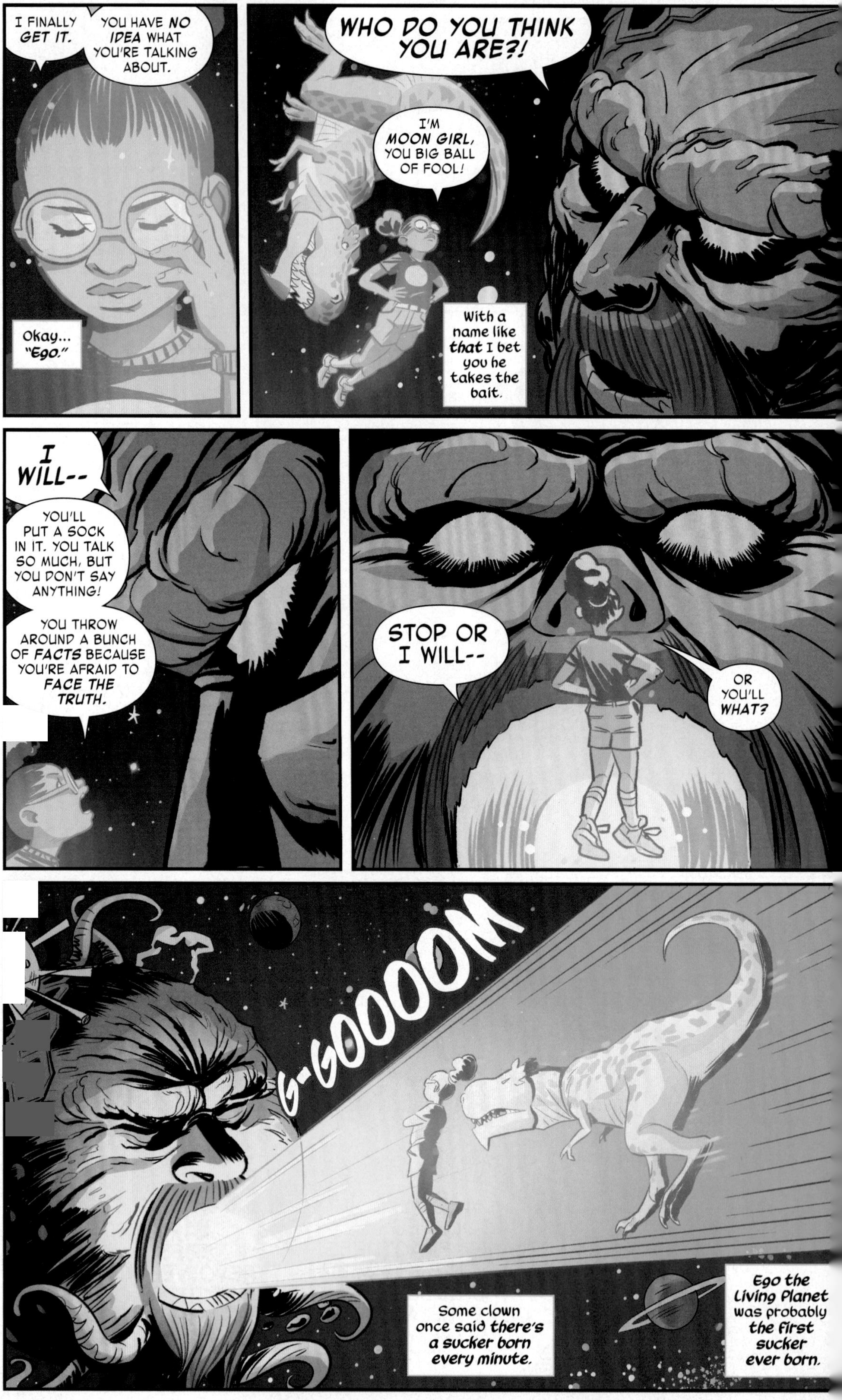
I FINALLY GET IT.
YOU HAVE NO IDEA WHAT YOU'RE TALKING ABOUT.
Okay... "Ego."
WHO DO YOU THINK YOU ARE?!
I'M MOON GIRL, YOU BIG BALL OF FOOL!
With a name like that I bet you he takes the bait.
I WILL--
YOU'LL PUT A SOCK IN IT. YOU TALK SO MUCH, BUT YOU DON'T SAY ANYTHING!
YOU THROW AROUND A BUNCH OF FACTS BECAUSE YOU'RE AFRAID TO FACE THE TRUTH.
STOP OR I WILL--
OR YOU'LL WHAT?
G-GOOOOM
Some clown once said there's a sucker born every minute.
Ego the Living Planet was probably the first sucker ever born.

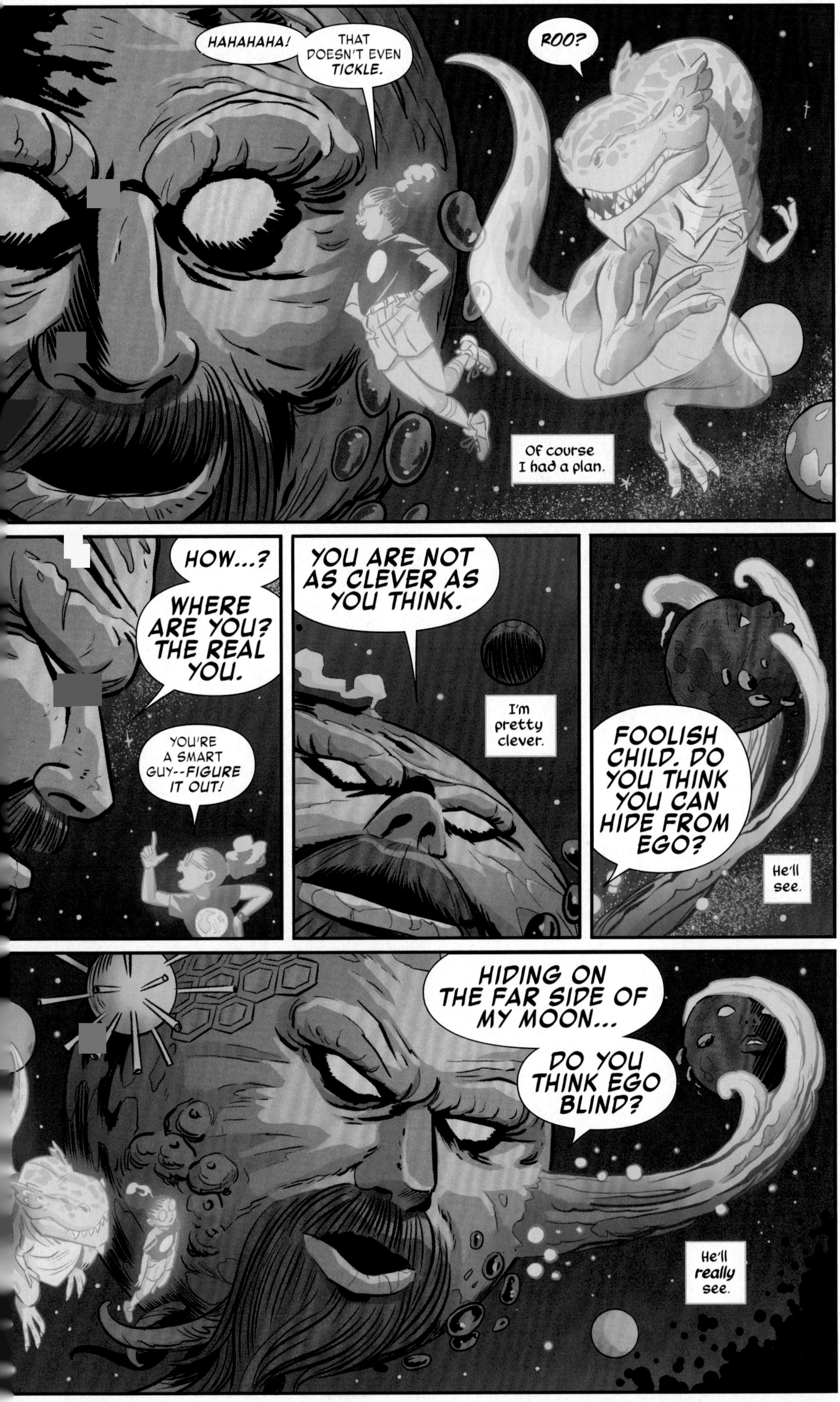
HAHAHAHA!
THAT DOESN'T EVEN TICKLE.
ROO?
Of course I had a plan.
HOW...?
WHERE ARE YOU? THE REAL YOU.
YOU'RE A SMART GUY--FIGURE IT OUT!
YOU ARE NOT AS CLEVER AS YOU THINK.
I'm pretty clever.
FOOLISH CHILD. DO YOU THINK YOU CAN HIDE FROM EGO?
He'll see.
HIDING ON THE FAR SIDE OF MY MOON...
DO YOU THINK EGO BLIND?
He'll really see.

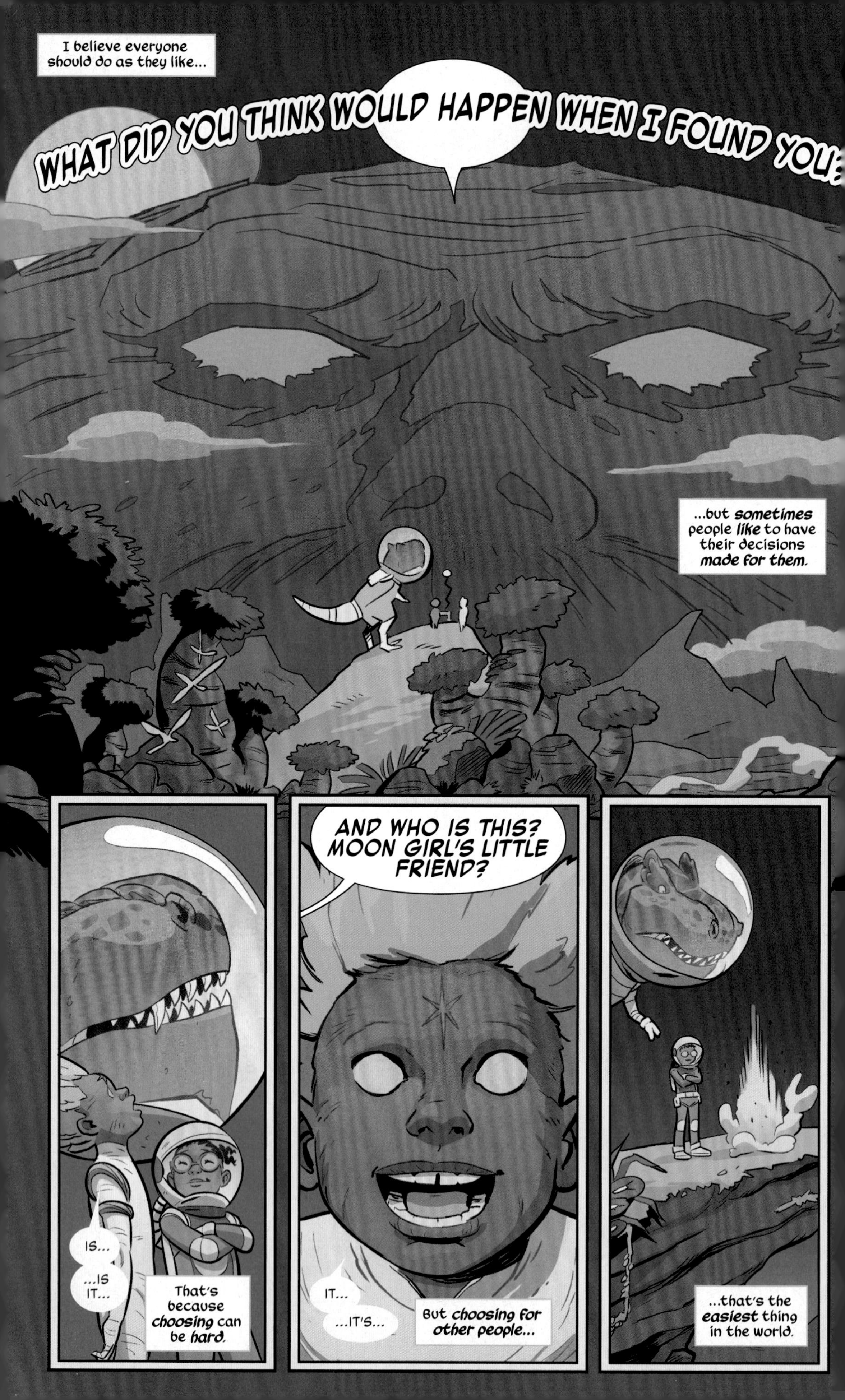

I believe everyone should do as they like...
WHAT DID YOU THINK WOULD HAPPEN WHEN I FOUND YOU?
...but sometimes people like to have their decisions made for them.
IS...
...IS IT...
That's because choosing can be hard.
AND WHO IS THIS? MOON GIRL'S LITTLE FRIEND?
IT...
...IT'S...
But choosing for other people...
...that's the easiest thing in the world.

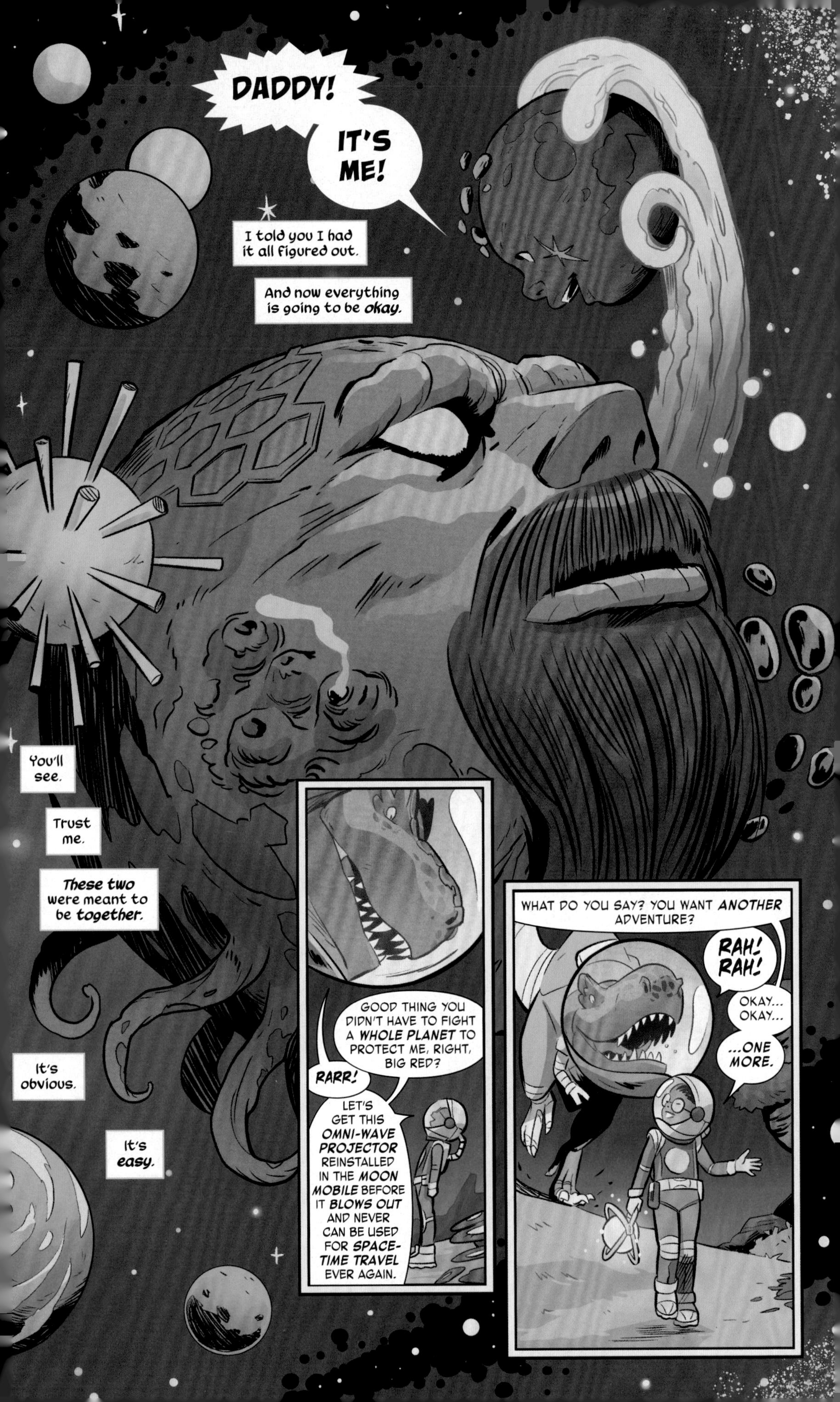

DADDY!
IT'S ME!
I told you I had it all figured out.
And now everything is going to be okay.
You'll see.
Trust me.
These two were meant to be together.
It's obvious.
It's easy.
GOOD THING YOU DIDN'T HAVE TO FIGHT A WHOLE PLANET TO PROTECT ME, RIGHT, BIG RED?
RARR!
LET'S GET THIS OMNI-WAVE PROJECTOR REINSTALLED IN THE MOON MOBILE BEFORE IT BLOWS OUT AND NEVER CAN BE USED FOR SPACE-TIME TRAVEL EVER AGAIN.
WHAT DO YOU SAY? YOU WANT ANOTHER ADVENTURE?
RAH! RAH!
OKAY... OKAY...
...ONE MORE.

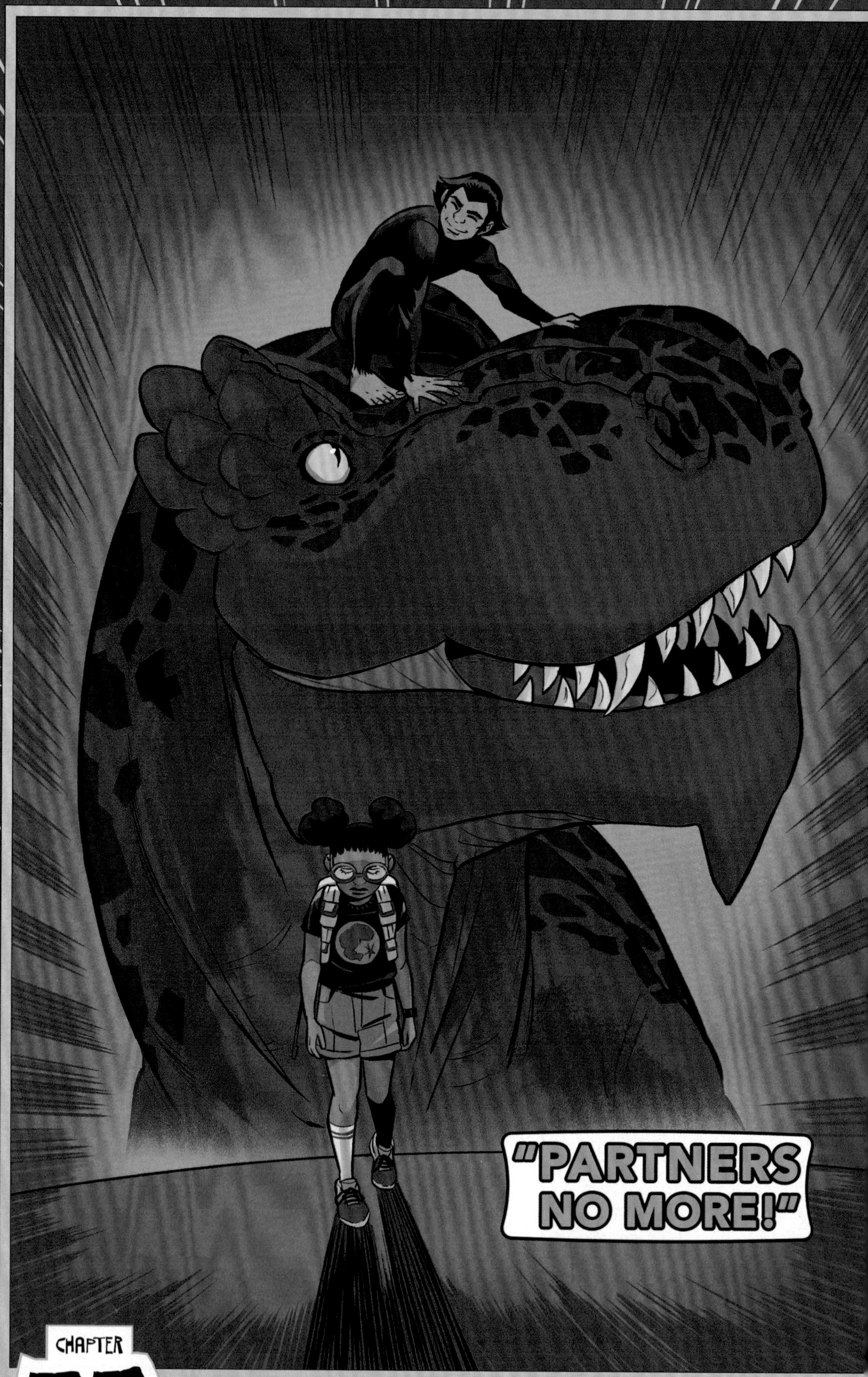
"PARTNERS NO MORE!"

CHAPTER 23

"THERE'S MORE THAN ONE WAY TO SKIN SCHRÖDINGER'S CAT"

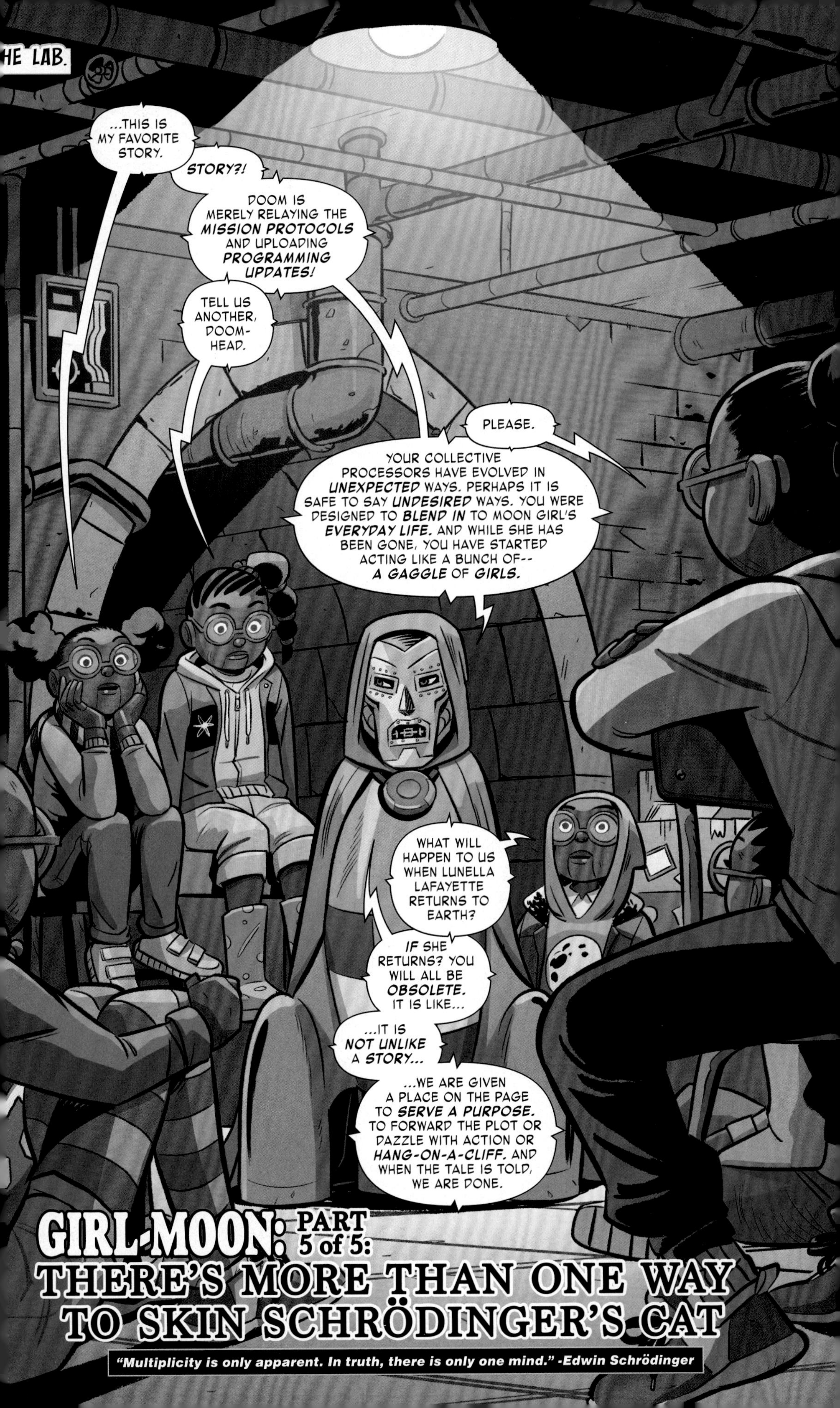
HE LAB.
...THIS IS MY FAVORITE STORY.
STORY?!
DOOM IS MERELY RELAYING THE MISSION PROTOCOLS AND UPLOADING PROGRAMMING UPDATES!
TELL US ANOTHER, DOOM-HEAD.
PLEASE.
YOUR COLLECTIVE PROCESSORS HAVE EVOLVED IN UNEXPECTED WAYS. PERHAPS IT IS SAFE TO SAY UNDESIRED WAYS. YOU WERE DESIGNED TO BLEND IN TO MOON GIRL'S EVERYDAY LIFE. AND WHILE SHE HAS BEEN GONE, YOU HAVE STARTED ACTING LIKE A BUNCH OF-- A GAGGLE OF GIRLS.
WHAT WILL HAPPEN TO US WHEN LUNELLA LAFAYETTE RETURNS TO EARTH?
IF SHE RETURNS? YOU WILL ALL BE OBSOLETE. IT IS LIKE...
...IT IS NOT UNLIKE A STORY...
...WE ARE GIVEN A PLACE ON THE PAGE TO SERVE A PURPOSE. TO FORWARD THE PLOT OR DAZZLE WITH ACTION OR HANG-ON-A-CLIFF. AND WHEN THE TALE IS TOLD, WE ARE DONE.
GIRL-MOON: PART 5 of 5:
THERE'S MORE THAN ONE WAY TO SKIN SCHRÖDINGER'S CAT
"Multiplicity is only apparent. In truth, there is only one mind." -Edwin Schrödinger

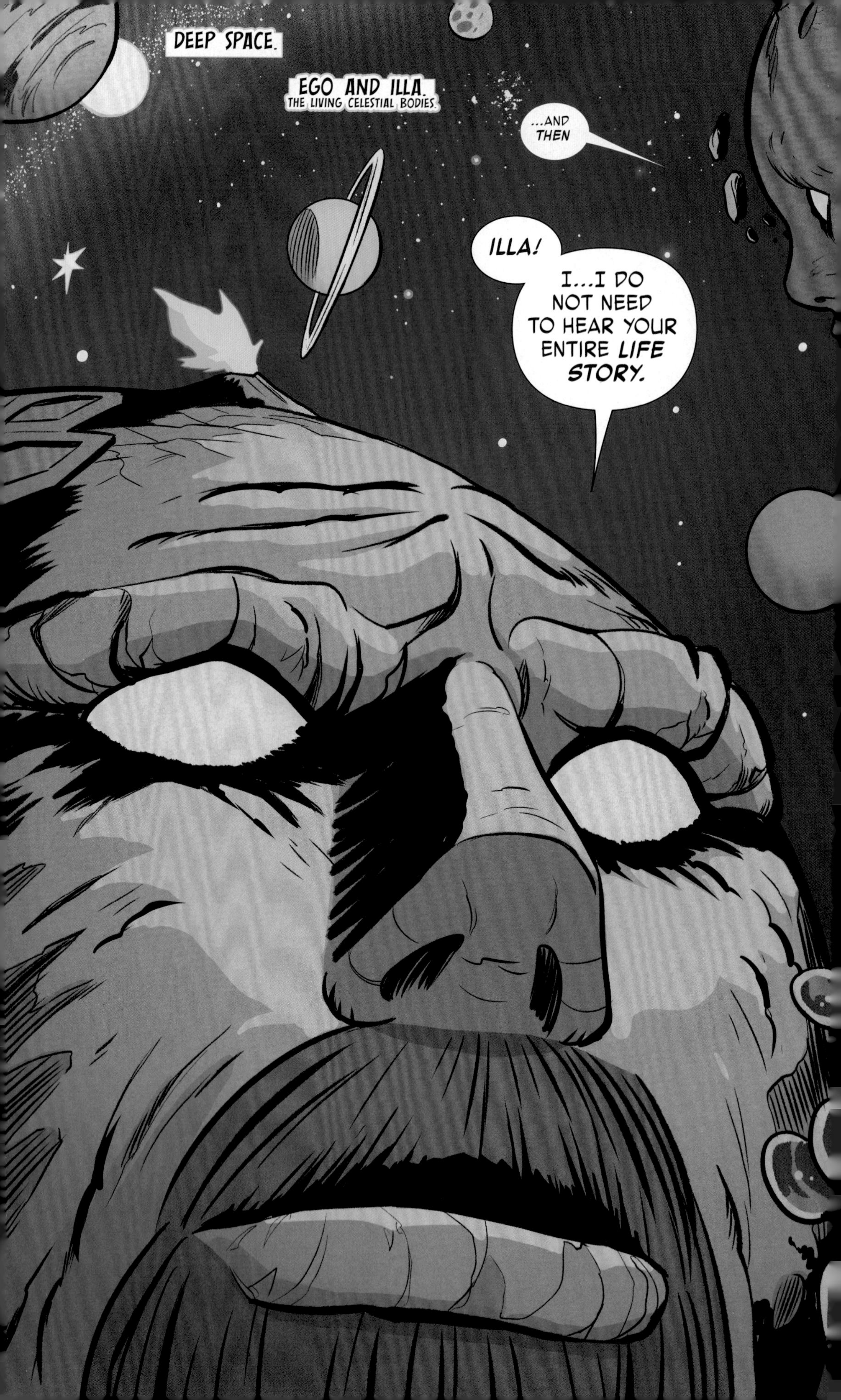
DEEP SPACE.
EGO AND ILLA. THE LIVING CELESTIAL BODIES.
...AND THEN
ILLA!
I...I DO NOT NEED TO HEAR YOUR ENTIRE LIFE STORY.

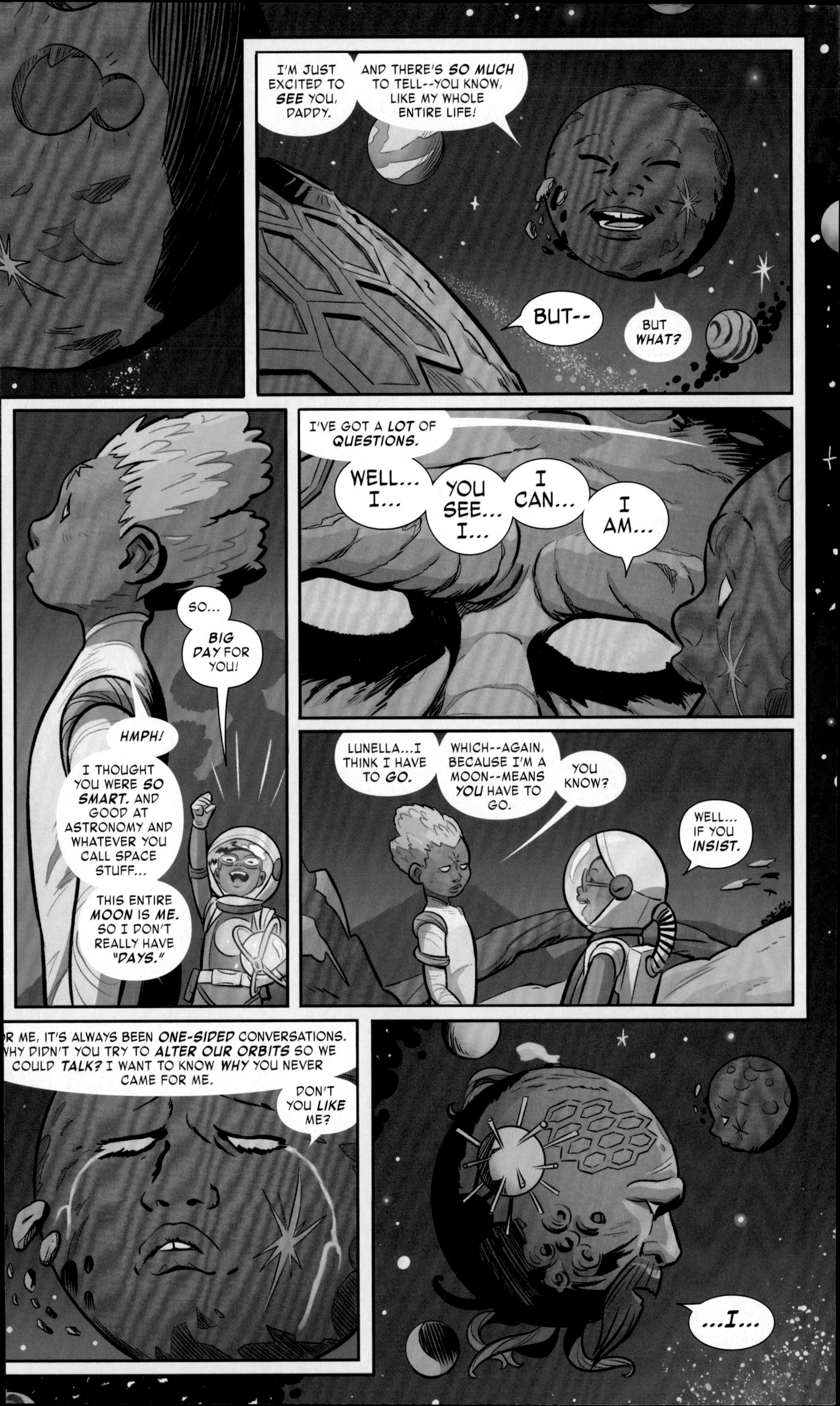
I'M JUST EXCITED TO SEE YOU, DADDY.
AND THERE'S SO MUCH TO TELL--YOU KNOW, LIKE MY WHOLE ENTIRE LIFE!
BUT--
BUT WHAT?
SO...
BIG DAY FOR YOU!
HMPH!
I THOUGHT YOU WERE SO SMART. AND GOOD AT ASTRONOMY AND WHATEVER YOU CALL SPACE STUFF...
THIS ENTIRE MOON IS ME. SO I DON'T REALLY HAVE "DAYS."
I'VE GOT A LOT OF QUESTIONS.
WELL... I...
YOU SEE... I...
I CAN...
I AM...
LUNELLA...I THINK I HAVE TO GO.
WHICH--AGAIN, BECAUSE I'M A MOON--MEANS YOU HAVE TO GO.
YOU KNOW?
WELL... IF YOU INSIST.
R ME, IT'S ALWAYS BEEN ONE-SIDED CONVERSATIONS. HY DIDN'T YOU TRY TO ALTER OUR ORBITS SO WE COULD TALK? I WANT TO KNOW WHY YOU NEVER CAME FOR ME.
DON'T YOU LIKE ME?
...I...

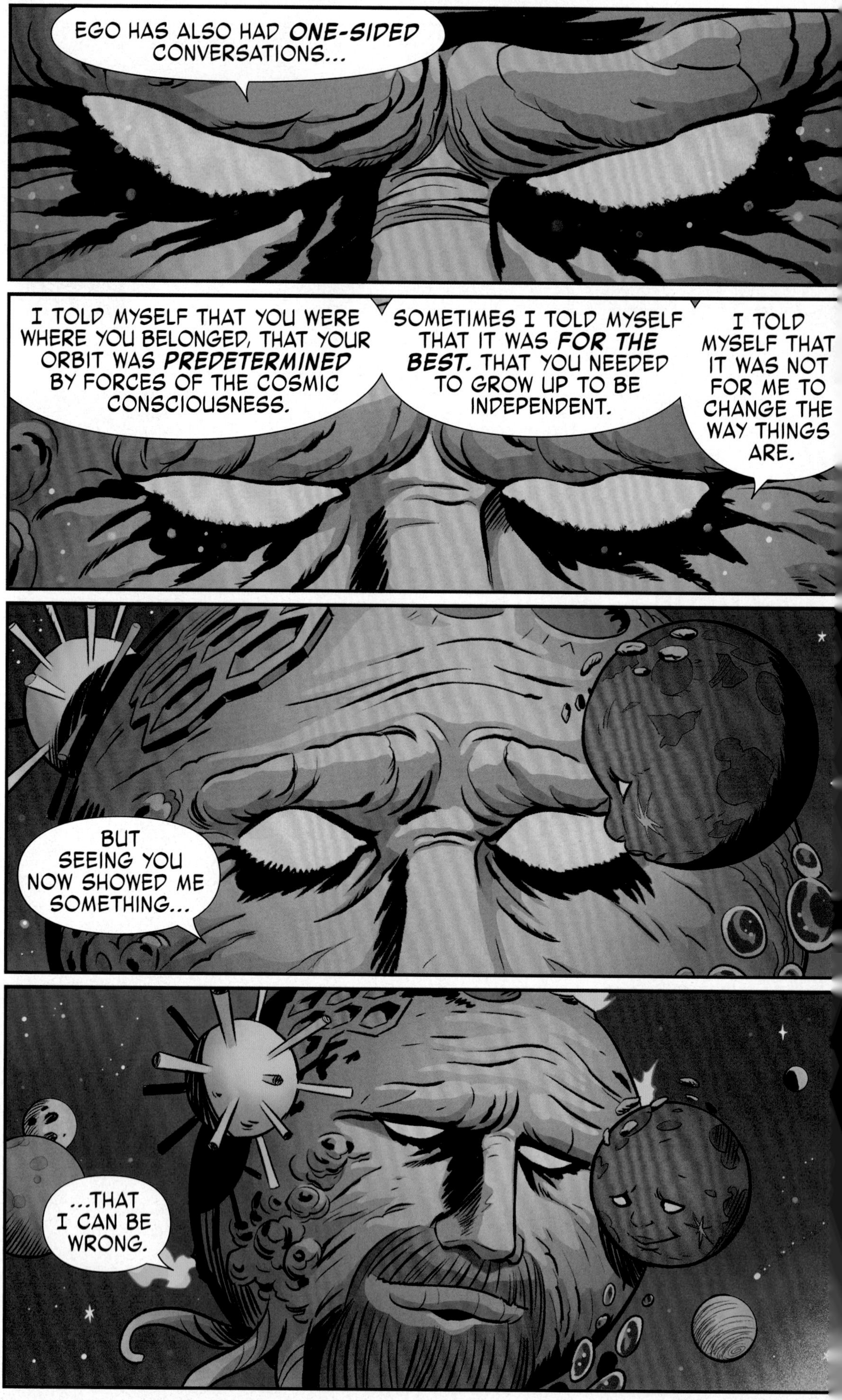
EGO HAS ALSO HAD *ONE-SIDED* CONVERSATIONS...
I TOLD MYSELF THAT YOU WERE WHERE YOU BELONGED, THAT YOUR ORBIT WAS *PREDETERMINED* BY FORCES OF THE COSMIC CONSCIOUSNESS.
SOMETIMES I TOLD MYSELF THAT IT WAS *FOR THE BEST.* THAT YOU NEEDED TO GROW UP TO BE INDEPENDENT.
I TOLD MYSELF THAT IT WAS NOT FOR ME TO CHANGE THE WAY THINGS ARE.
BUT SEEING YOU NOW SHOWED ME SOMETHING...
...THAT I CAN BE WRONG.

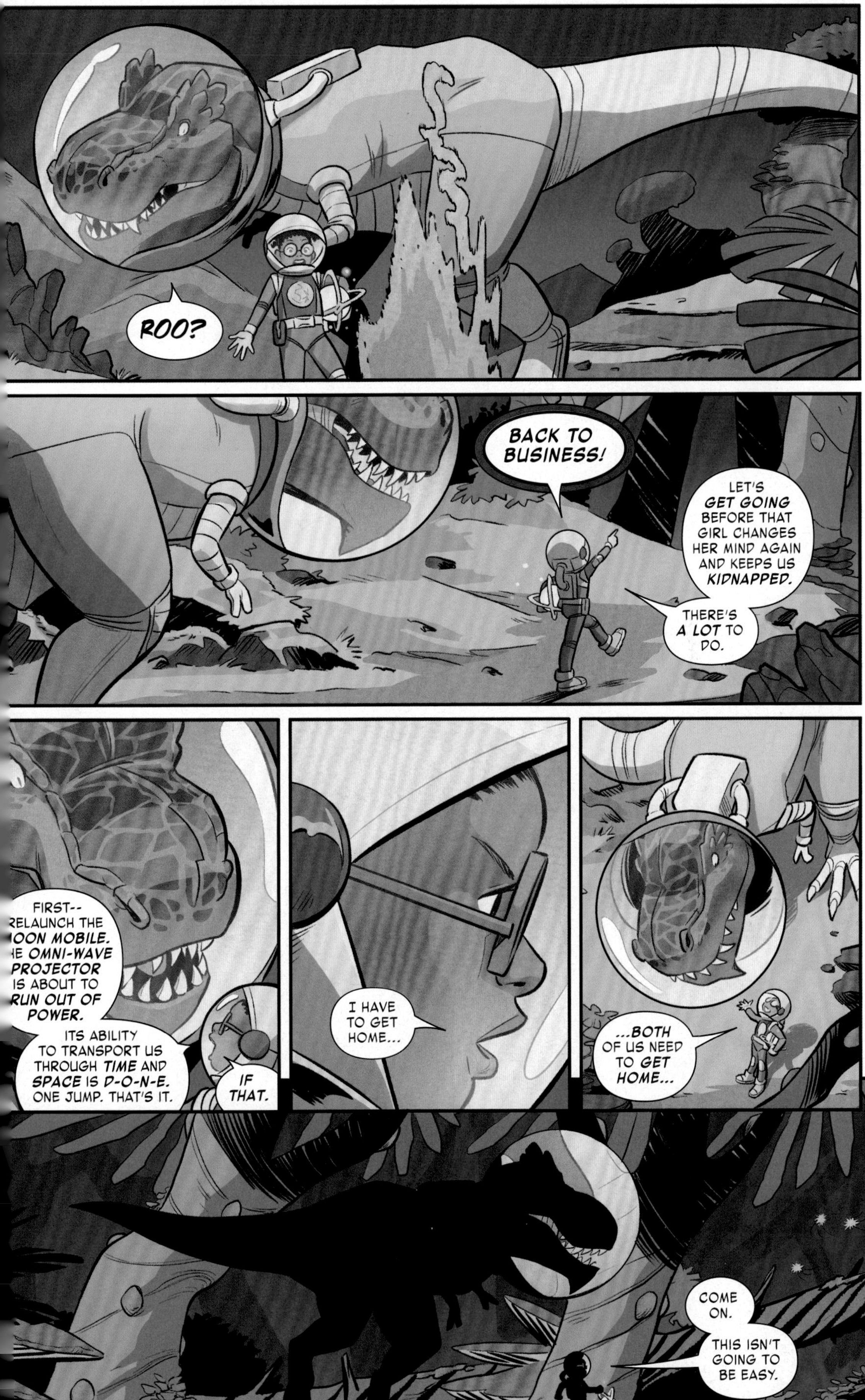
ROO?
BACK TO BUSINESS!
LET'S GET GOING BEFORE THAT GIRL CHANGES HER MIND AGAIN AND KEEPS US KIDNAPPED.
THERE'S A LOT TO DO.
FIRST-- RELAUNCH THE MOON MOBILE. THE OMNI-WAVE PROJECTOR IS ABOUT TO RUN OUT OF POWER.
ITS ABILITY TO TRANSPORT US THROUGH TIME AND SPACE IS D-O-N-E. ONE JUMP. THAT'S IT.
IF THAT.
I HAVE TO GET HOME...
...BOTH OF US NEED TO GET HOME...
COME ON.
THIS ISN'T GOING TO BE EASY.

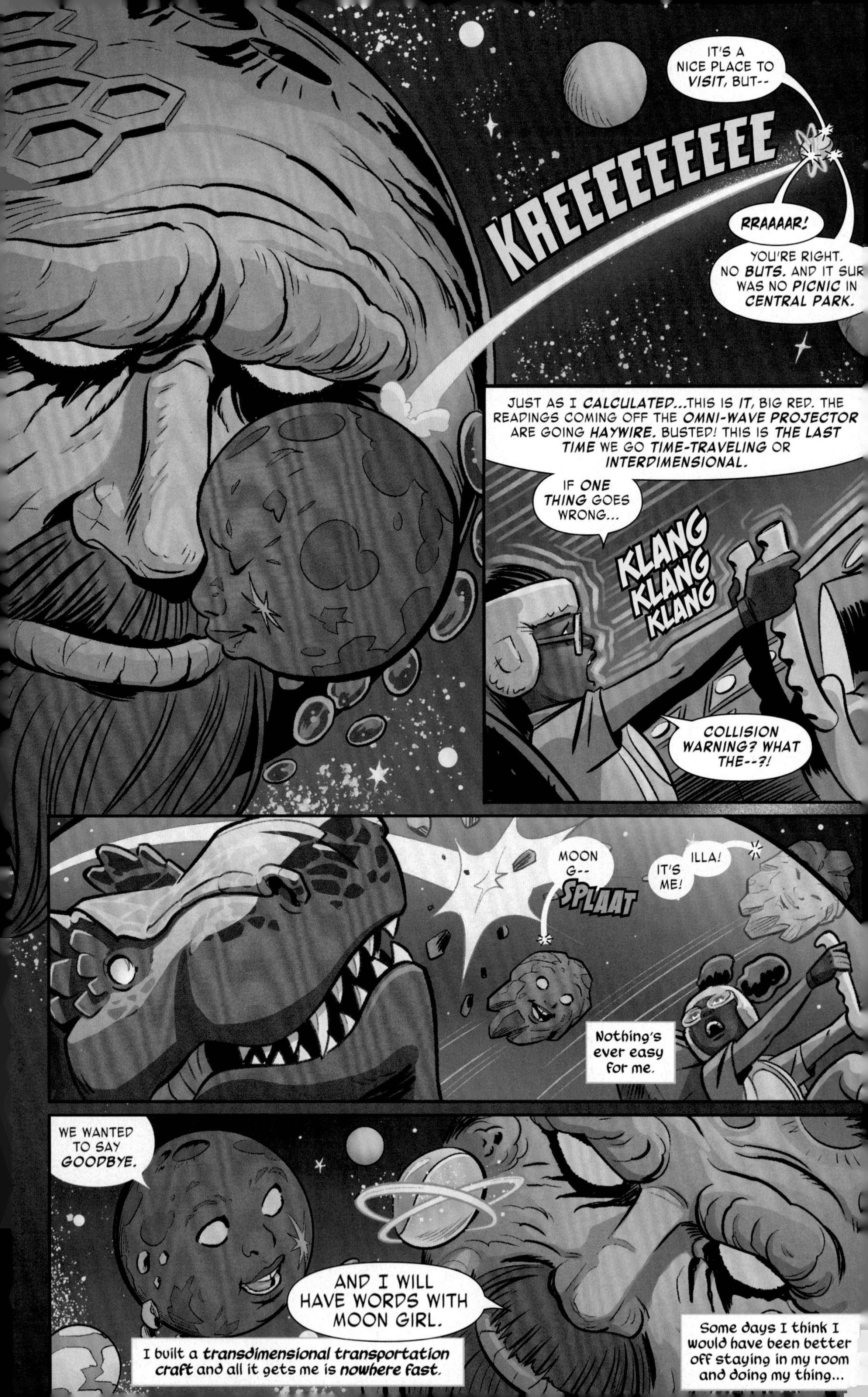
IT'S A NICE PLACE TO VISIT, BUT--
KREEEEEEEEE
RRAAAAR!
YOU'RE RIGHT. NO BUTS. AND IT SUR WAS NO PICNIC IN CENTRAL PARK.
JUST AS I CALCULATED...THIS IS IT, BIG RED. THE READINGS COMING OFF THE OMNI-WAVE PROJECTOR ARE GOING HAYWIRE. BUSTED! THIS IS THE LAST TIME WE GO TIME-TRAVELING OR INTERDIMENSIONAL.
IF ONE THING GOES WRONG...
KLANG KLANG KLANG
COLLISION WARNING? WHAT THE--?!
MOON G--
SPLAAT
IT'S ME!
ILLA!
Nothing's ever easy for me.
WE WANTED TO SAY GOODBYE.
AND I WILL HAVE WORDS WITH MOON GIRL.
I built a transdimensional transportation craft and all it gets me is nowhere fast.
Some days I think I would have been better off staying in my room and doing my thing...

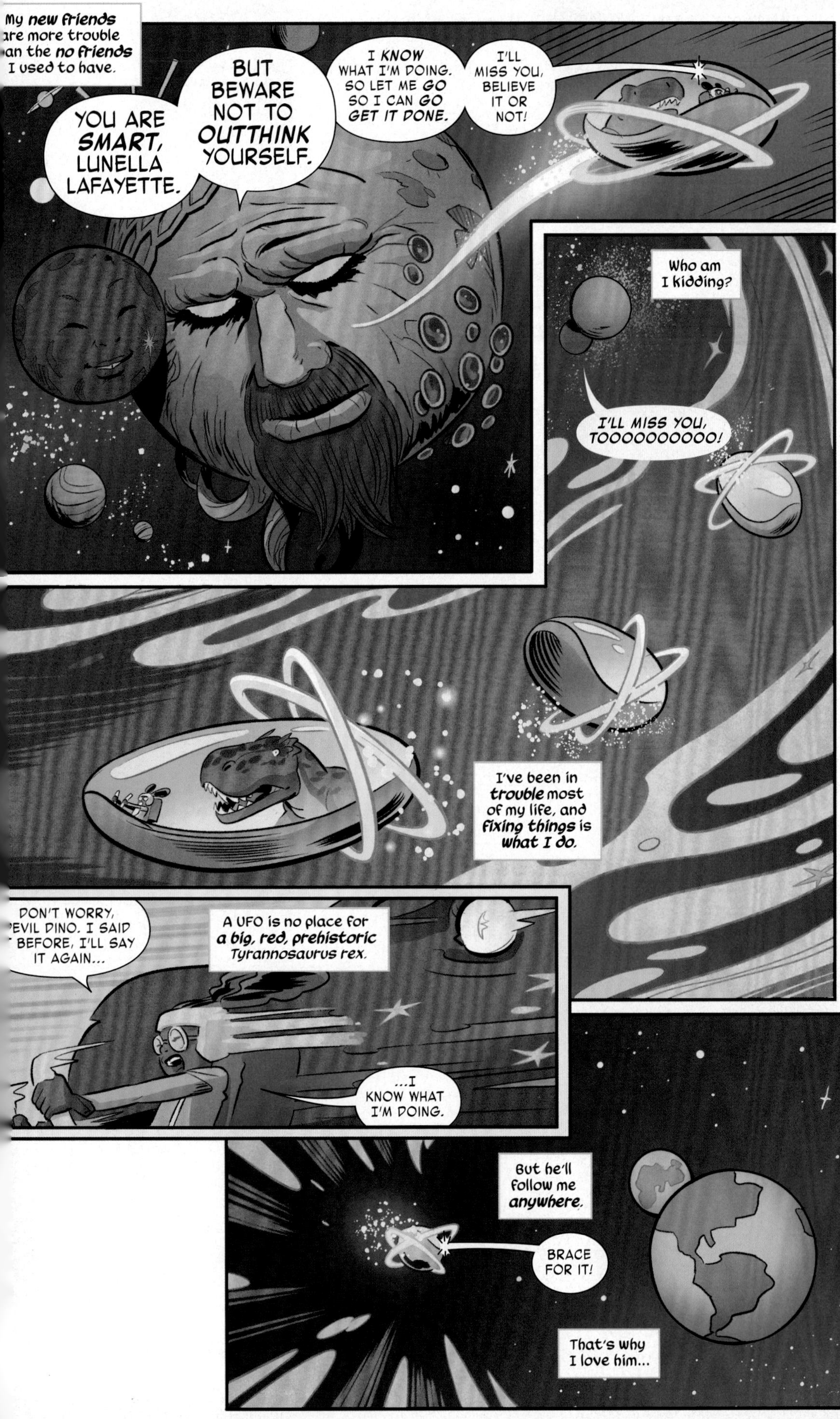

My new friends are more trouble than the no friends I used to have.
YOU ARE SMART, LUNELLA LAFAYETTE.
BUT BEWARE NOT TO OUTTHINK YOURSELF.
I KNOW WHAT I'M DOING. SO LET ME GO SO I CAN GO GET IT DONE.
I'LL MISS YOU, BELIEVE IT OR NOT!
Who am I kidding?
I'LL MISS YOU, TOOOOOOOOOO!
I've been in trouble most of my life, and fixing things is what I do.
DON'T WORRY, DEVIL DINO. I SAID IT BEFORE, I'LL SAY IT AGAIN...
A UFO is no place for a big, red, prehistoric Tyrannosaurus rex.
...I KNOW WHAT I'M DOING.
But he'll follow me anywhere.
BRACE FOR IT!
That's why I love him...

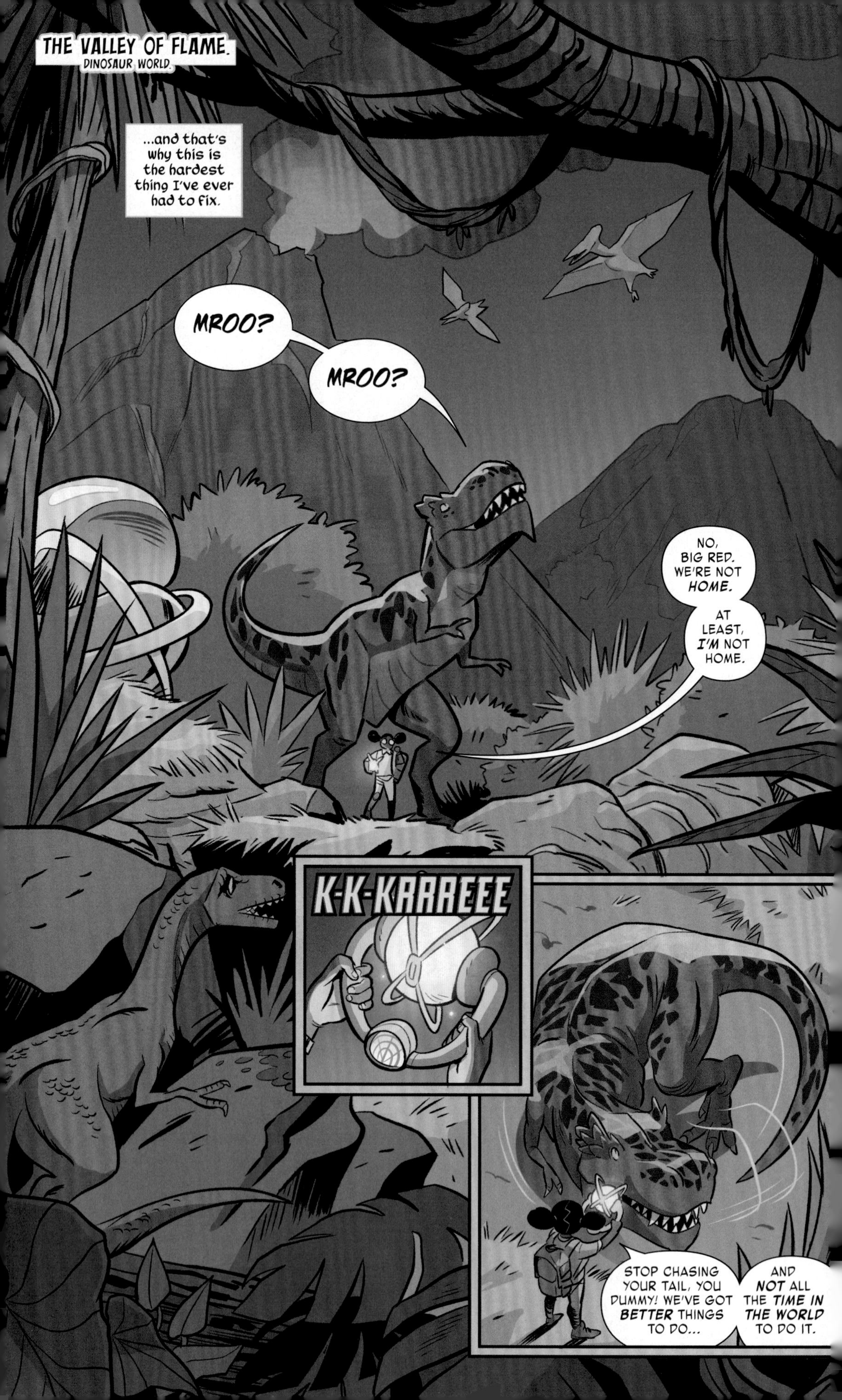
THE VALLEY OF FLAME.
DINOSAUR WORLD.
...and that's why this is the hardest thing I've ever had to fix.
MROO?
MROO?
NO, BIG RED. WE'RE NOT HOME.
AT LEAST, I'M NOT HOME.
K-K-KRRREEE
STOP CHASING YOUR TAIL, YOU DUMMY! WE'VE GOT BETTER THINGS TO DO...
AND NOT ALL THE TIME IN THE WORLD TO DO IT.

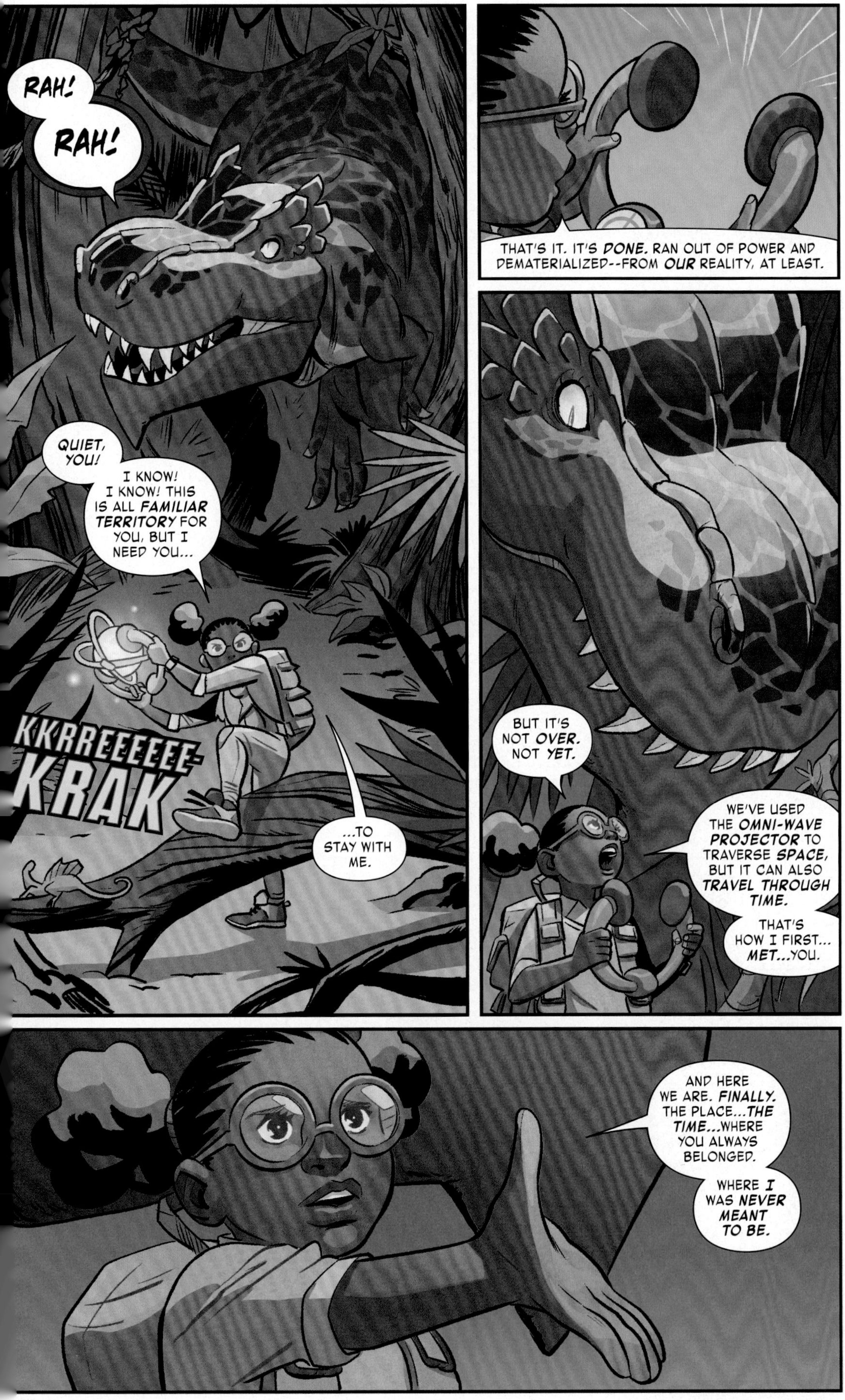
RAH!
RAH!
QUIET, YOU!
I KNOW! I KNOW! THIS IS ALL FAMILIAR TERRITORY FOR YOU, BUT I NEED YOU...
KKRREEEEEEE-KRAK
...TO STAY WITH ME.
THAT'S IT. IT'S DONE. RAN OUT OF POWER AND DEMATERIALIZED--FROM OUR REALITY, AT LEAST.
BUT IT'S NOT OVER. NOT YET.
WE'VE USED THE OMNI-WAVE PROJECTOR TO TRAVERSE SPACE, BUT IT CAN ALSO TRAVEL THROUGH TIME.
THAT'S HOW I FIRST... MET...YOU.
AND HERE WE ARE. FINALLY. THE PLACE...THE TIME...WHERE YOU ALWAYS BELONGED.
WHERE I WAS NEVER MEANT TO BE.

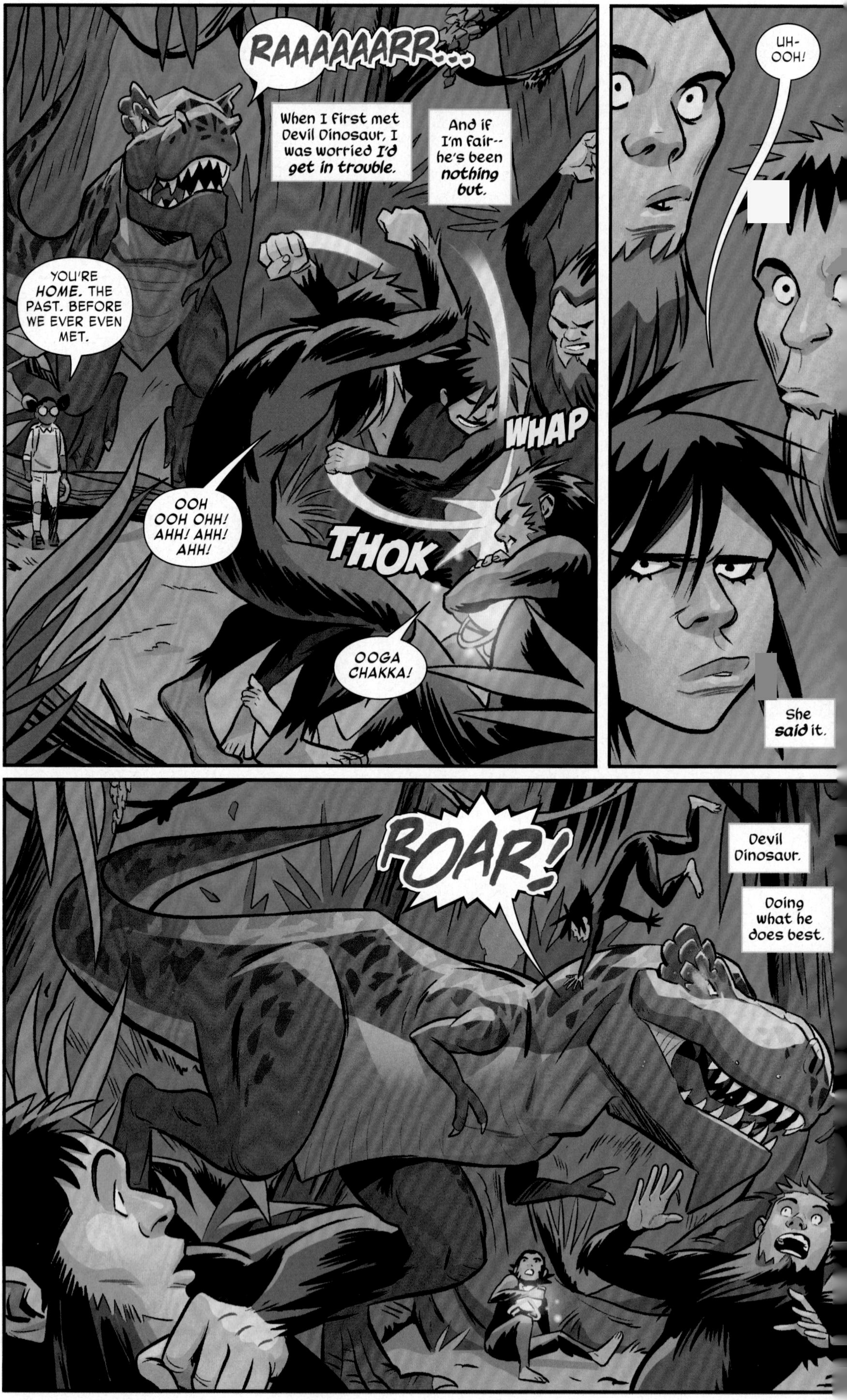
RAAAAAARR...
When I first met Devil Dinosaur, I was worried I'd get in trouble.
And if I'm fair--he's been nothing but.
YOU'RE HOME. THE PAST. BEFORE WE EVER EVEN MET.
WHAP
OOH OOH OHH! AHH! AHH! AHH!
THOK
OOGA CHAKKA!
UH-OOH!
She said it.
ROAR!
Devil Dinosaur.
Doing what he does best.

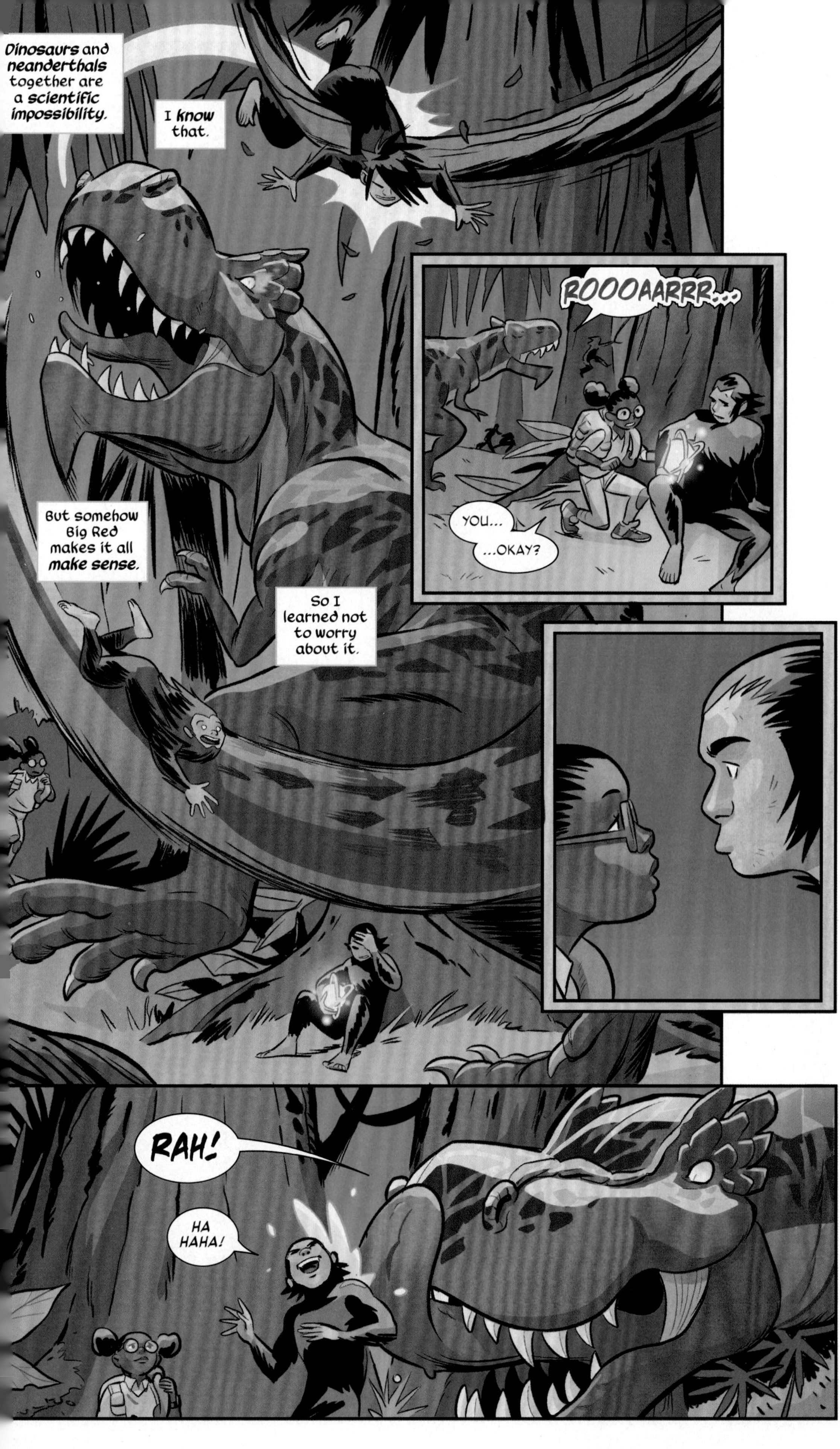

Dinosaurs and neanderthals together are a scientific impossibility.
I know that.
But somehow Big Red makes it all make sense.
So I learned not to worry about it.
ROOOAARRR...
YOU...
...OKAY?
RAH!
HA HAHA!

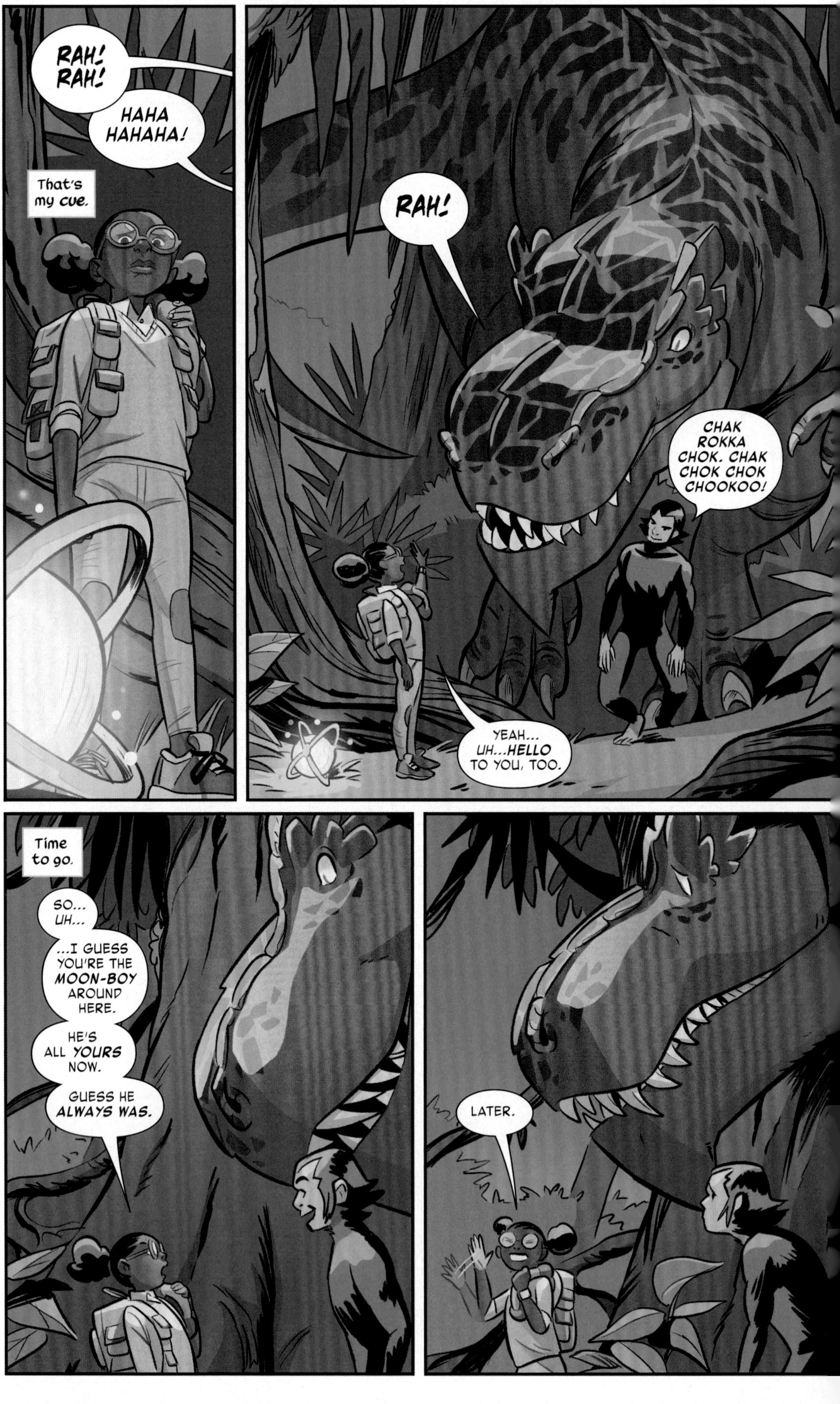
RAH! RAH!
HAHA HAHAHA!
That's my cue.
RAH!
CHAK ROKKA CHOK. CHAK CHOK CHOK CHOOKOO!
YEAH... UH...HELLO TO YOU, TOO.
Time to go.
SO... UH...
...I GUESS YOU'RE THE MOON-BOY AROUND HERE.
HE'S ALL YOURS NOW.
GUESS HE ALWAYS WAS.
LATER.

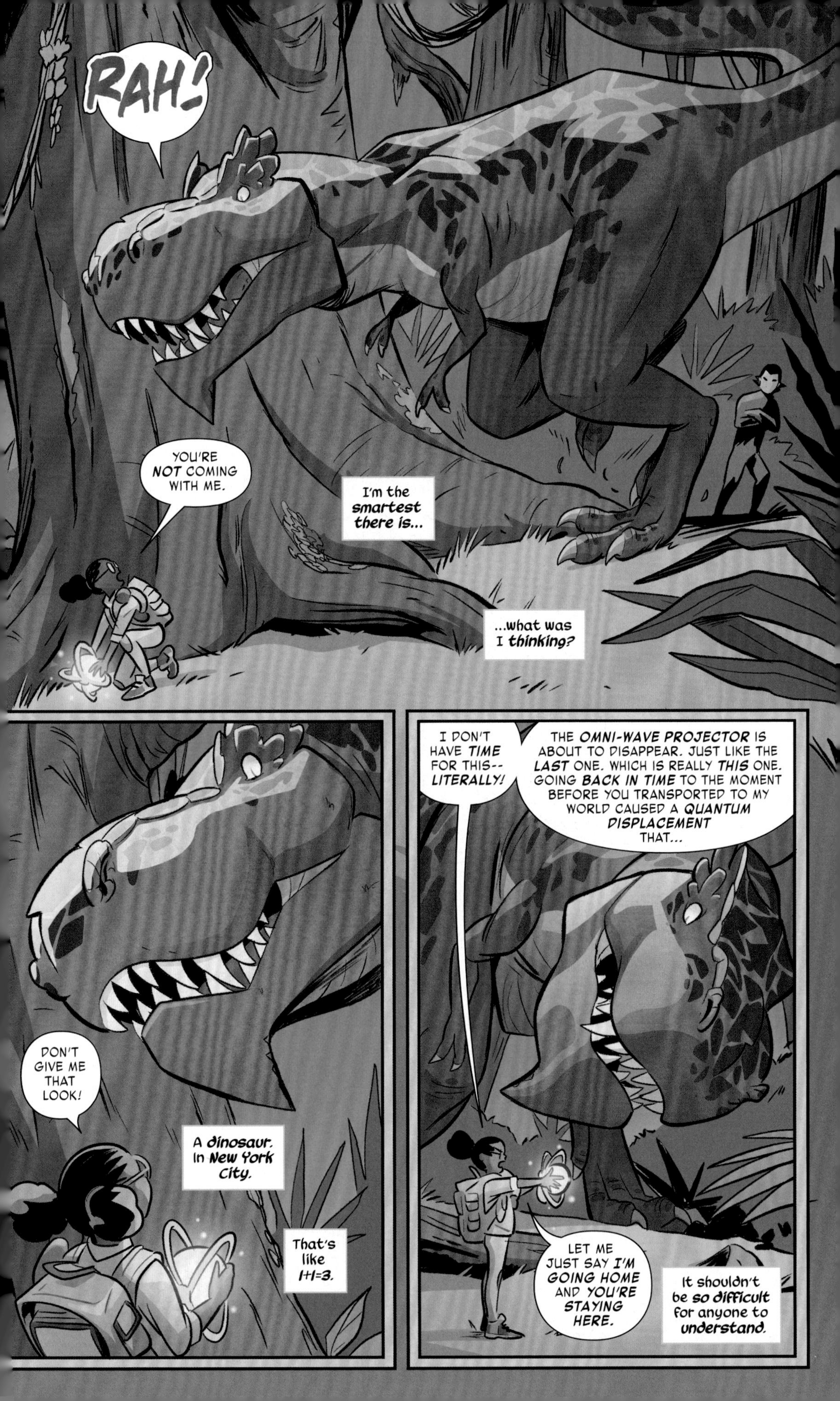
RAH!
YOU'RE NOT COMING WITH ME.
I'm the smartest there is...
...what was I thinking?
DON'T GIVE ME THAT LOOK!
A dinosaur. In New York City.
That's like 1+1=3.
I DON'T HAVE TIME FOR THIS-- LITERALLY!
THE OMNI-WAVE PROJECTOR IS ABOUT TO DISAPPEAR. JUST LIKE THE LAST ONE. WHICH IS REALLY THIS ONE. GOING BACK IN TIME TO THE MOMENT BEFORE YOU TRANSPORTED TO MY WORLD CAUSED A QUANTUM DISPLACEMENT THAT...
LET ME JUST SAY I'M GOING HOME AND YOU'RE STAYING HERE.
It shouldn't be so difficult for anyone to understand.

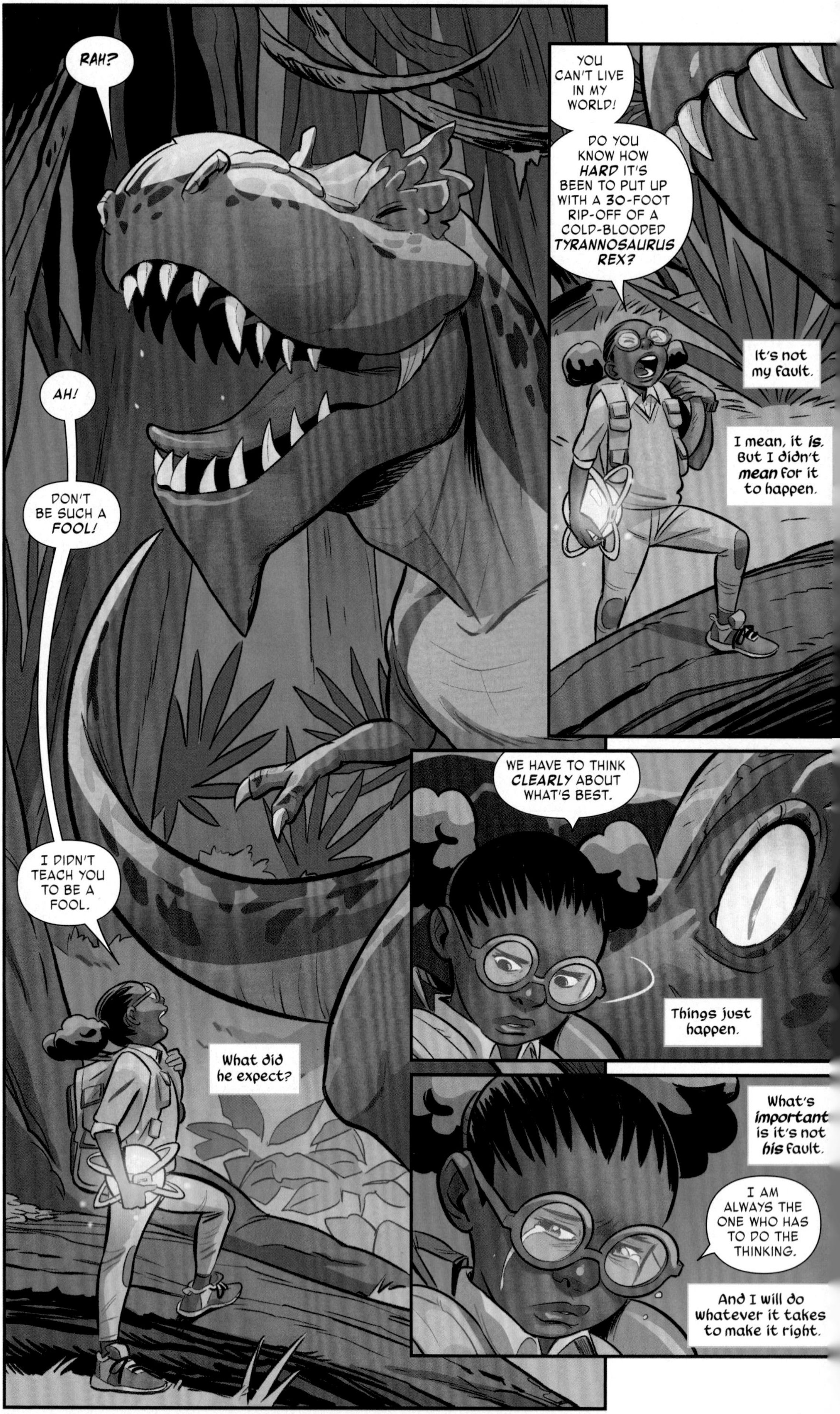
RAH?
AH!
DON'T BE SUCH A FOOL!
I DIDN'T TEACH YOU TO BE A FOOL.
What did he expect?
YOU CAN'T LIVE IN MY WORLD!
DO YOU KNOW HOW HARD IT'S BEEN TO PUT UP WITH A 30-FOOT RIP-OFF OF A COLD-BLOODED TYRANNOSAURUS REX?
It's not my fault.
I mean, it is. But I didn't mean for it to happen.
WE HAVE TO THINK CLEARLY ABOUT WHAT'S BEST.
Things just happen.
What's important is it's not his fault.
I AM ALWAYS THE ONE WHO HAS TO DO THE THINKING.
And I will do whatever it takes to make it right.

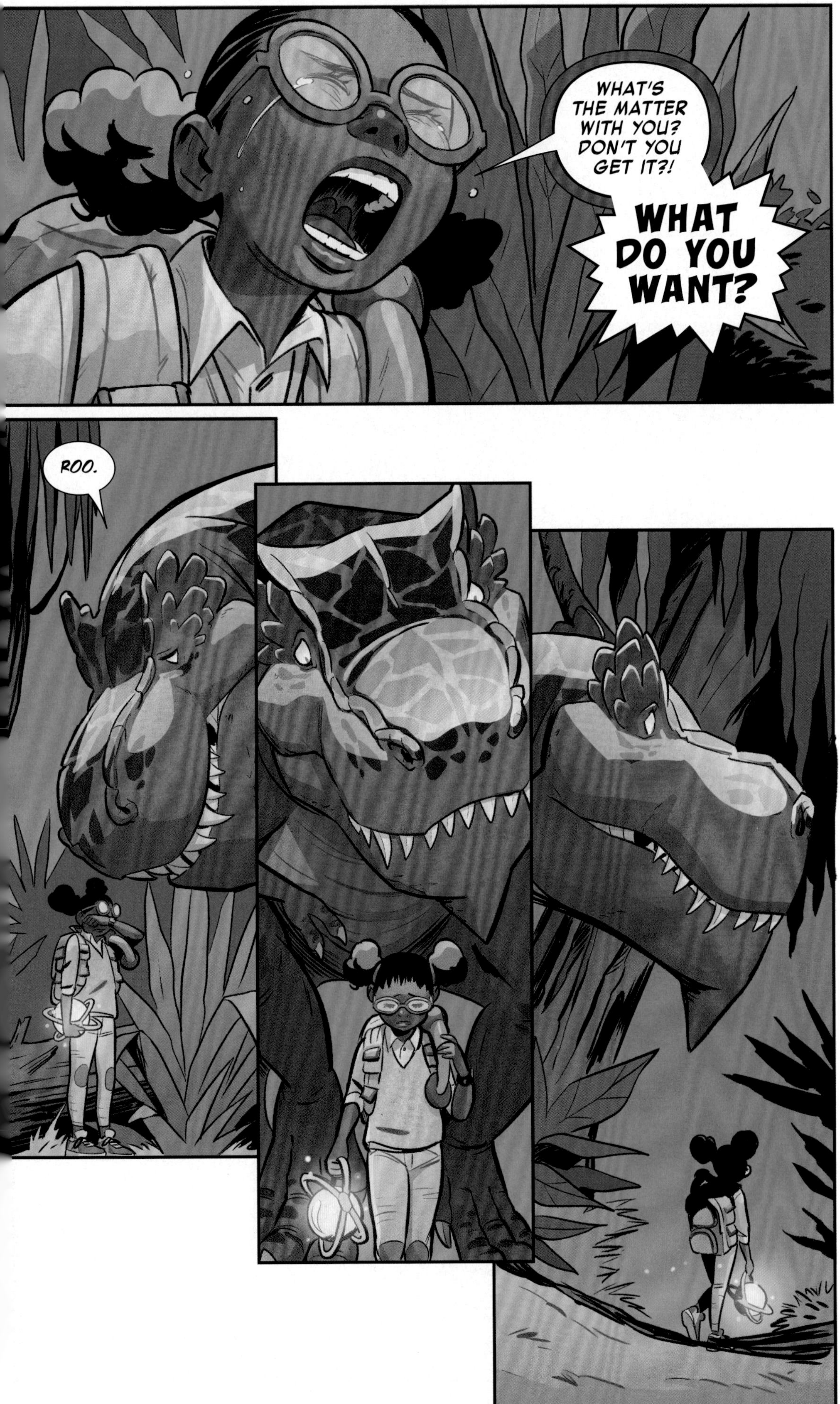
WHAT'S THE MATTER WITH YOU? DON'T YOU GET IT?!
WHAT DO YOU WANT?
ROO.

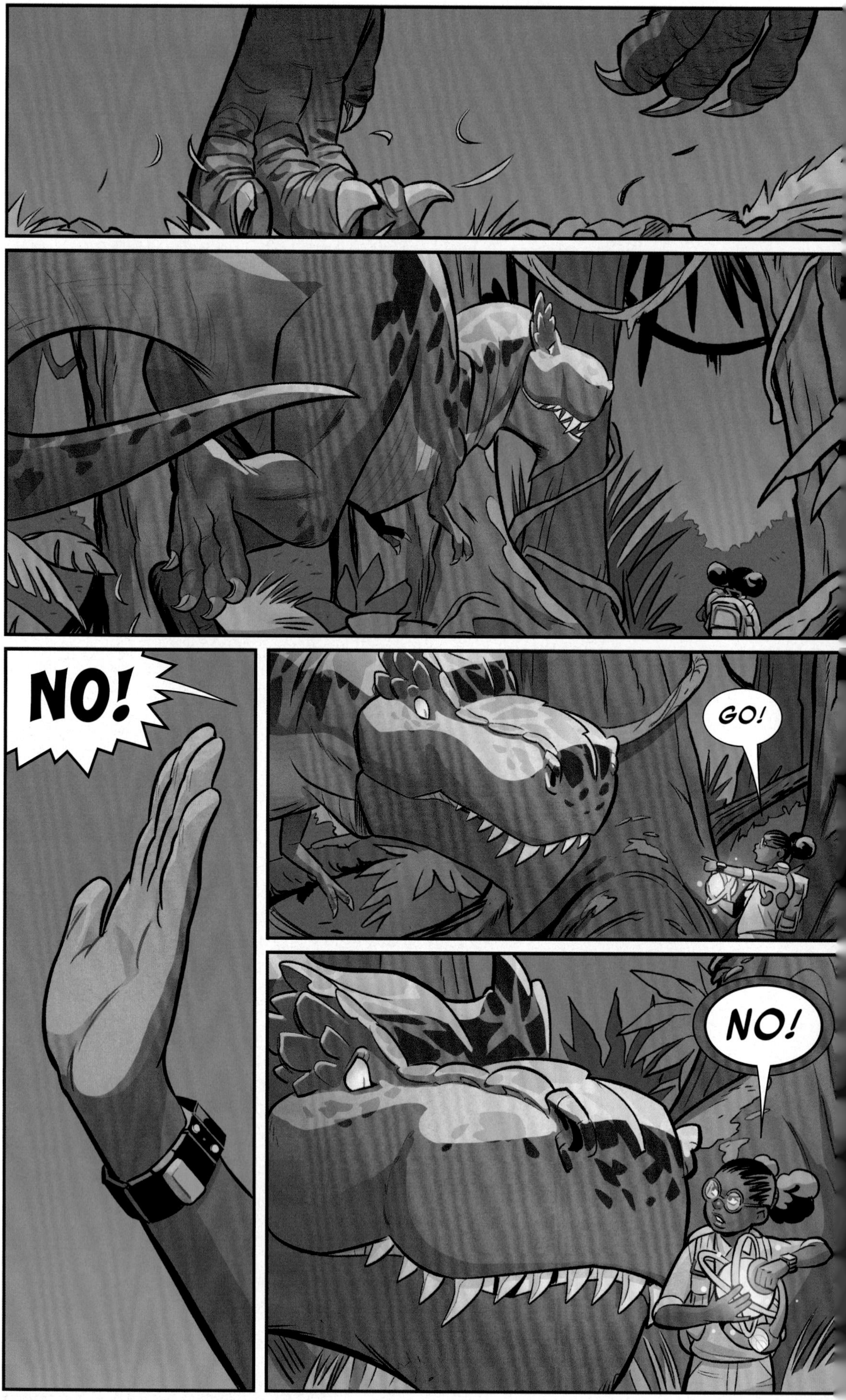
NO!
GO!
NO!

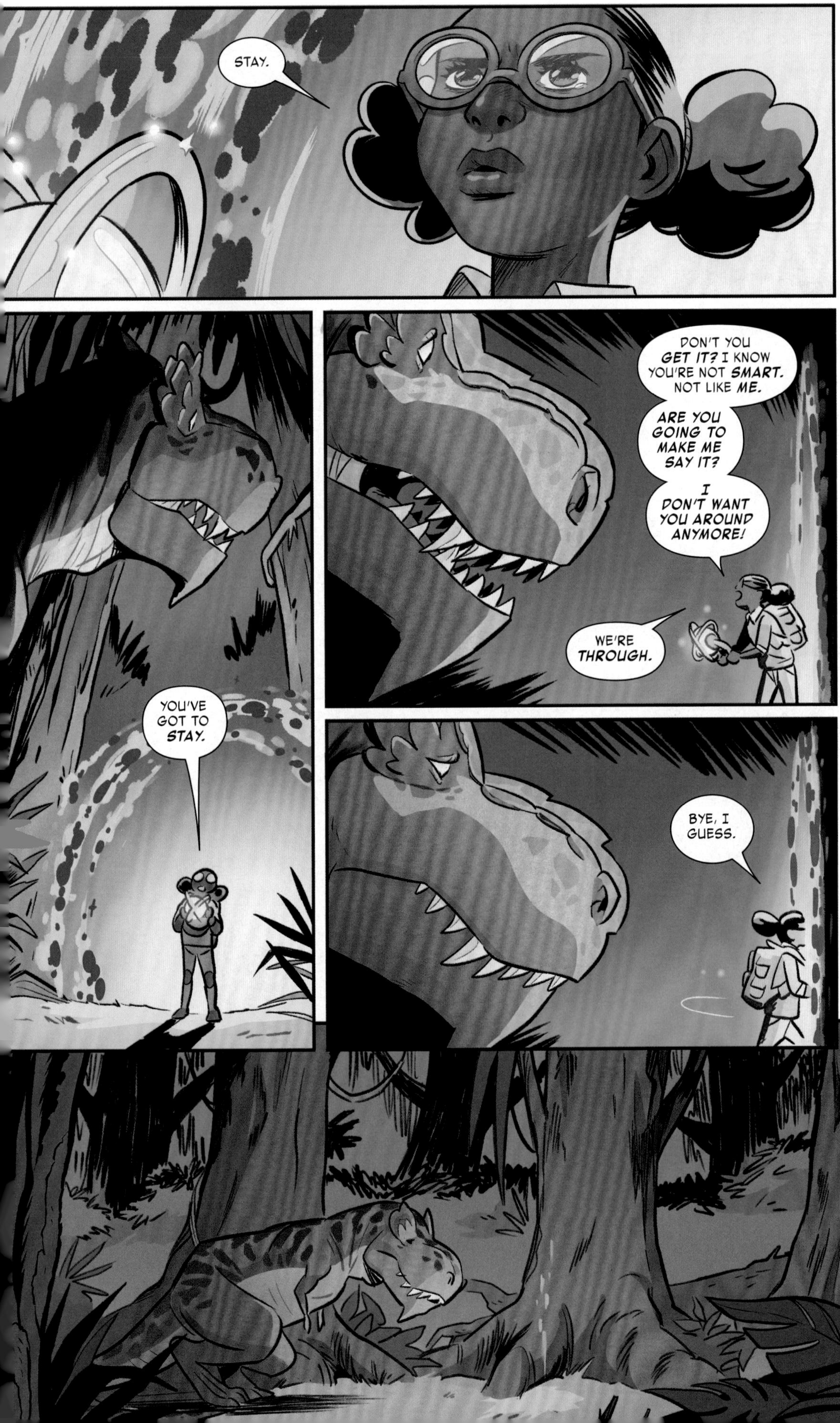
STAY.
YOU'VE GOT TO STAY.
DON'T YOU GET IT? I KNOW YOU'RE NOT SMART. NOT LIKE ME.
ARE YOU GOING TO MAKE ME SAY IT?
I DON'T WANT YOU AROUND ANYMORE!
WE'RE THROUGH.
BYE, I GUESS.

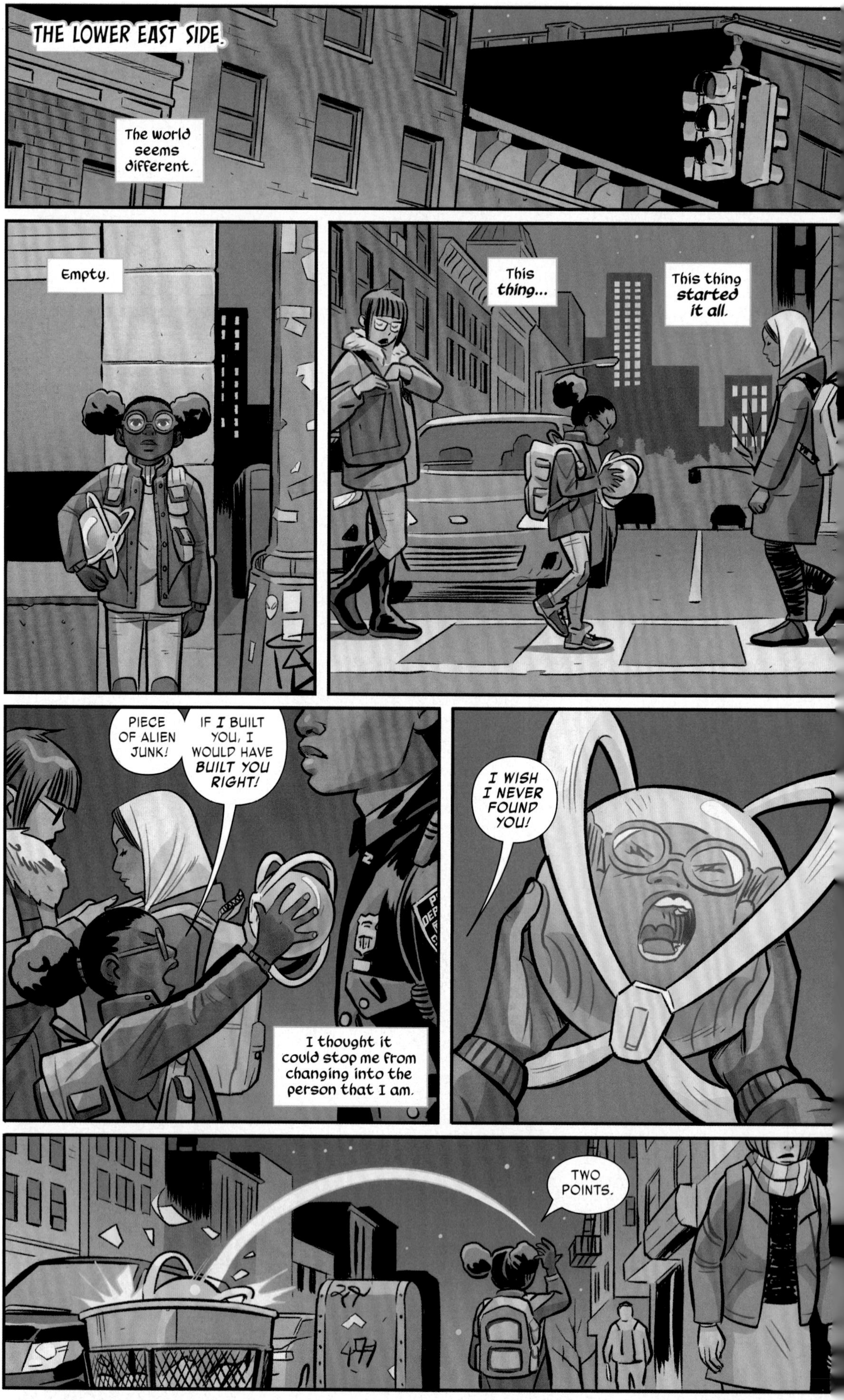

THE LOWER EAST SIDE.
The world seems different.
Empty.
This *thing*...
This thing ***started it all.***
PIECE OF ALIEN JUNK!
IF *I* BUILT YOU, I WOULD HAVE ***BUILT YOU RIGHT!***
I thought it could stop me from changing into the person that I am.
I WISH I NEVER FOUND YOU!
TWO POINTS.

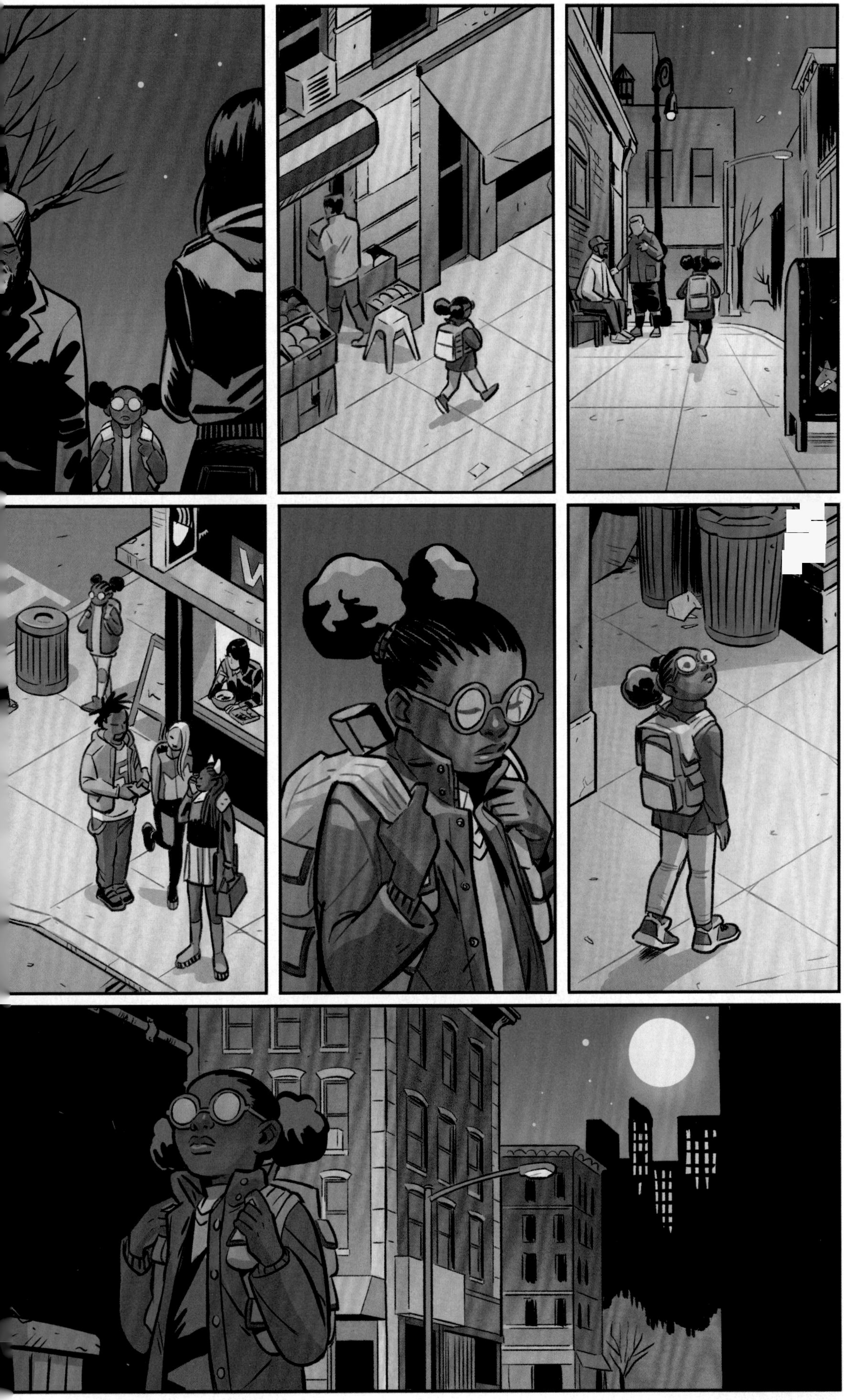

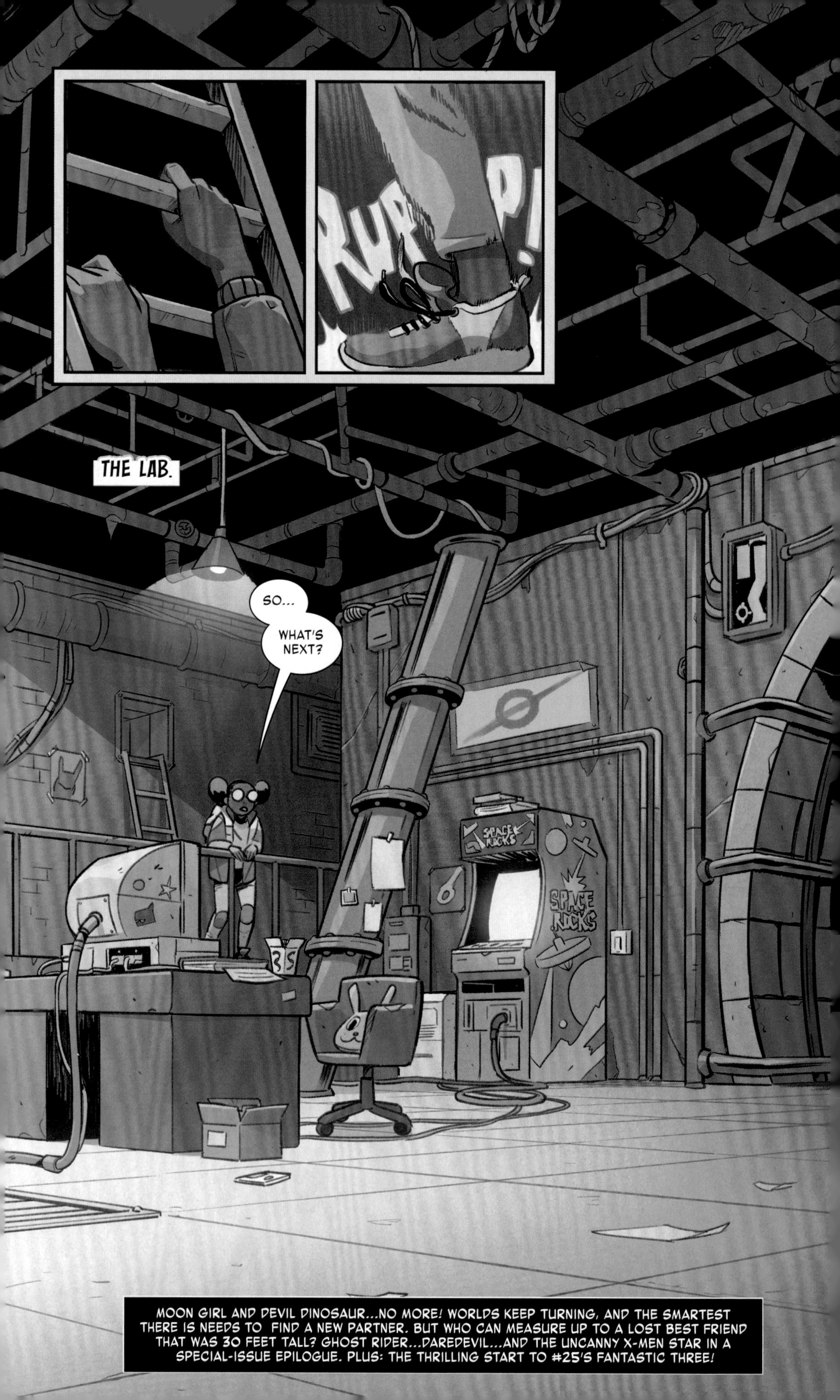
RUPP!
THE LAB.
SO...
WHAT'S NEXT?
SPACE ROCKS
SPACE ROCKS
MOON GIRL AND DEVIL DINOSAUR...NO MORE! WORLDS KEEP TURNING, AND THE SMARTEST THERE IS NEEDS TO FIND A NEW PARTNER. BUT WHO CAN MEASURE UP TO A LOST BEST FRIEND THAT WAS 30 FEET TALL? GHOST RIDER...DAREDEVIL...AND THE UNCANNY X-MEN STAR IN A SPECIAL-ISSUE EPILOGUE. PLUS: THE THRILLING START TO #25'S FANTASTIC THREE!

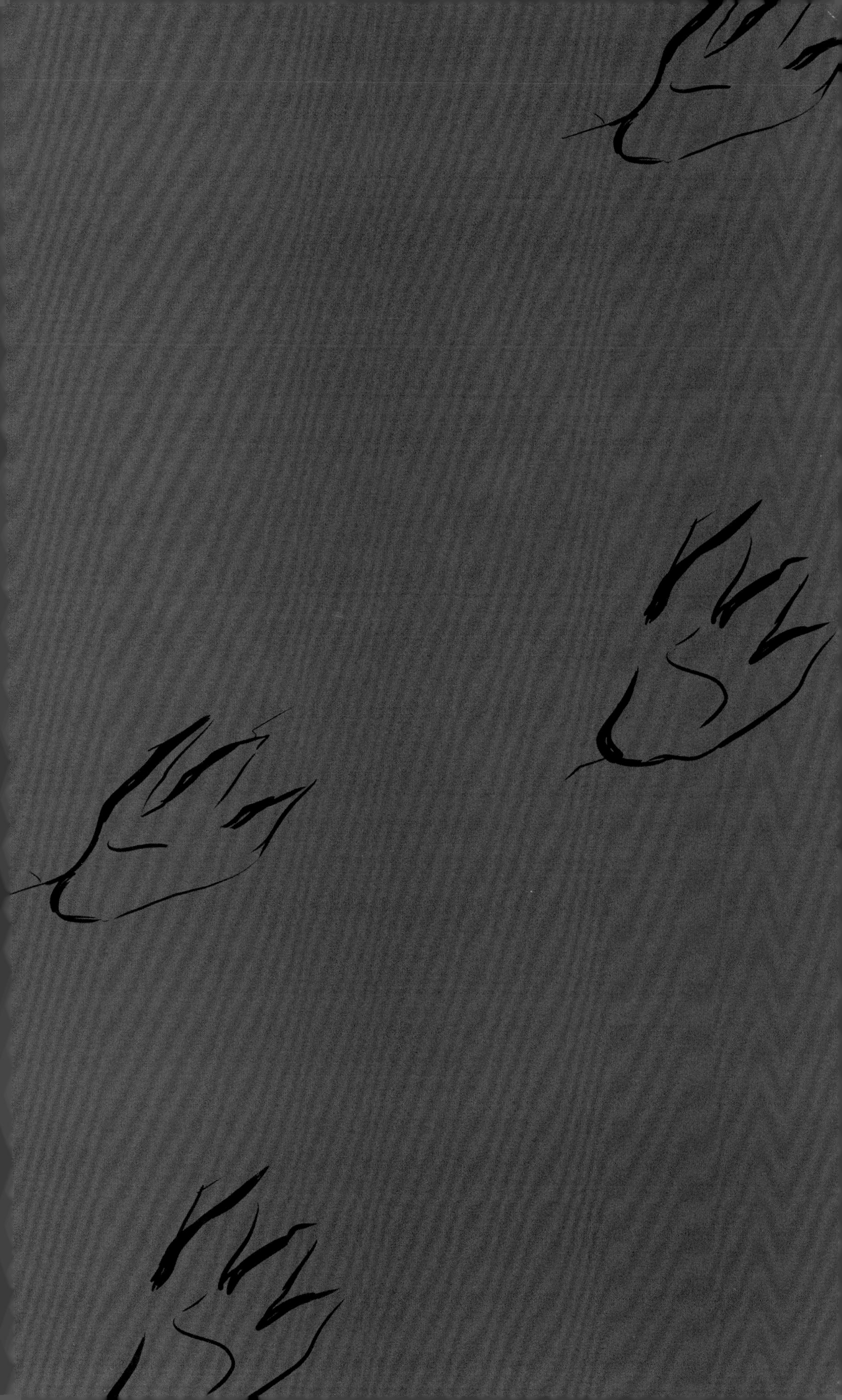

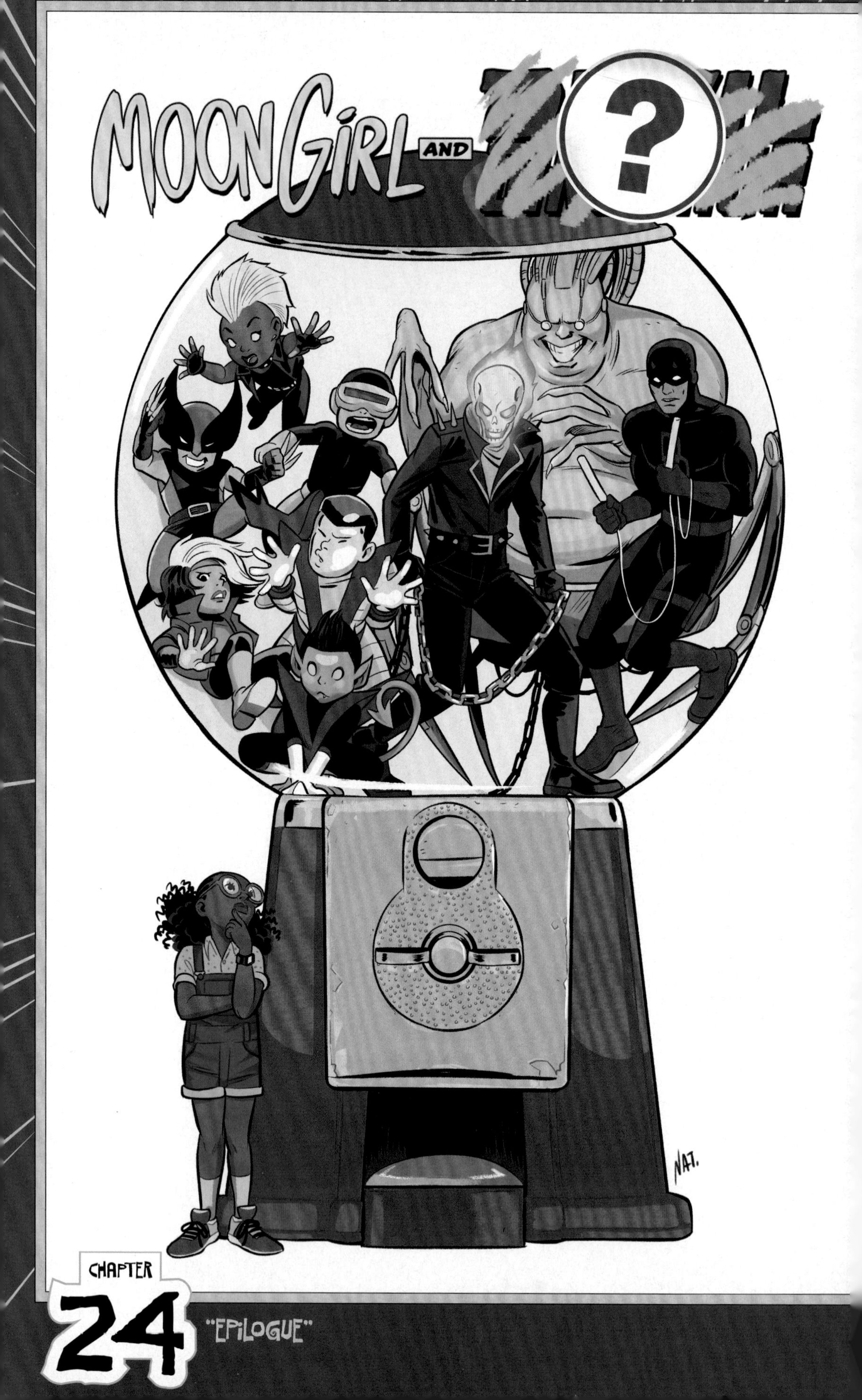
MOON GIRL AND ?
NAT.

CHAPTER
24
"EPILOGUE"

GIRL-MOON: EPILOGUE

HOW DOES THE ***WORLD'S GREATEST COMIC TEAM*** CARRY ON WHEN YOU'RE SHORT A 30-FOOT-TALL PARTNER? MOON GIRL ***WITHOUT*** DEVIL DINOSAUR--LUNELLA LAFAYETTE NEEDS A NEW SIDEKICK. A SPECIAL TALE TOLD IN THREE PARTS...

"Maybe I became a mathematician because I was so crummy at housework." --Cathleen Morawetz

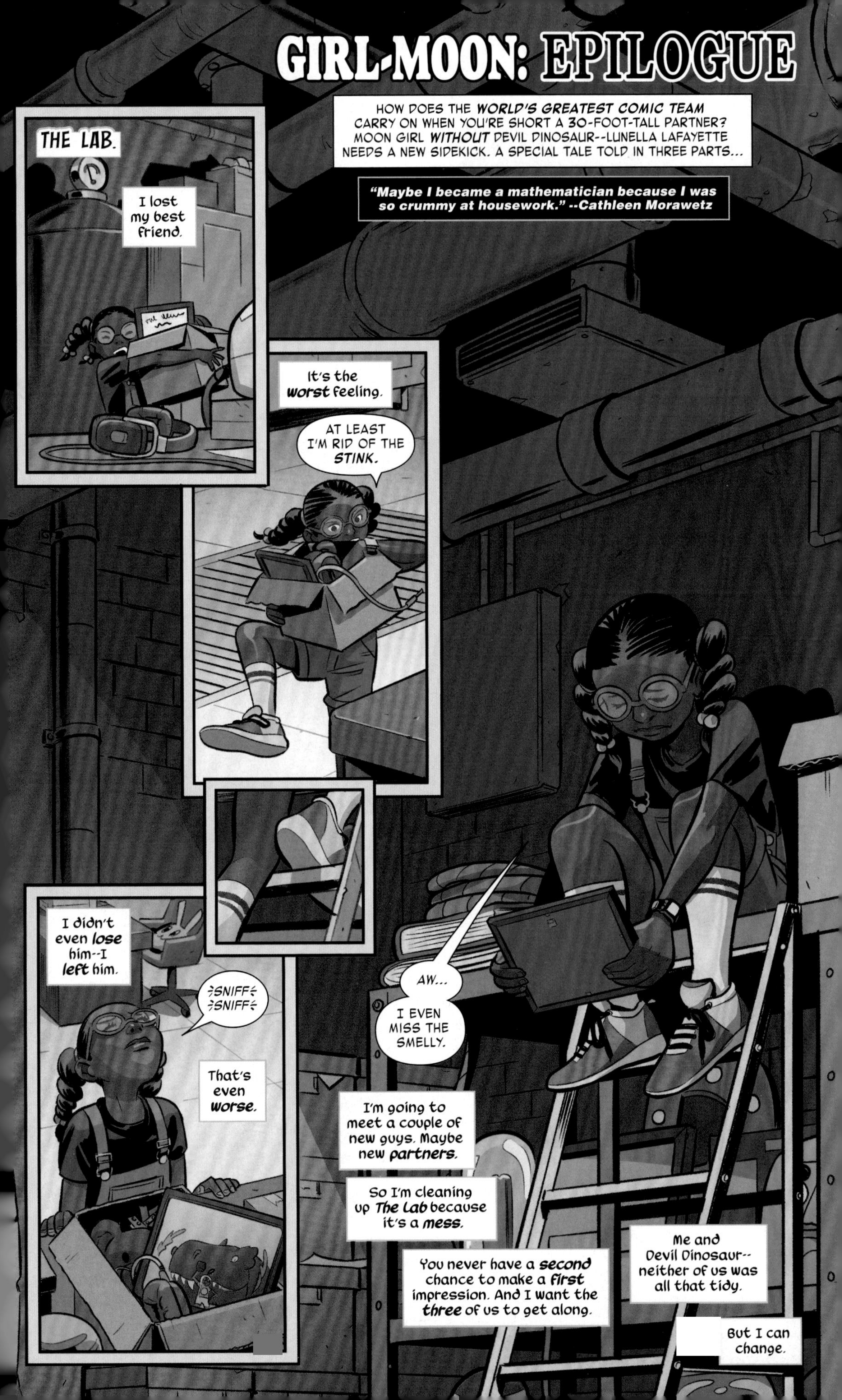

THE LAB.
I lost my best friend.
It's the worst feeling.
AT LEAST I'M RID OF THE STINK.
I didn't even lose him--I left him.
SNIFF SNIFF
That's even worse.
AW...
I EVEN MISS THE SMELLY.
I'm going to meet a couple of new guys. Maybe new partners.
So I'm cleaning up The Lab because it's a mess.
You never have a second chance to make a first impression. And I want the three of us to get along.
Me and Devil Dinosaur--neither of us was all that tidy.
But I can change.

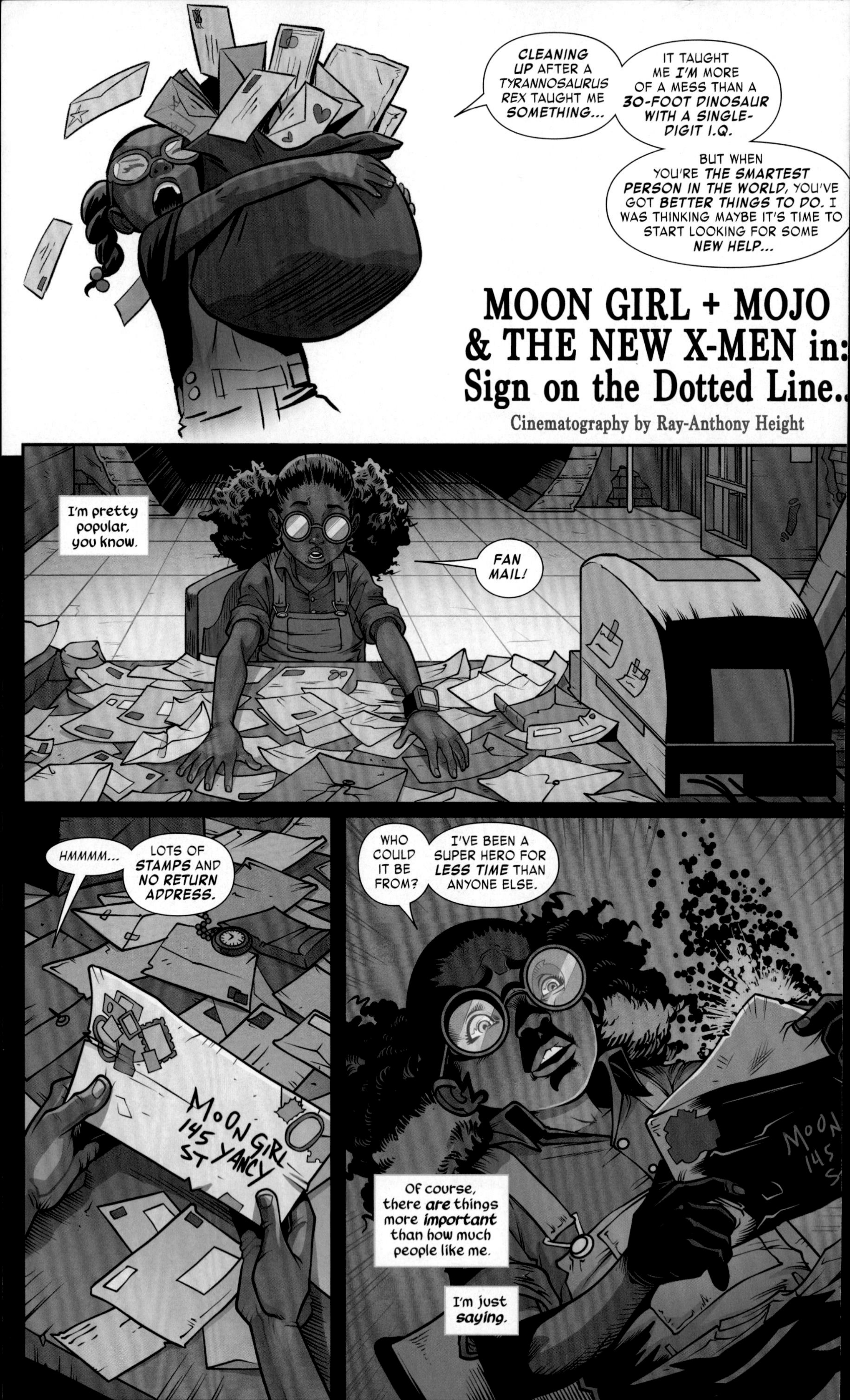

CLEANING UP AFTER A TYRANNOSAURUS REX TAUGHT ME SOMETHING...
IT TAUGHT ME I'M MORE OF A MESS THAN A 30-FOOT DINOSAUR WITH A SINGLE-DIGIT I.Q.
BUT WHEN YOU'RE THE SMARTEST PERSON IN THE WORLD, YOU'VE GOT BETTER THINGS TO DO. I WAS THINKING MAYBE IT'S TIME TO START LOOKING FOR SOME NEW HELP...
MOON GIRL + MOJO & THE NEW X-MEN in: Sign on the Dotted Line..
Cinematography by Ray-Anthony Height
I'm pretty popular, you know.
FAN MAIL!
HMMMM...
LOTS OF STAMPS AND NO RETURN ADDRESS.
MOON GIRL 145 ST YANCY
WHO COULD IT BE FROM?
I'VE BEEN A SUPER HERO FOR LESS TIME THAN ANYONE ELSE.
Of course, there are things more important than how much people like me.
I'm just saying.

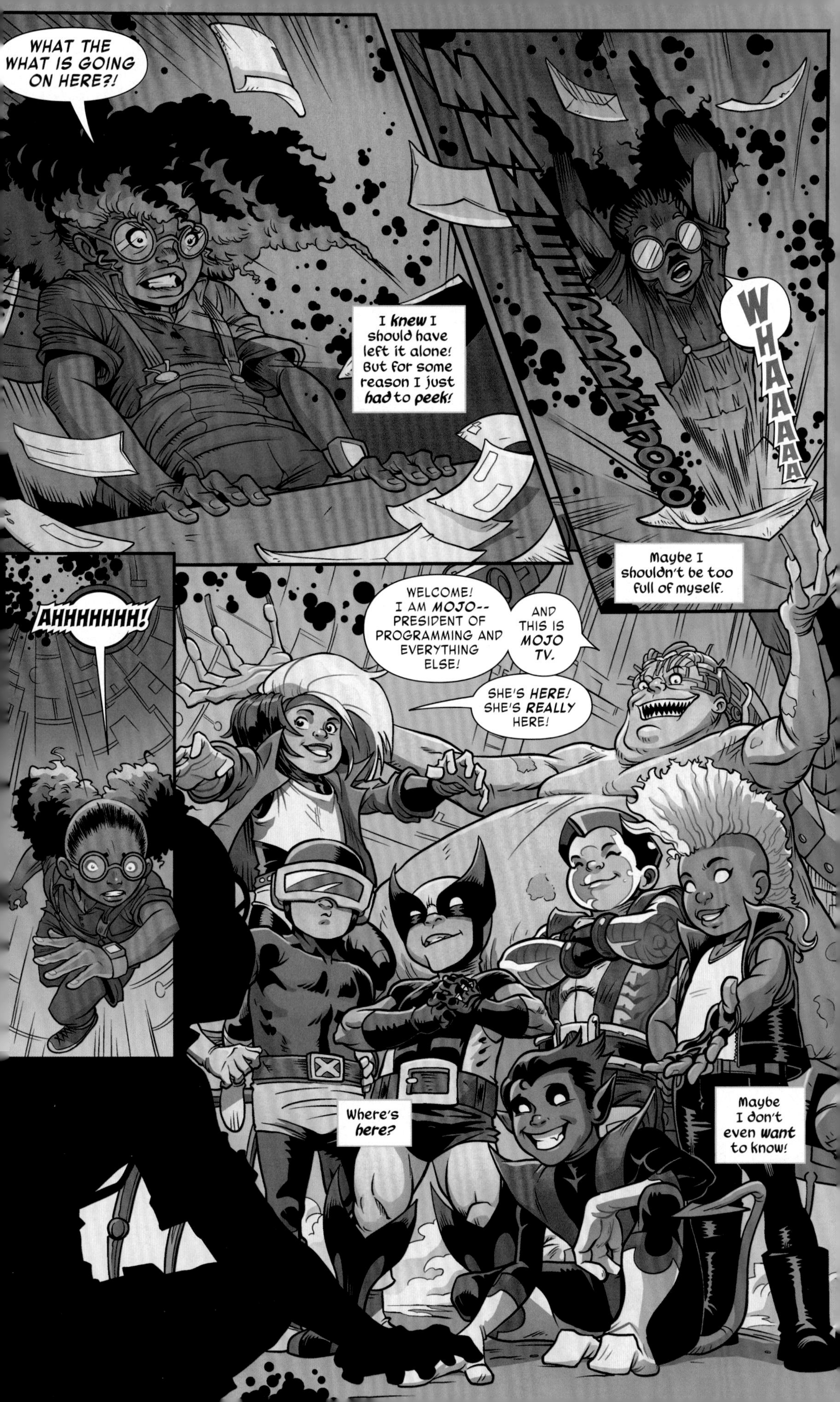
WHAT THE WHAT IS GOING ON HERE?!
I *knew* I should have left it alone! But for some reason I just *had* to *peek!*
MMEEERRRRR'POOO
WHAAAAAA
Maybe I shouldn't be too full of myself.
AHHHHHHHH!
WELCOME! I AM *MOJO*-- PRESIDENT OF PROGRAMMING AND EVERYTHING ELSE!
AND THIS IS *MOJO TV.*
SHE'S *HERE!* SHE'S *REALLY* HERE!
Where's *here?*
Maybe I don't even *want* to know!

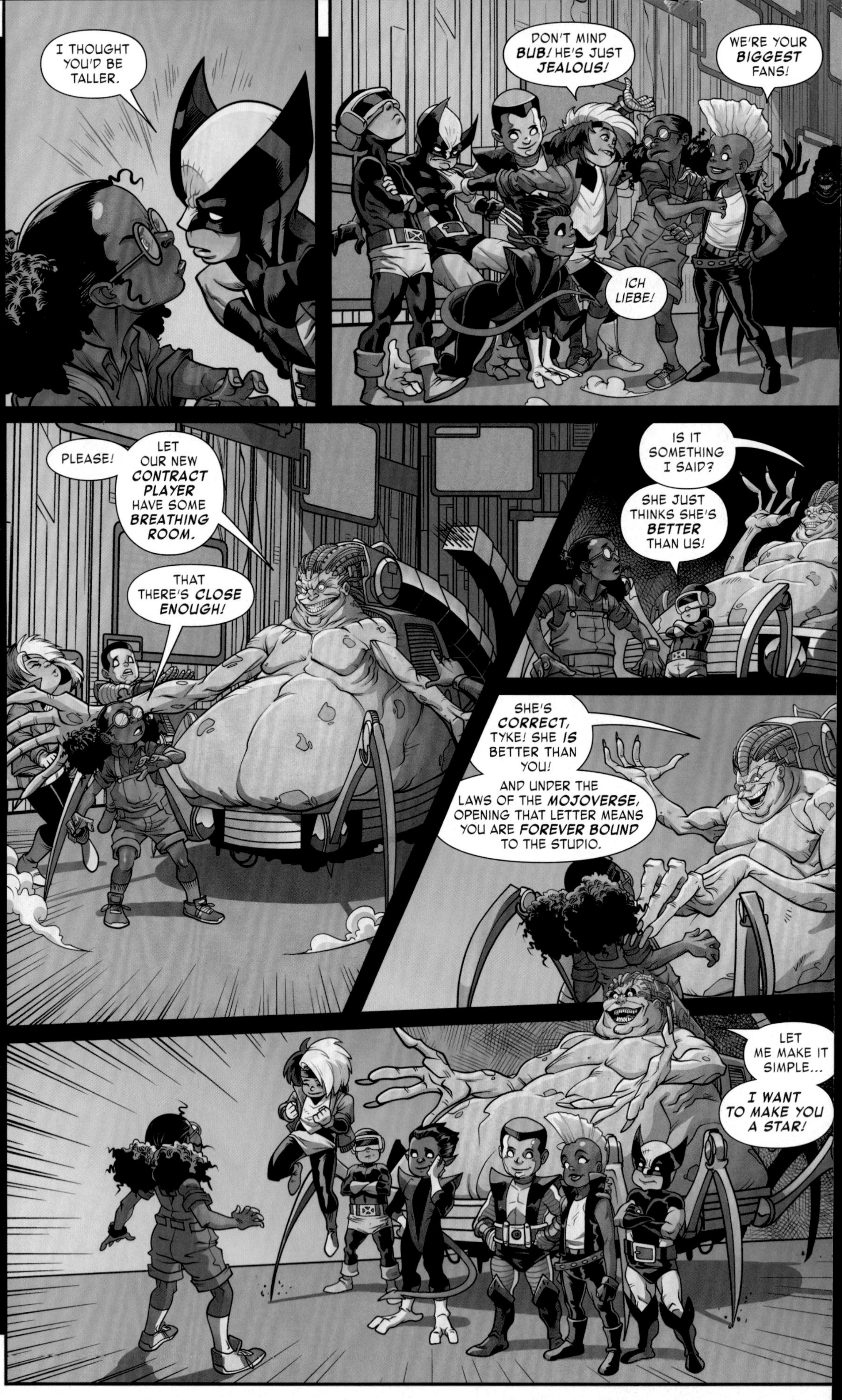

I THOUGHT YOU'D BE TALLER.
DON'T MIND BUB! HE'S JUST JEALOUS!
WE'RE YOUR BIGGEST FANS!
ICH LIEBE!
PLEASE!
LET OUR NEW CONTRACT PLAYER HAVE SOME BREATHING ROOM.
THAT THERE'S CLOSE ENOUGH!
IS IT SOMETHING I SAID?
SHE JUST THINKS SHE'S BETTER THAN US!
SHE'S CORRECT, TYKE! SHE IS BETTER THAN YOU!
AND UNDER THE LAWS OF THE MOJOVERSE, OPENING THAT LETTER MEANS YOU ARE FOREVER BOUND TO THE STUDIO.
LET ME MAKE IT SIMPLE...
I WANT TO MAKE YOU A STAR!

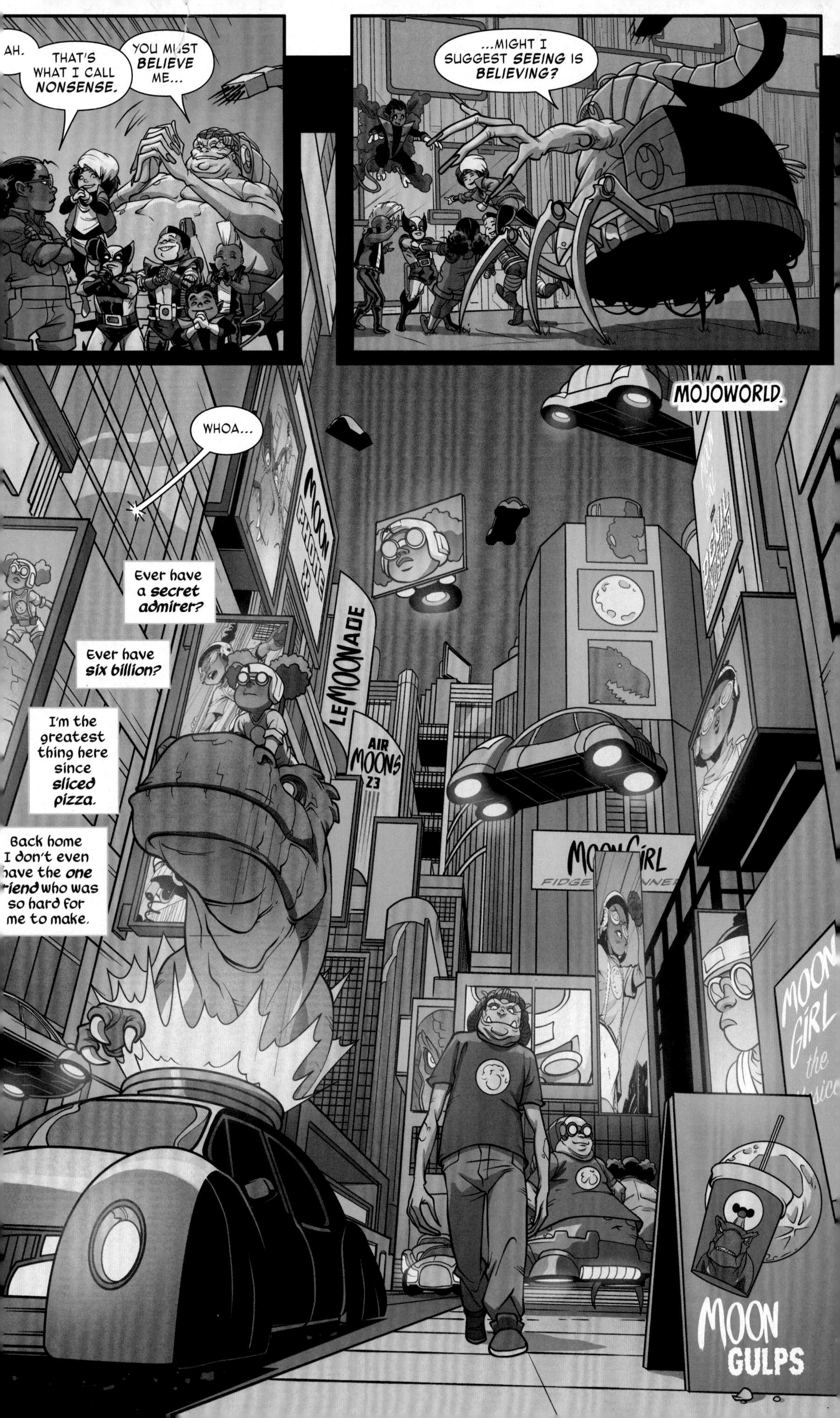

AH.
THAT'S WHAT I CALL NONSENSE.
YOU MUST BELIEVE ME...
...MIGHT I SUGGEST SEEING IS BELIEVING?
MOJOWORLD.
WHOA...
Ever have a secret admirer?
Ever have six billion?
I'm the greatest thing here since sliced pizza.
Back home I don't even have the one friend who was so hard for me to make.
LEMOONADE
AIR MOONS 23
MOON GIRL
MOON GIRL the
MOON GULPS

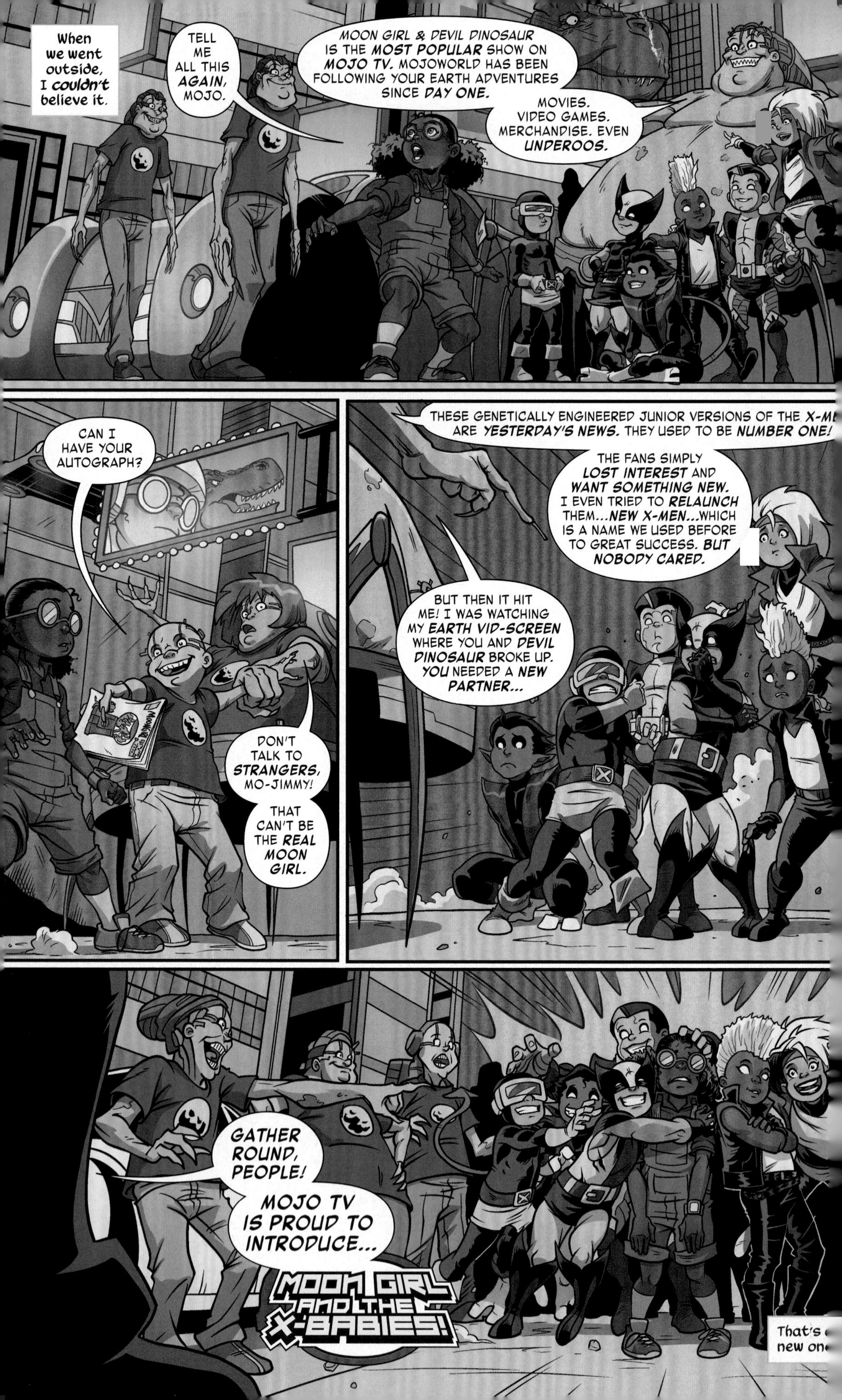

When we went outside, I couldn't believe it.
TELL ME ALL THIS AGAIN, MOJO.
MOON GIRL & DEVIL DINOSAUR IS THE MOST POPULAR SHOW ON MOJO TV. MOJOWORLD HAS BEEN FOLLOWING YOUR EARTH ADVENTURES SINCE DAY ONE.
MOVIES. VIDEO GAMES. MERCHANDISE. EVEN UNDEROOS.
CAN I HAVE YOUR AUTOGRAPH?
DON'T TALK TO STRANGERS, MO-JIMMY!
THAT CAN'T BE THE REAL MOON GIRL.
THESE GENETICALLY ENGINEERED JUNIOR VERSIONS OF THE X-M
ARE YESTERDAY'S NEWS. THEY USED TO BE NUMBER ONE!
THE FANS SIMPLY LOST INTEREST AND WANT SOMETHING NEW. I EVEN TRIED TO RELAUNCH THEM...NEW X-MEN...WHICH IS A NAME WE USED BEFORE TO GREAT SUCCESS. BUT NOBODY CARED.
BUT THEN IT HIT ME! I WAS WATCHING MY EARTH VID-SCREEN WHERE YOU AND DEVIL DINOSAUR BROKE UP. YOU NEEDED A NEW PARTNER...
GATHER ROUND, PEOPLE!
MOJO TV IS PROUD TO INTRODUCE...
MOON GIRL AND THE X-BABIES!
That's
new on

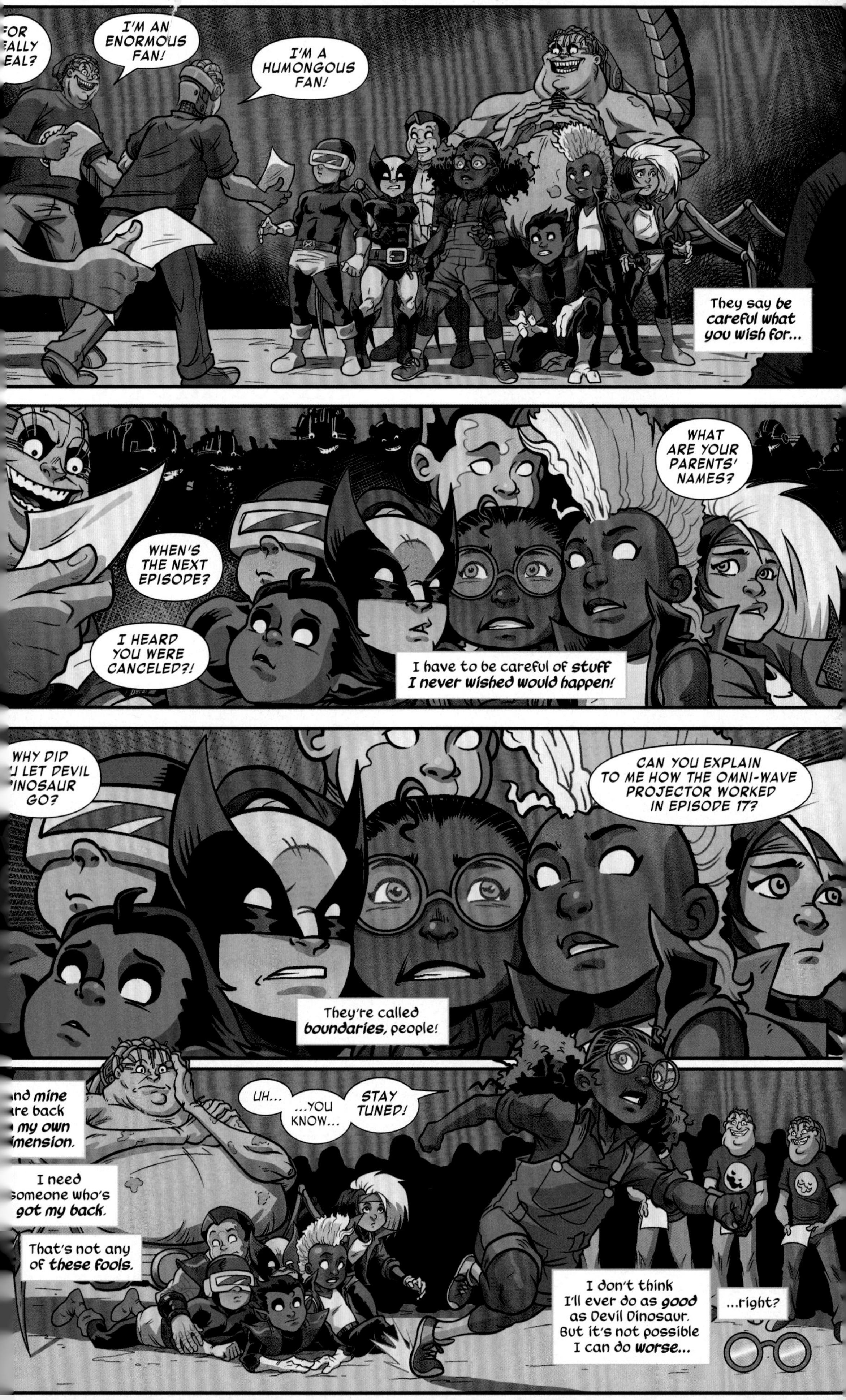

FOR
ALLY
EAL?
I'M AN ENORMOUS FAN!
I'M A HUMONGOUS FAN!
They say be careful what you wish for...
WHEN'S THE NEXT EPISODE?
I HEARD YOU WERE CANCELED?!
WHAT ARE YOUR PARENTS' NAMES?
I have to be careful of stuff I never wished would happen!
WHY DID
LET DEVIL
INOSAUR
GO?
CAN YOU EXPLAIN TO ME HOW THE OMNI-WAVE PROJECTOR WORKED IN EPISODE 17?
They're called boundaries, people!
nd mine
re back
my own
imension.
I need
omeone who's
got my back.
That's not any of these fools.
UH...
...YOU KNOW...
STAY TUNED!
I don't think I'll ever do as good as Devil Dinosaur. But it's not possible I can do worse...
...right?

EVER TRY TO *CATCH A CAB* AT *RUSH HOUR?* WAIT IN *CROSSTOWN TRAFFIC* ON A *BUS?* THE SUBWAY DOESN'T TAKE ME *WHERE I WANT TO GO.* I USED TO *GO IN STYLE* ON THE BACK OF A FIERY RED *DINOSAUR* NAMED *DEVIL.*

NOW I NEED A NEW RIDE.

MOON GIRL + GHOST RIDER in: Think Fast!

Pit crewed by Domo Stanton

TALLY-HO!

THE RACE IS AFOOT!

LET'S ROLL!

I HAVE AN APPOINTMENT-- AND *THAT GUY* CHARGES BY THE HOUR!

DO I LOOK LIKE A *CHAUFFEUR?*

WELL... KINDA...BUT EITHER WAY-- I'M LATE.

SO MAKE ROOM!

EVERY *SOLSTICE* CERTAIN *GHOST RIDERS* ARE SUMMONED *TO RACE* ACROSS *VAST DIMENSIONS* TO TEST THEIR *SPEED.* THE LOSER SUFFERS NOT JUST *INDIGNITY,* BUT UNSPEAKABLE...

WELL...IT'S *UNSPEAKABLE.*

THIS TIME THE *HELLTRACK* IS *YANCY STREET,* BURNING DOWN THE QUARTER-MILE FROM *ESSEX* TO *HOUSTON.*

HOUSTON STREET IS ON THE WAY.

YANCY ST.

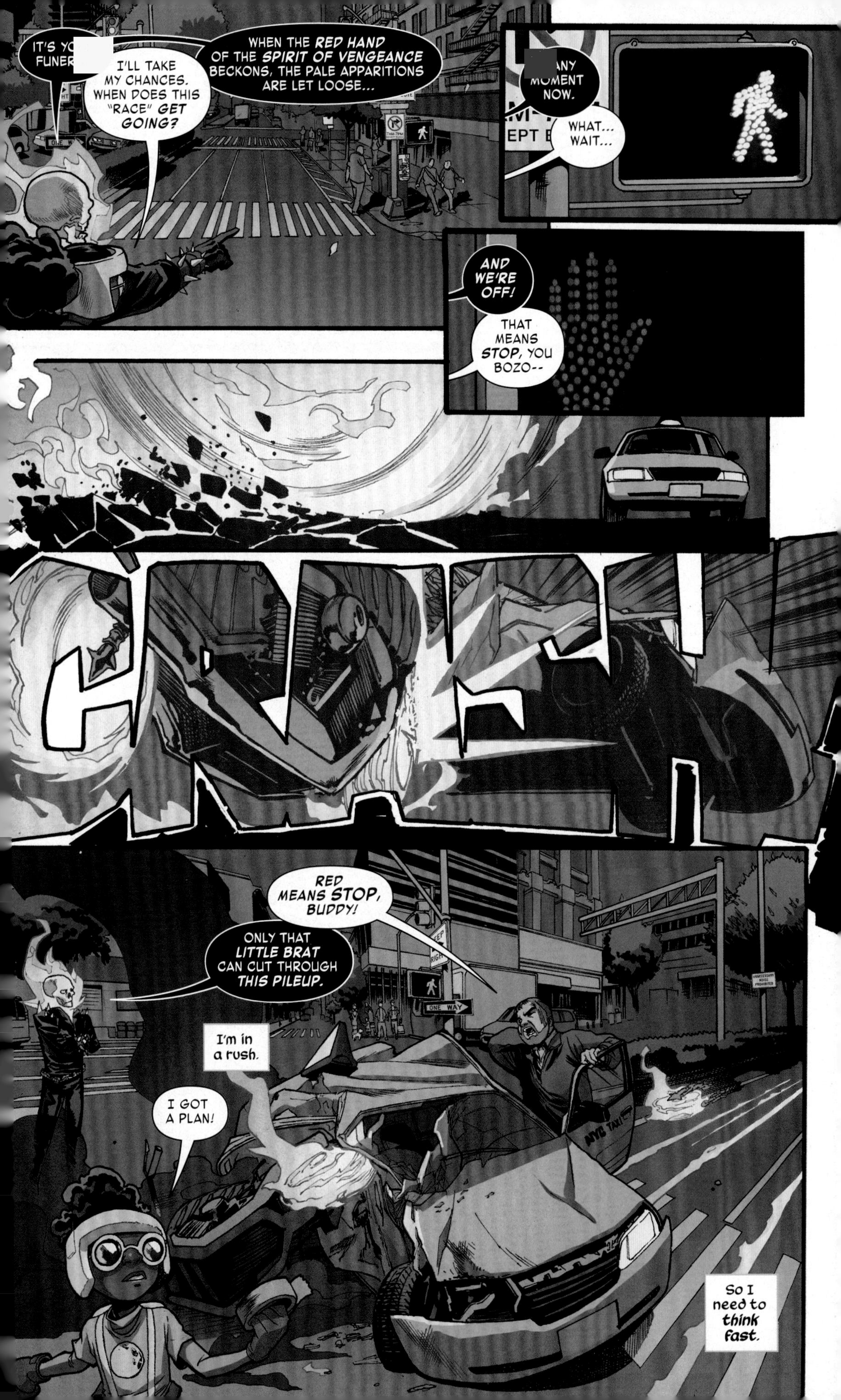

I'LL TAKE MY CHANCES. WHEN DOES THIS "RACE" GET GOING?
WHEN THE RED HAND OF THE SPIRIT OF VENGEANCE BECKONS, THE PALE APPARITIONS ARE LET LOOSE...
[redacted] ANY MOMENT NOW.
WHAT... WAIT...
AND WE'RE OFF!
THAT MEANS STOP, YOU BOZO--
RED MEANS STOP, BUDDY!
ONLY THAT LITTLE BRAT CAN CUT THROUGH THIS PILEUP.
I'm in a rush.
I GOT A PLAN!
So I need to think fast.

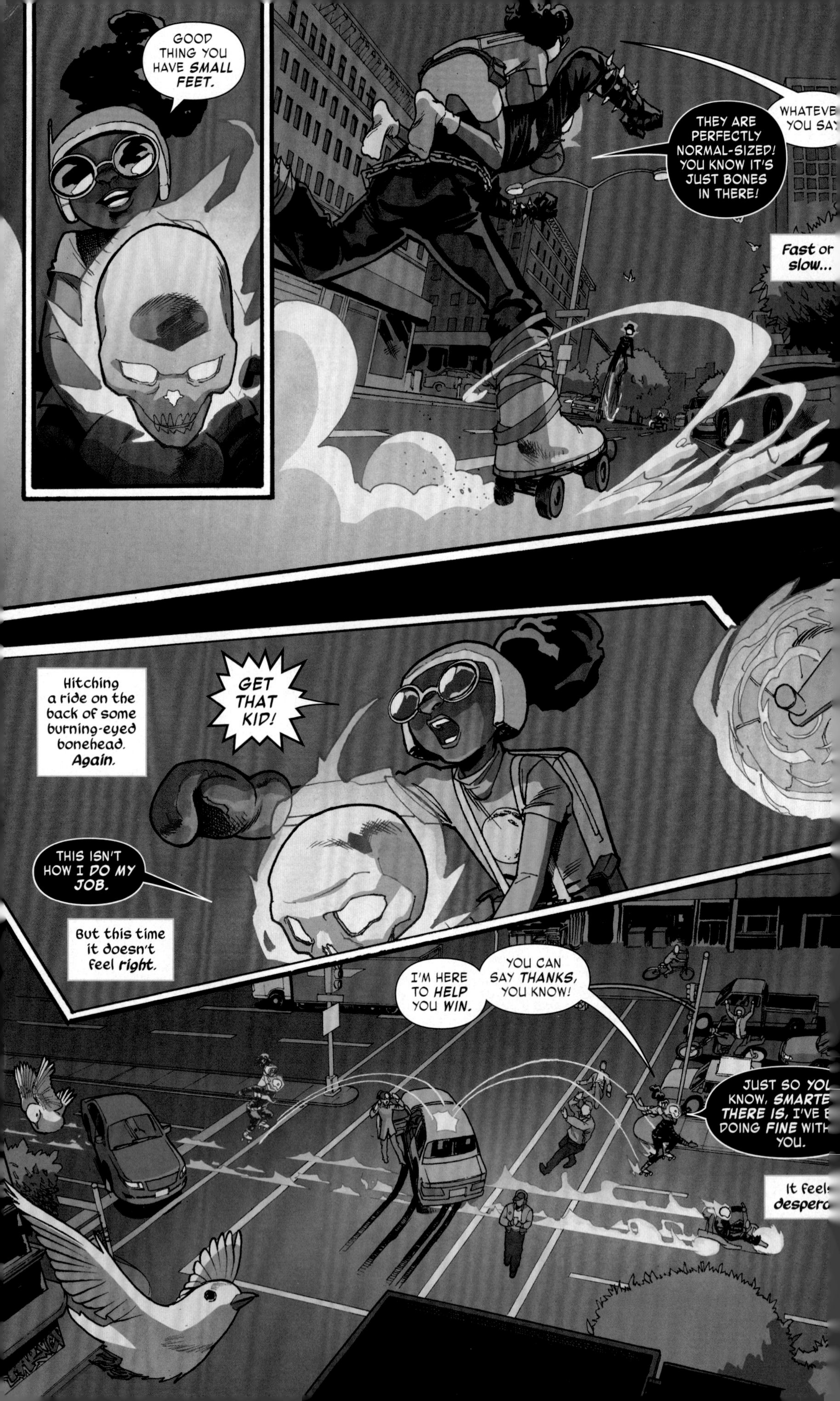
GOOD THING YOU HAVE SMALL FEET.
THEY ARE PERFECTLY NORMAL-SIZED! YOU KNOW IT'S JUST BONES IN THERE!
WHATEVE YOU SA
Fast or slow...
Hitching a ride on the back of some burning-eyed bonehead. Again.
GET THAT KID!
THIS ISN'T HOW I DO MY JOB.
But this time it doesn't feel right.
I'M HERE TO HELP YOU WIN.
YOU CAN SAY THANKS, YOU KNOW!
JUST SO YO KNOW, SMARTE THERE IS, I'VE DOING FINE WITH YOU.
It feels despera

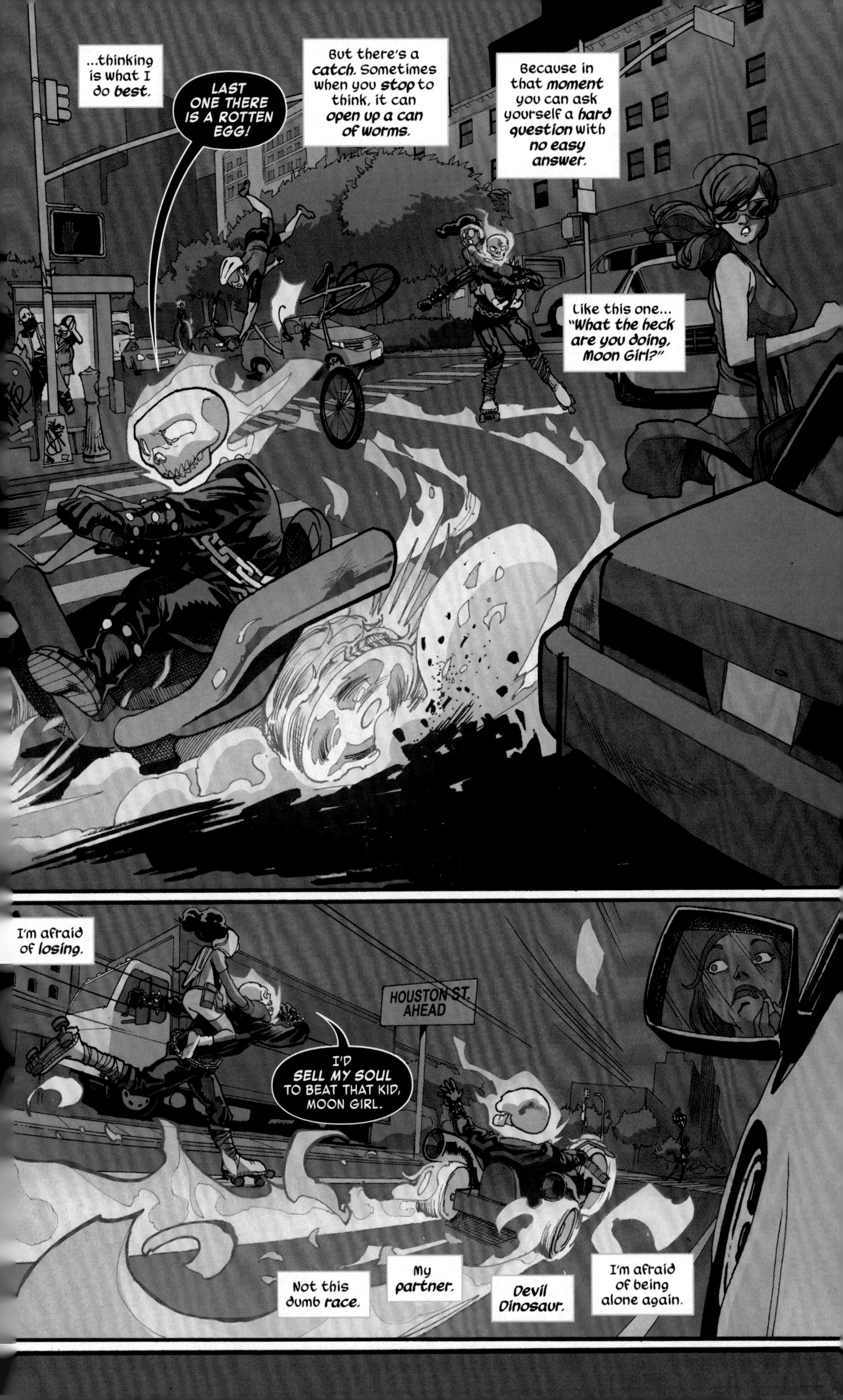

...thinking is what I do best.
LAST ONE THERE IS A ROTTEN EGG!
But there's a catch. Sometimes when you stop to think, it can open up a can of worms.
Because in that moment you can ask yourself a hard question with no easy answer.
Like this one... "What the heck are you doing, Moon Girl?"
I'm afraid of losing.
HOUSTON ST. AHEAD
I'D SELL MY SOUL TO BEAT THAT KID, MOON GIRL.
Not this dumb race.
My partner.
Devil Dinosaur.
I'm afraid of being alone again.

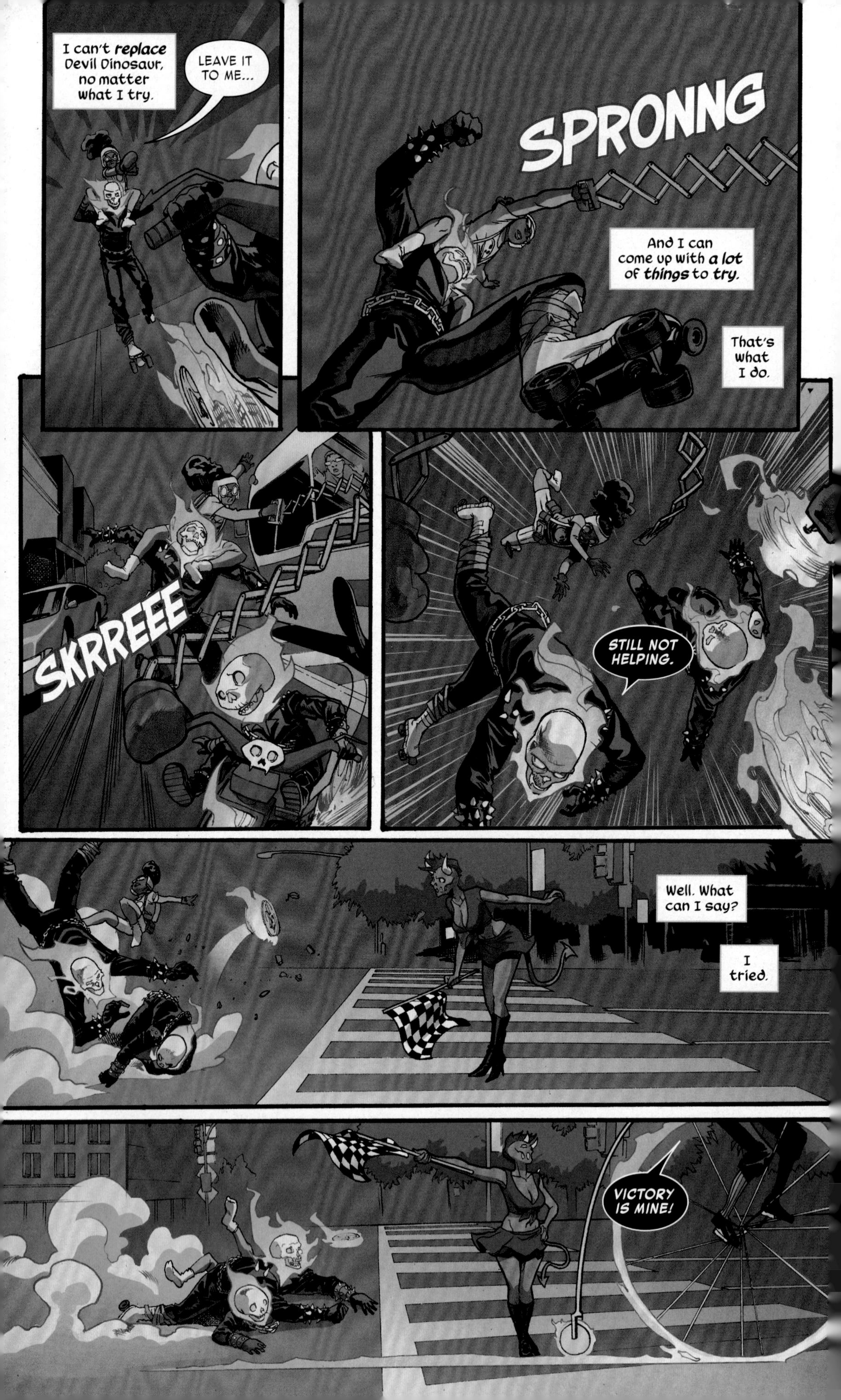
I can't *replace* Devil Dinosaur, no matter what I try.
LEAVE IT TO ME...
SPRONNG
And I can come up with *a lot* of *things* to *try*.
That's what I do.
SKRREEE
STILL NOT HELPING.
Well. What can I say?
I tried.
VICTORY IS MINE!

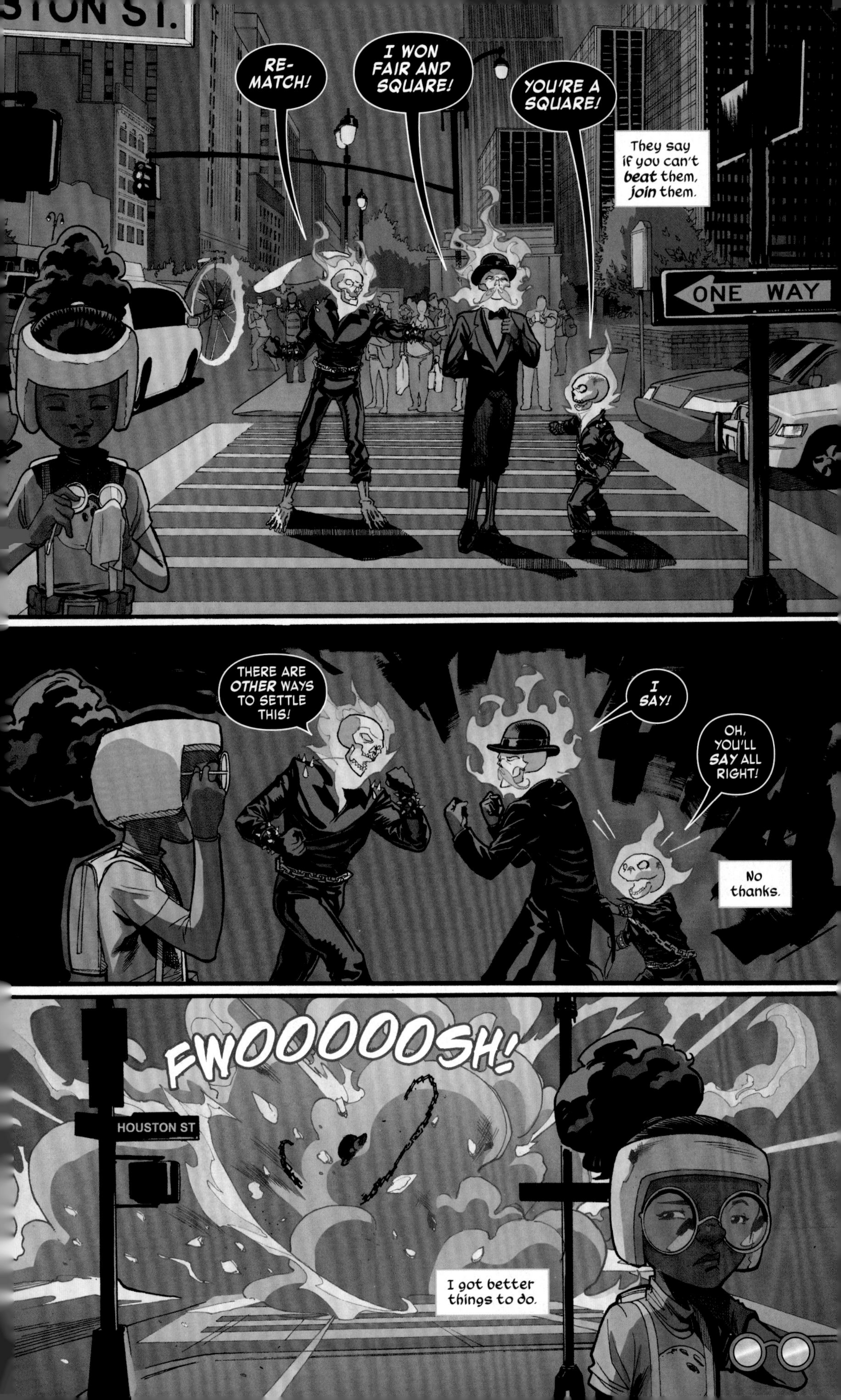
STON ST.
RE-MATCH!
I WON FAIR AND SQUARE!
YOU'RE A SQUARE!
They say if you can't beat them, join them.
ONE WAY
THERE ARE OTHER WAYS TO SETTLE THIS!
I SAY!
OH, YOU'LL SAY ALL RIGHT!
No thanks.
FWOOOOOOSH!
HOUSTON ST
I got better things to do.

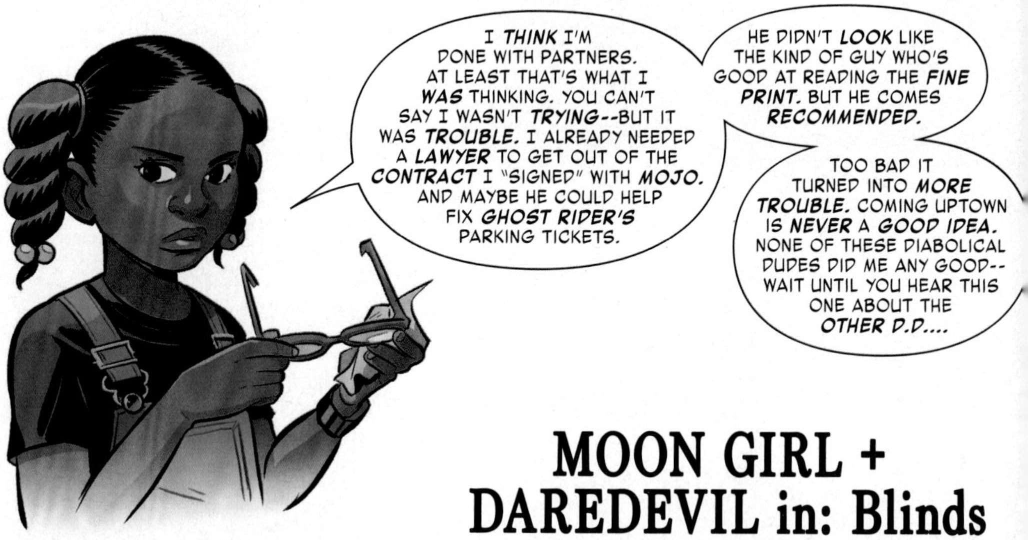
I THINK I'M DONE WITH PARTNERS. AT LEAST THAT'S WHAT I WAS THINKING. YOU CAN'T SAY I WASN'T TRYING--BUT IT WAS TROUBLE. I ALREADY NEEDED A LAWYER TO GET OUT OF THE CONTRACT I "SIGNED" WITH MOJO. AND MAYBE HE COULD HELP FIX GHOST RIDER'S PARKING TICKETS.
HE DIDN'T LOOK LIKE THE KIND OF GUY WHO'S GOOD AT READING THE FINE PRINT. BUT HE COMES RECOMMENDED.
TOO BAD IT TURNED INTO MORE TROUBLE. COMING UPTOWN IS NEVER A GOOD IDEA. NONE OF THESE DIABOLICAL DUDES DID ME ANY GOOD--WAIT UNTIL YOU HEAR THIS ONE ABOUT THE OTHER D.D....

MOON GIRL + DAREDEVIL in: Blinds

Courtroom sketches by Michael Shelfer

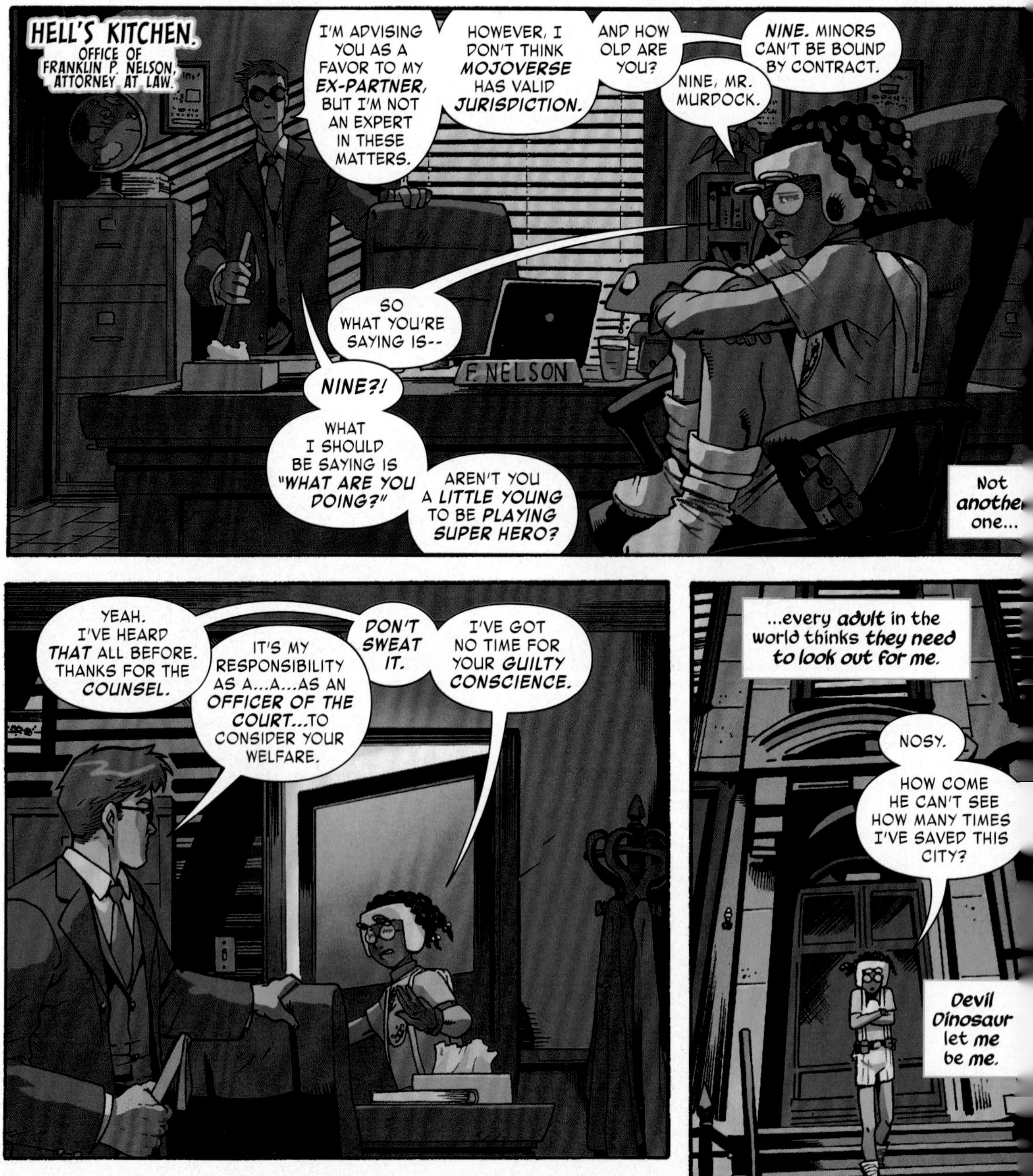
HELL'S KITCHEN.
OFFICE OF FRANKLIN P. NELSON, ATTORNEY AT LAW.
I'M ADVISING YOU AS A FAVOR TO MY EX-PARTNER, BUT I'M NOT AN EXPERT IN THESE MATTERS.
HOWEVER, I DON'T THINK MOJOVERSE HAS VALID JURISDICTION.
AND HOW OLD ARE YOU?
NINE. MINORS CAN'T BE BOUND BY CONTRACT.
NINE, MR. MURDOCK.
SO WHAT YOU'RE SAYING IS--
F. NELSON
NINE?!
WHAT I SHOULD BE SAYING IS "WHAT ARE YOU DOING?"
AREN'T YOU A LITTLE YOUNG TO BE PLAYING SUPER HERO?
Not anothe
one...
YEAH. I'VE HEARD THAT ALL BEFORE. THANKS FOR THE COUNSEL.
IT'S MY RESPONSIBILITY AS A...A...AS AN OFFICER OF THE COURT...TO CONSIDER YOUR WELFARE.
DON'T SWEAT IT.
I'VE GOT NO TIME FOR YOUR GUILTY CONSCIENCE.
...every adult in the world thinks they need to look out for me.
NOSY.
HOW COME HE CAN'T SEE HOW MANY TIMES I'VE SAVED THIS CITY?
Devil Dinosaur let me be me.

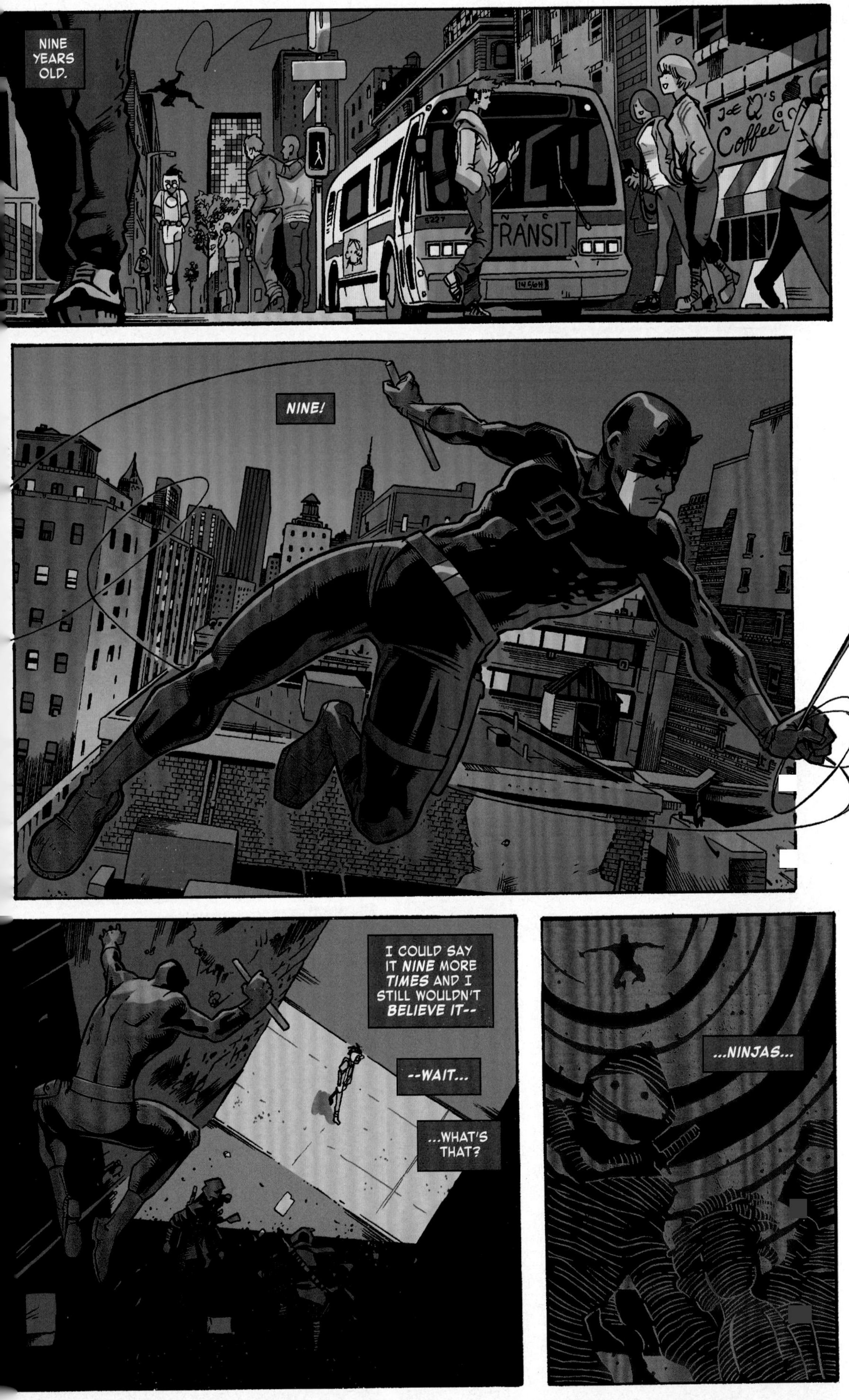
NINE YEARS OLD.
JOE Q's
Coffee
NYC
TRANSIT
NINE!
I COULD SAY IT NINE MORE TIMES AND I STILL WOULDN'T BELIEVE IT--
--WAIT...
...WHAT'S THAT?
...NINJAS...

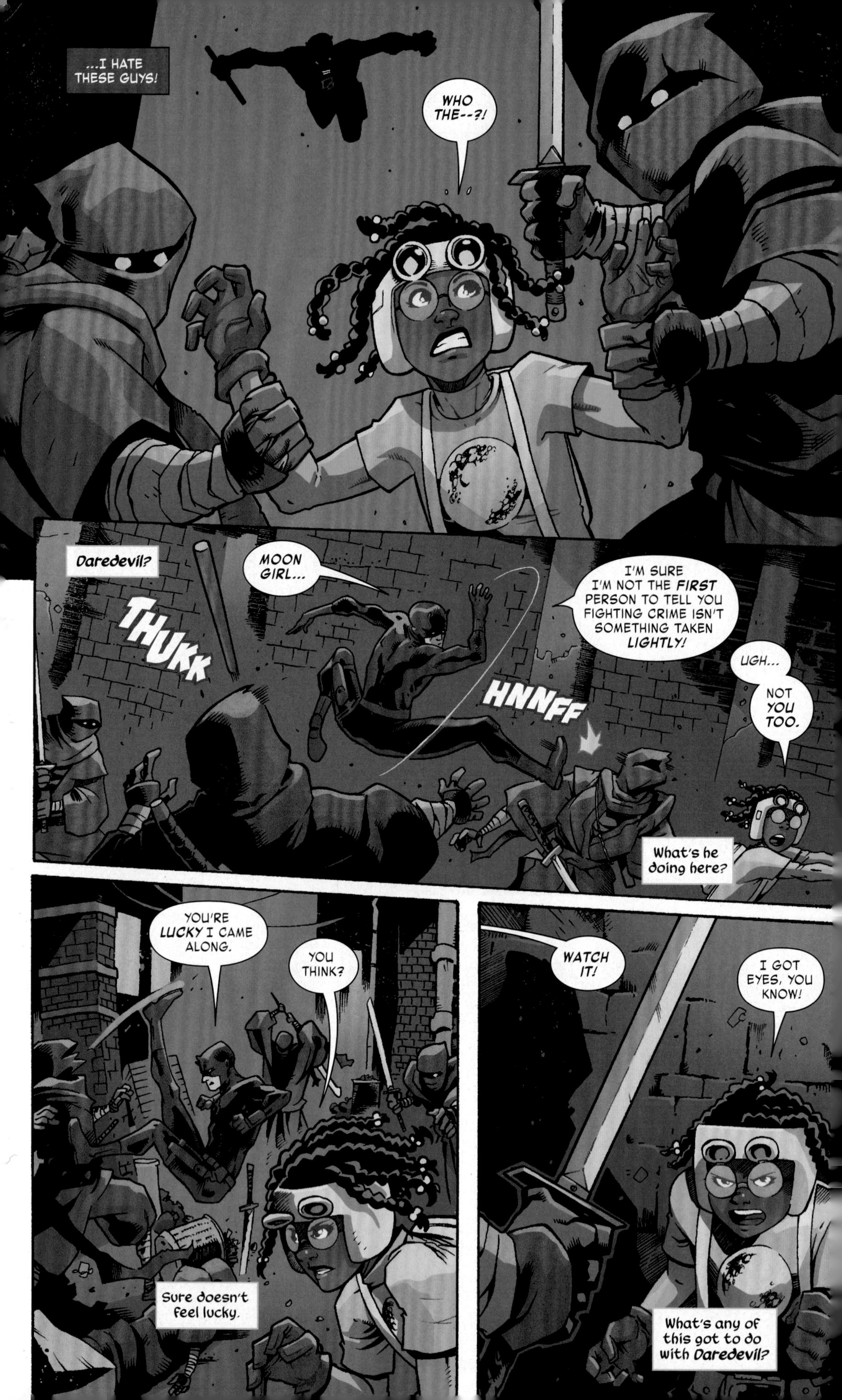

...I HATE THESE GUYS!
WHO THE--?!
Daredevil?
MOON GIRL...
THUKK
I'M SURE I'M NOT THE FIRST PERSON TO TELL YOU FIGHTING CRIME ISN'T SOMETHING TAKEN LIGHTLY!
HNNFF
UGH...
NOT YOU TOO.
What's he doing here?
YOU'RE LUCKY I CAME ALONG.
YOU THINK?
Sure doesn't feel lucky.
WATCH IT!
I GOT EYES, YOU KNOW!
What's any of this got to do with Daredevil?

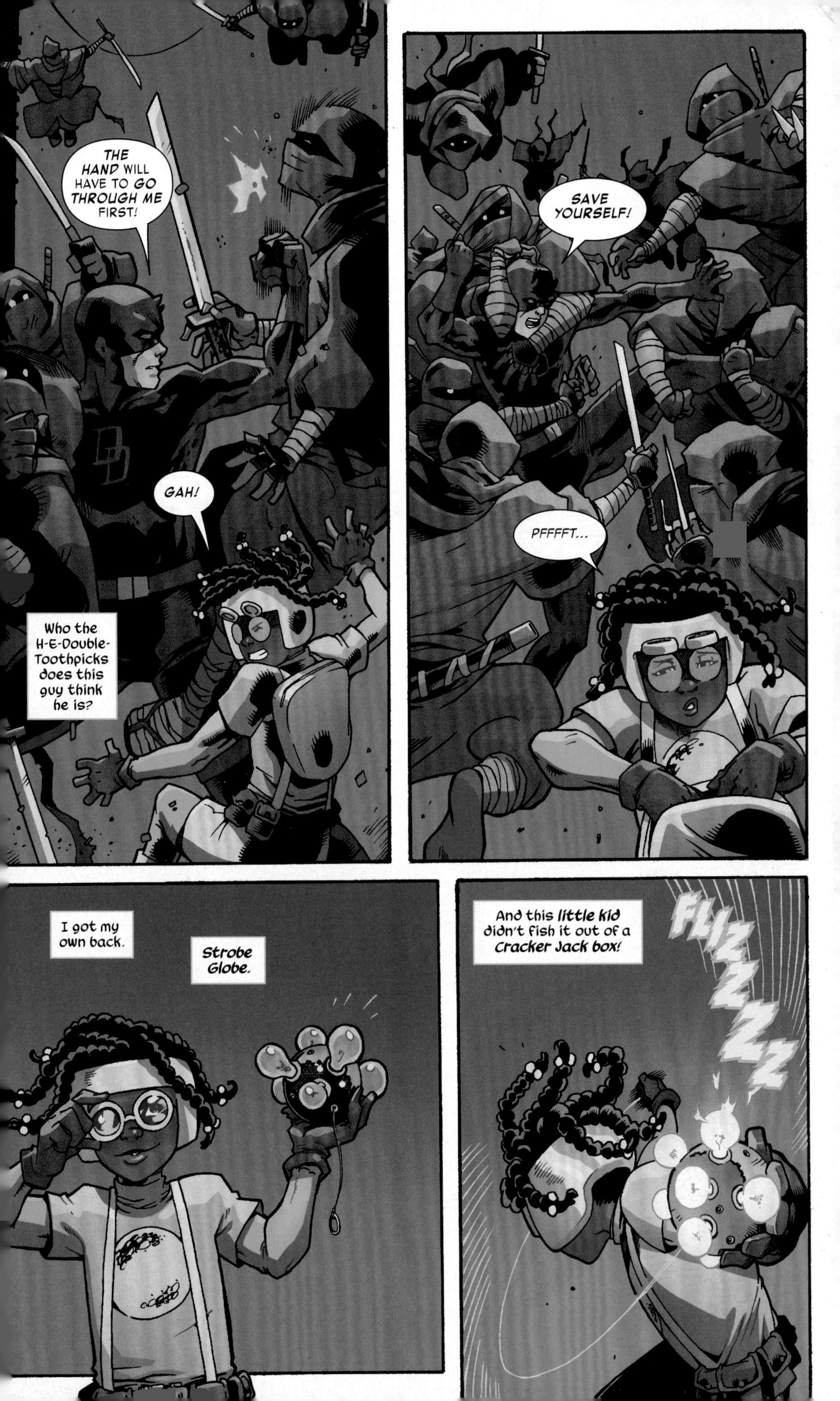

THE HAND WILL HAVE TO GO THROUGH ME FIRST!
GAH!
Who the H-E-Double-Toothpicks does this guy think he is?
SAVE YOURSELF!
PFFFFT...
I got my own back.
Strobe Globe.
And this little kid didn't fish it out of a Cracker Jack box!
FLIZZZZ

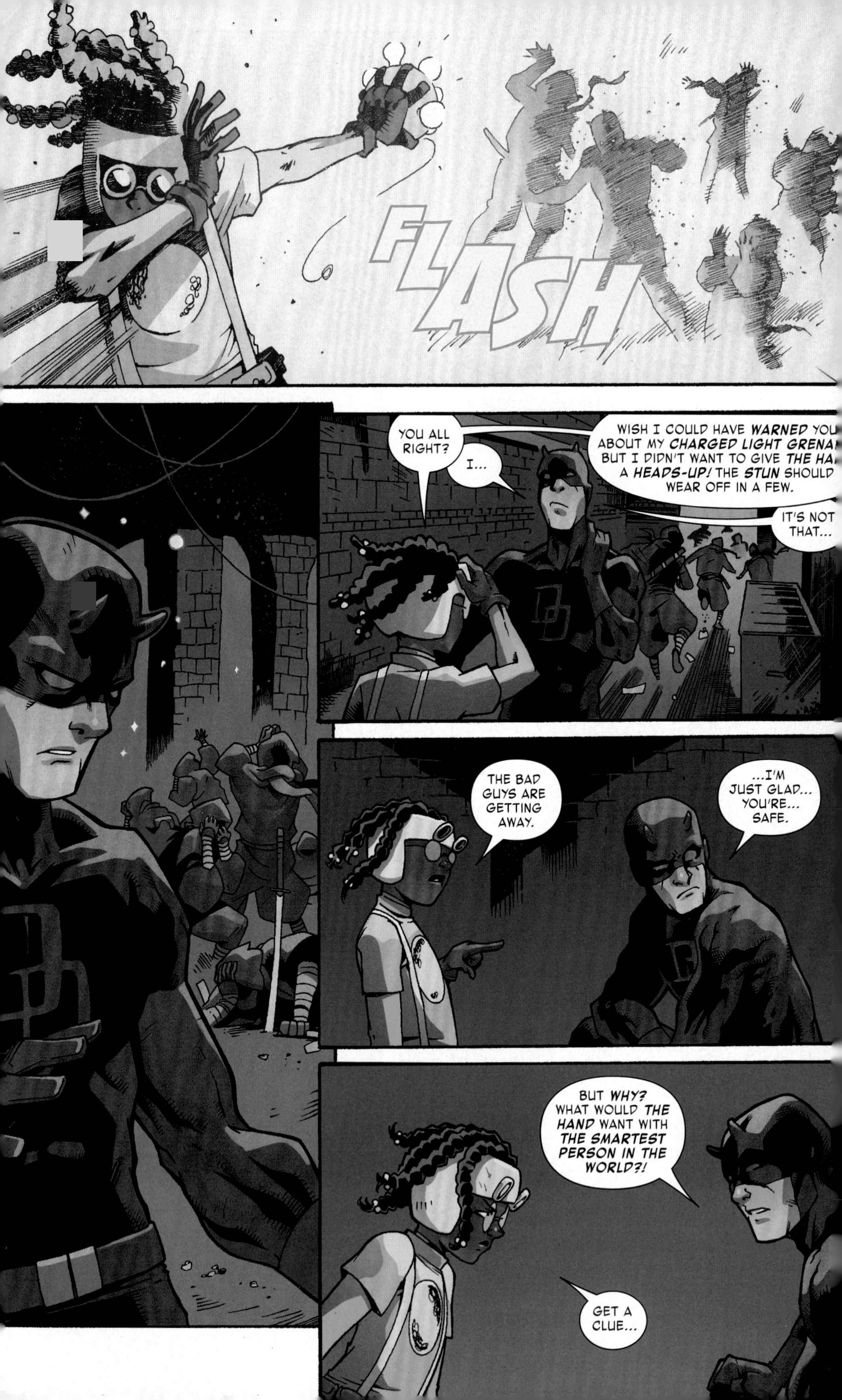
FLASH
YOU ALL RIGHT?
I...
WISH I COULD HAVE WARNED YOU ABOUT MY CHARGED LIGHT GRENA BUT I DIDN'T WANT TO GIVE THE HA A HEADS-UP! THE STUN SHOULD WEAR OFF IN A FEW.
IT'S NOT THAT...
THE BAD GUYS ARE GETTING AWAY.
...I'M JUST GLAD... YOU'RE... SAFE.
BUT WHY? WHAT WOULD THE HAND WANT WITH THE SMARTEST PERSON IN THE WORLD?!
GET A CLUE...

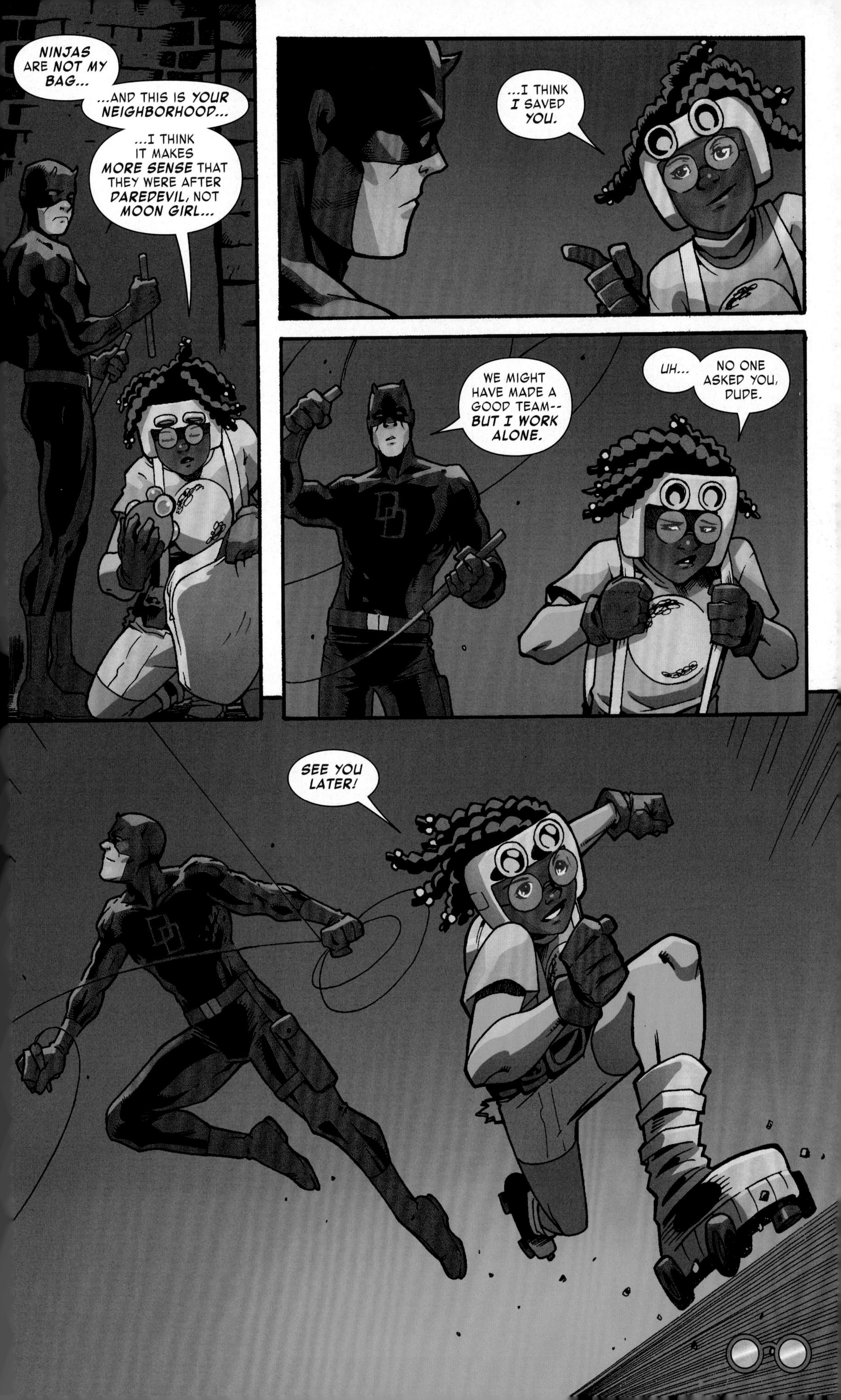

NINJAS ARE NOT MY BAG...
...AND THIS IS YOUR NEIGHBORHOOD...
...I THINK IT MAKES MORE SENSE THAT THEY WERE AFTER DAREDEVIL, NOT MOON GIRL...
...I THINK I SAVED YOU.
WE MIGHT HAVE MADE A GOOD TEAM-- BUT I WORK ALONE.
UH...
NO ONE ASKED YOU, DUDE.
SEE YOU LATER!

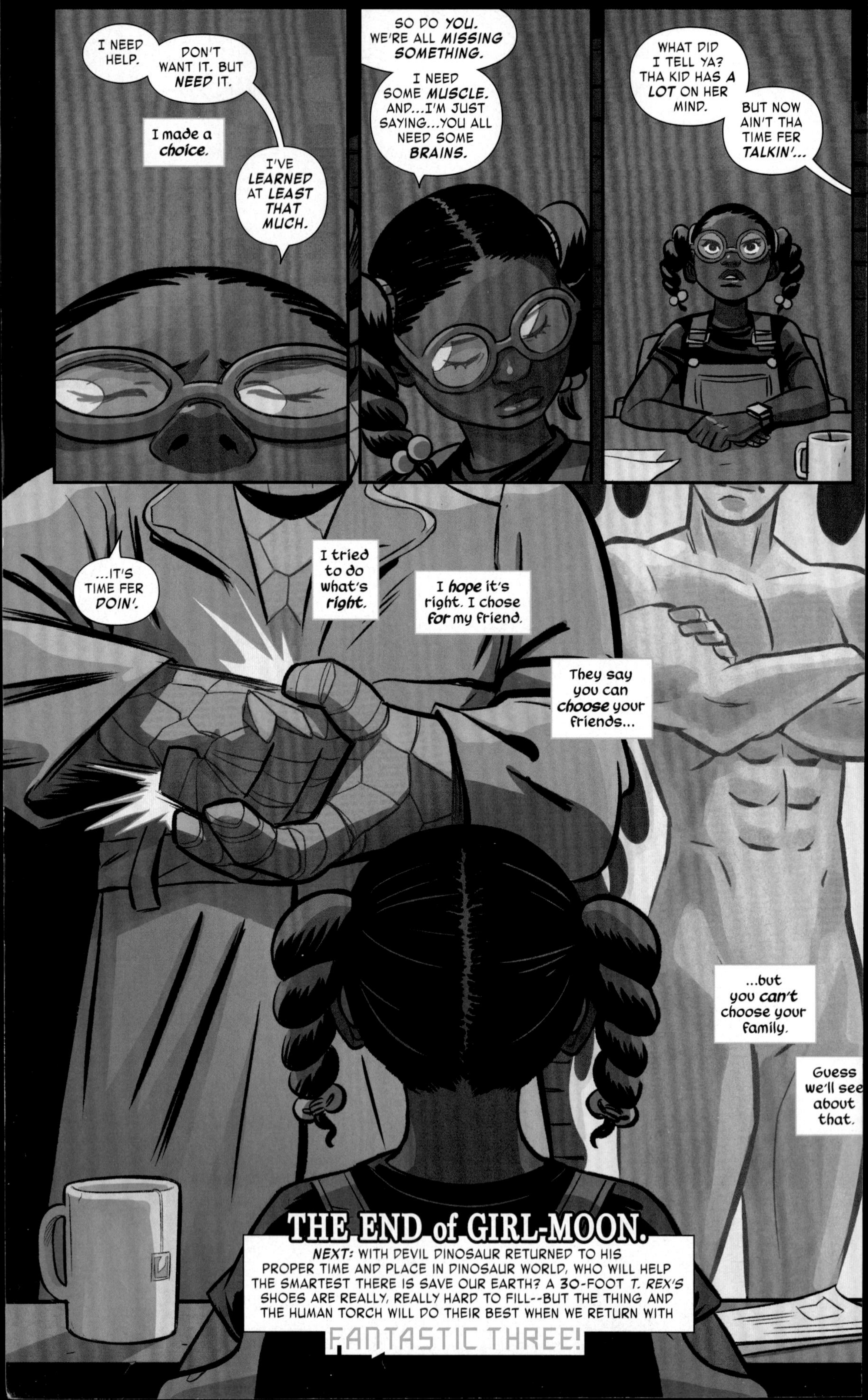

I NEED HELP.
DON'T WANT IT. BUT NEED IT.
I made a choice.
I'VE LEARNED AT LEAST THAT MUCH.
SO DO YOU. WE'RE ALL MISSING SOMETHING.
I NEED SOME MUSCLE. AND...I'M JUST SAYING...YOU ALL NEED SOME BRAINS.
WHAT DID I TELL YA? THA KID HAS A LOT ON HER MIND.
BUT NOW AIN'T THA TIME FER TALKIN'...
...IT'S TIME FER DOIN'.
I tried to do what's right.
I hope it's right. I chose for my friend.
They say you can choose your friends...
...but you can't choose your family.
Guess we'll see about that.
THE END of GIRL-MOON.
NEXT: WITH DEVIL DINOSAUR RETURNED TO HIS PROPER TIME AND PLACE IN DINOSAUR WORLD, WHO WILL HELP THE SMARTEST THERE IS SAVE OUR EARTH? A 30-FOOT T. REX'S SHOES ARE REALLY, REALLY HARD TO FILL--BUT THE THING AND THE HUMAN TORCH WILL DO THEIR BEST WHEN WE RETURN WITH
FANTASTIC THREE!

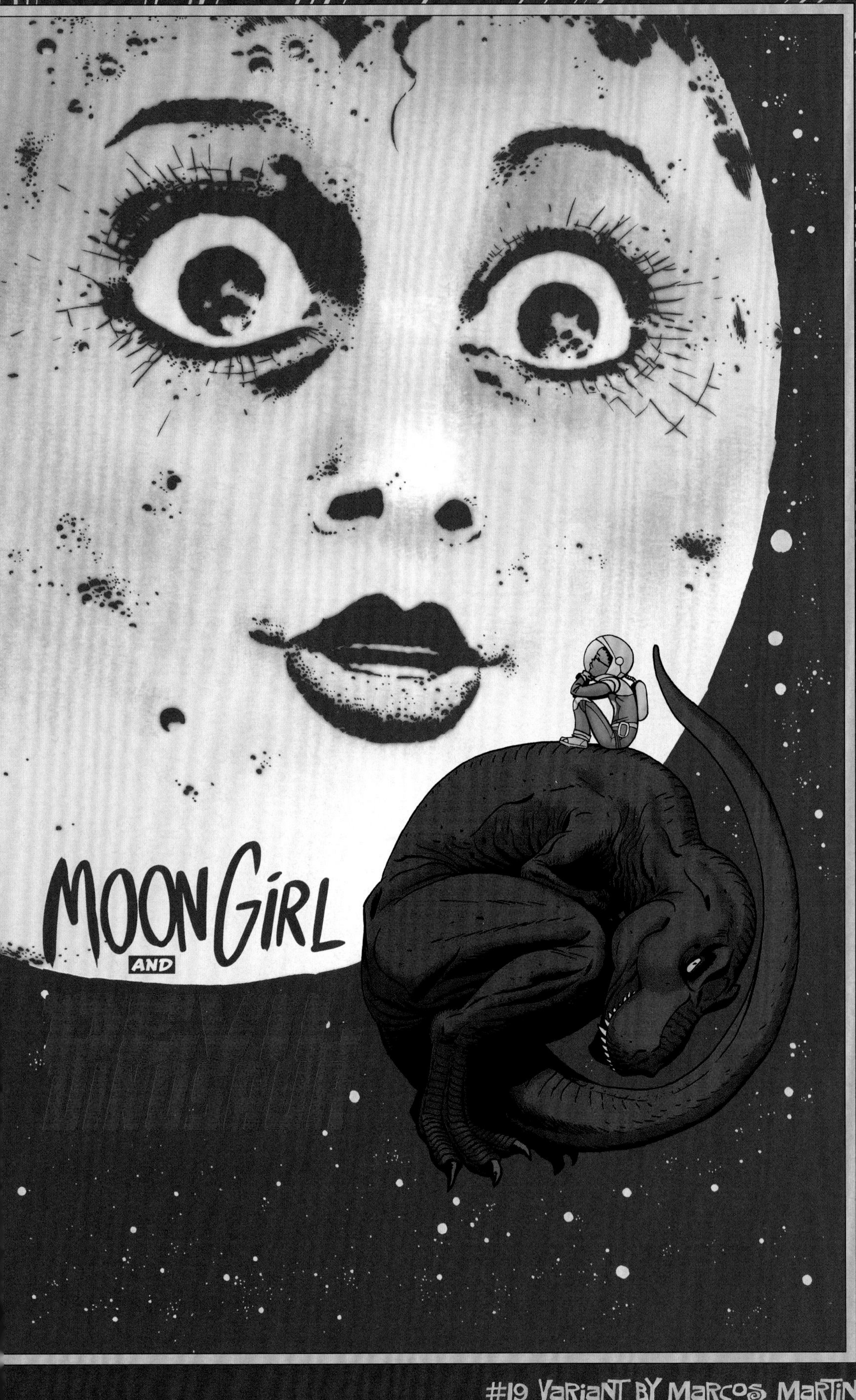
MOON GIRL
AND

#19 VARIANT BY MARCOS MARTIN

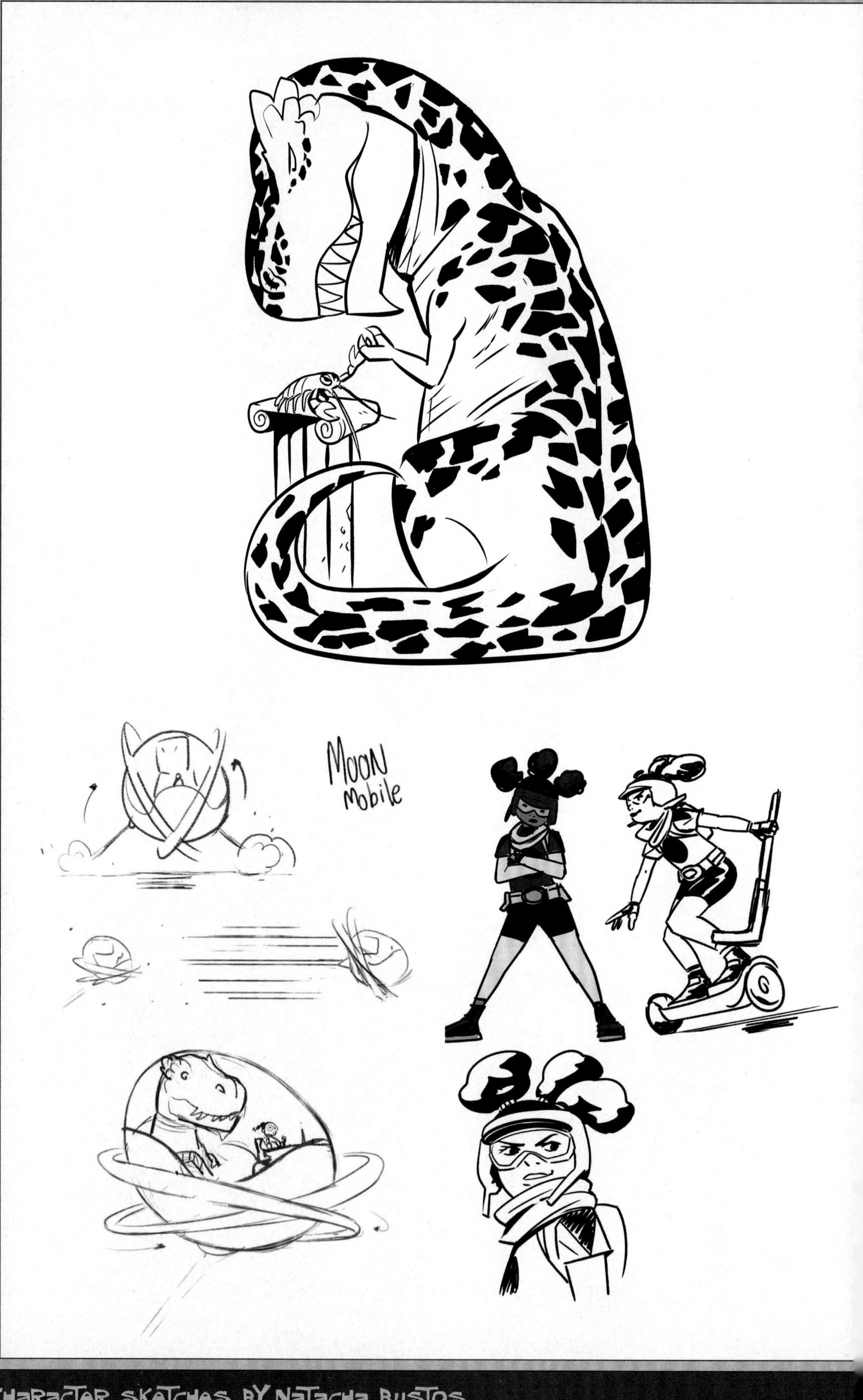
MOON
Mobile

CHARACTER SKETCHES BY NATACHA BUSTOS

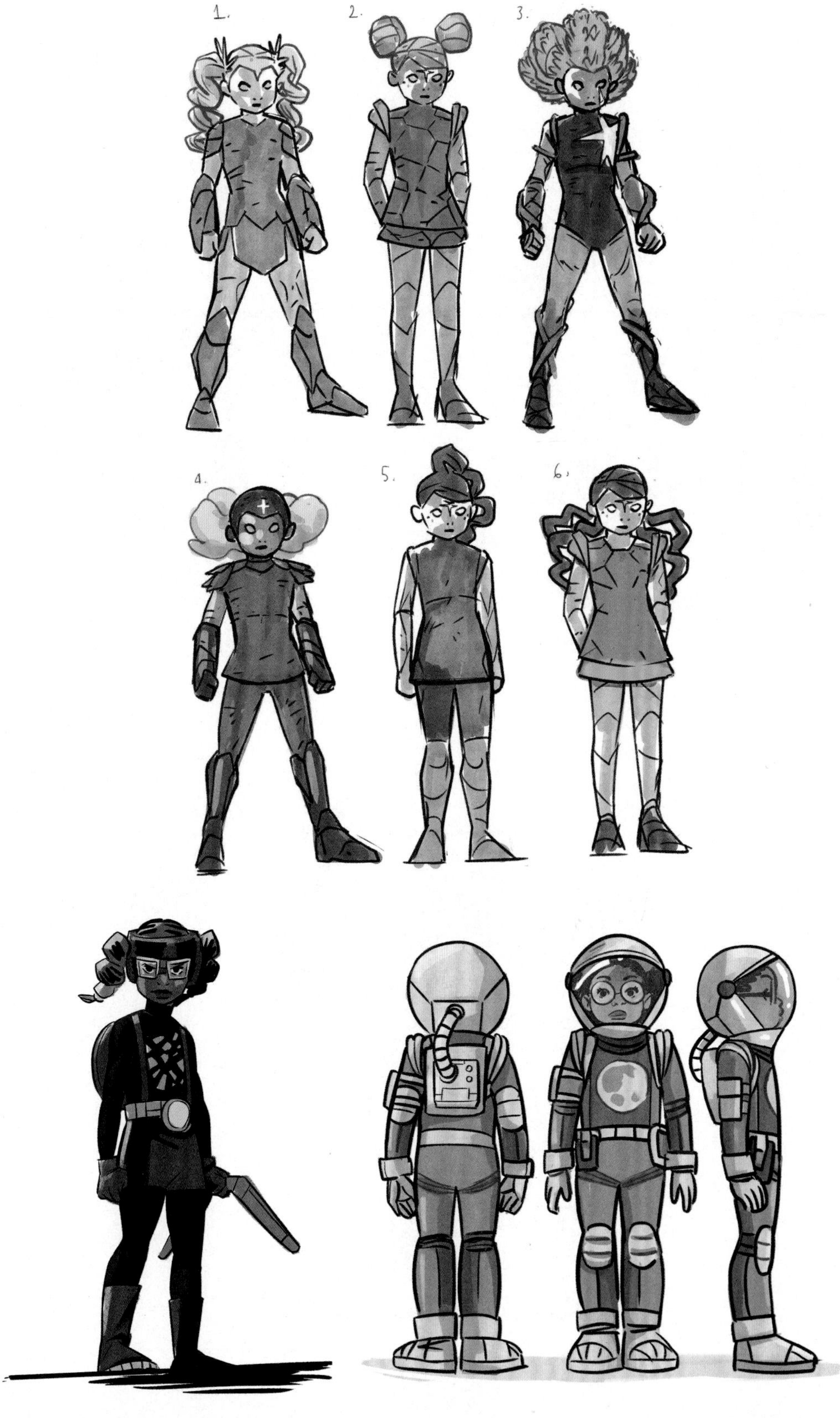
1.
2.
3.
4.
5.
6.

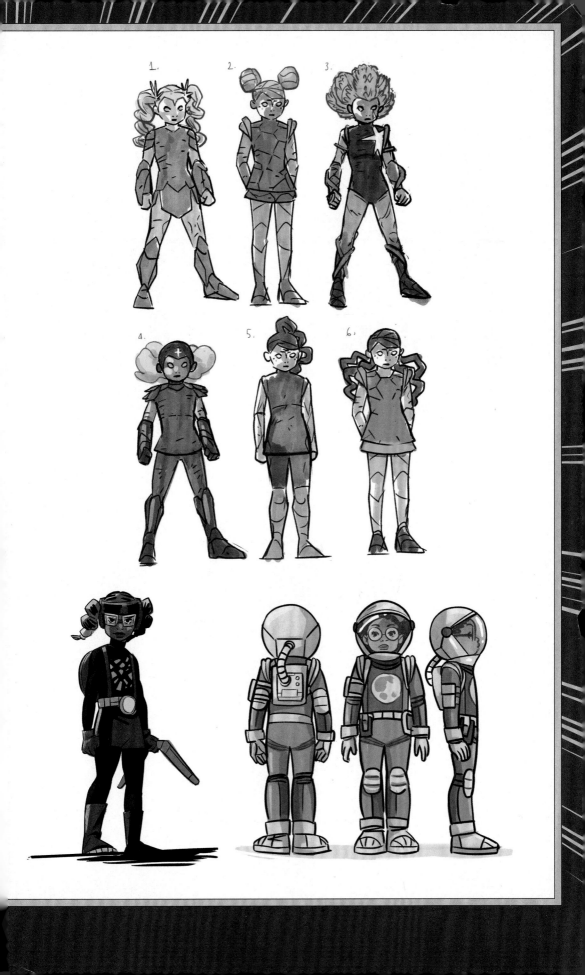

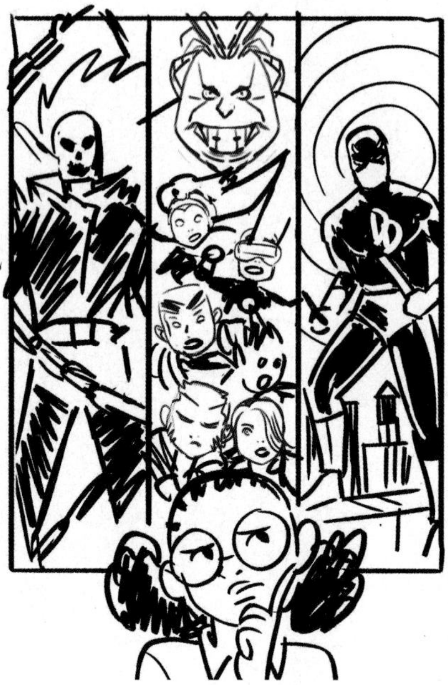

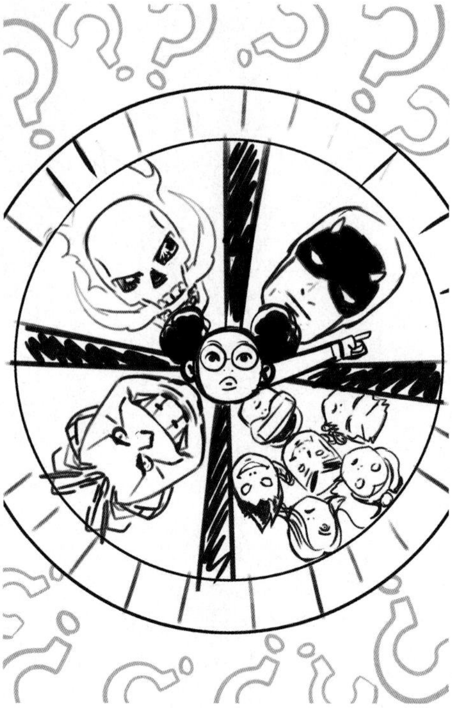

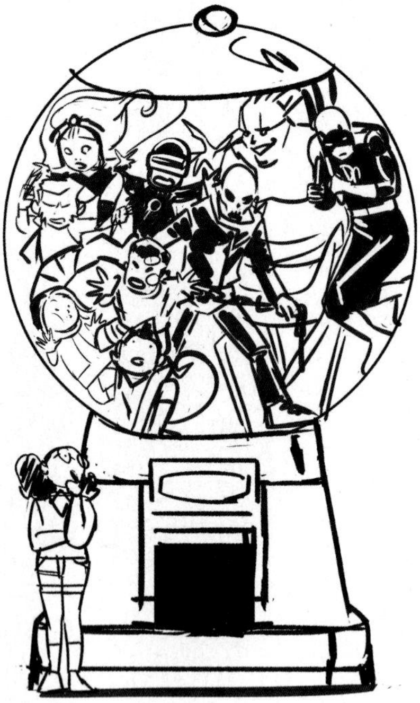

#24 COVER SKETCHES BY NATACHA BUSTOS